# RICH KIDS, POOR PARENTS

PERSONAL FINANCE GUIDE TO RAISING CHILDREN WHILE BALANCING YOUR RETIREMENT SAVINGS

# RICH KIDS POOR PARENTS

THEIR FUTURE MATTERS

SO DOES YOURS

RAISE INDEPENDENT CHILDREN WITHOUT SACRIFICING YOUR FINANCIAL FUTURE

M. E. PARKINSON, PHD

Healthy Planet Press
Website: healthyplanetpress.com

First published in 2026.


Paperback ISBN: 978-1-950856-26-8
eBook ISBN: 978-1-950856-27-5

# Table of Contents

INTRODUCTION

# FINDING *Balance*

*The more you have,*
*the more you are occupied.*

*The less you have,*
*the freer you are.*

— MOTHER TERESA

Before we talk about kids, phones, sports, schools, childcare, or retirement, we need to start somewhere honest—not inspirational, not motivational, just honest. Most Americans don't have money to invest. According to the Federal Reserve's Survey of Consumer Finances, over 40% of

Americans do not have $1000 in savings. Most parents are drowning in debt and overwhelmed in their children's needs and wants. Most money books on Amazon focus on how, where and what to invest in, tax strategy for investing, index funds and how to withdrawal. Titles like how to retire rich, ultimate guide to investing. These books assume that you have money to invest in retirement. What many families are experiencing today is that they do not have money to invest. And this is not random, and it is not simply the result of social media or technology. Those things amplify behavior and raise expectations, but they are not the root cause. What's actually happening is quieter, slower, and far more familiar than most people want to admit.

What families are feeling—often without naming it—is the weight of patterns that have been building over time. Patterns of accommodation that gradually turn into expectation, and then into something that feels surprisingly difficult to undo. It doesn't arrive with a dramatic moment or a clear warning sign. Instead, it shows up in small decisions that feel reasonable, loving, and harmless. The problem is that those decisions don't stay small . . . they stack.

This book uses real-life case studies of how families spend money on their children, paired with the math and psychology behind those decisions—showing not just what was spent, why the parent spent the money, but what those same dollars could have become if redirected toward retirement. The stories in this book are true. Names have been changed, details adjusted, and timelines softened where necessary, but the patterns are real. Some of these stories reflect my own life—an overindulgent mother who, with the best intentions, drove further down the road of consumerism than I ever planned. I was not a passenger in that process. I was driving the car, occasionally speeding, and almost always convinced that what I was doing was helpful, loving, justified, or simply keeping up with what everyone else seemed to be doing—which, as it turns out, is not a financial strategy. Other stories come from friends, family, and conversations that have been shared with me over decades, sometimes with frustration, and occasionally with a kind of honesty that only shows up after the fact. Looking back, the patterns are obvious. Looking forward is where the opportunity is. Because at some point, every parent will look back and evaluate the decisions they made along the way. **This book is not written for that moment.**

This book is written for the moment before that, while decisions are still being made in real time. It is written to offer structure, awareness, and a way to shift direction early enough to change the outcome—not just for your children, but for your own financial future as well.

Throughout this book, I am not saying don't give to your children, or don't create experiences, or don't enjoy the life you are working so hard to build. What I am saying is consider the alternatives. Consider why you are giving. Consider the messages you are sending, both intentionally and unintentionally. Consider your financial and psychological patterns associated with money. And most importantly, ask whether your decisions regarding your children are reinforcing dependence, entitlement, and long-term financial pressure or building independence.

This book assesses real case examples of spending, showing the psychological patterns of why parents make these decisions, and recommendations for how to do something different. The financial models presented were intentionally built using conservative assumptions. In each chapter, the examples assume that money spent on a particular expense was instead redirected and invested, earning an average annual return of 7 percent. The twenty-year values shown in the chapter illustrations were selected to provide an easy-to-understand comparison, not to maximize the financial results. Twenty years of compounding interest may significantly understate the true opportunity cost of these decisions. Retirement accounts, brokerage accounts, Roth IRAs, and other long-term investments are often held for thirty, forty, or even more years. A parent making spending decisions in their thirties or forties may not access those funds until their sixties or seventies. Therefore, the table in Chapter 17, *The True Cost of Choices*, extends the chapter examples by showing the potential 30-year and 40-year compounded values of the spending decisions throughout this book.

While you are reading, skip to the places that matter most to you right now. Maybe you are having a baby, deciding childcare, preschool, dealing with preteen clothes and phones, buying a teenager a car, dealing with high school failure, vacation planning, college planning, contributing to a wedding, contributing to a home purchase. Read what is important to you and what could make a difference in your future retirement savings because children are expensive.

## The Cost of Children

Raising children today comes with a high baseline cost. For a middle-income family in the United States, the estimated cost to raise a child to age 18 is $325,486, or roughly $17,000 per year based on adjusting the USDA 2015 chart for 2026 inflation. That number reflects the essentials: housing, food, transportation, clothing, healthcare, and education-related basics. In other words, that's the cost of doing a responsible job. But very few families stop at responsible.

Once you add in everything that has become "normal" such as travel sports, phones, gaming systems, a plethora of toys, and the occasional "we needed this vacation because if we heard 'I'm bored' one more time I would go crazy," the number doesn't just rise, it drifts into a completely different category. These expenses rarely show up as a single decision. They appear one at a time, each one justified, each one "not that big of a deal." The objective used to be raising capable, independent adults who could handle discomfort, solve problems, and take responsibility for themselves.

Somewhere along the way, the goal shifted without anyone formally agreeing to the change. That shift doesn't happen overnight, and it doesn't happen because parents are careless. It happens because parents are responsive, attentive, and trying to make life smoother for their children. It feels like good parenting wrapped in love. It just happens to be expensive love with a surprisingly flexible definition of "need" versus "want." A small inconvenience gets removed here, a frustration gets softened there, and before long, the environment becomes highly optimized for comfort. Unfortunately, growth does not thrive in highly optimized comfort. It thrives in friction, and friction has become something many households unintentionally engineer out of daily life.

Now we have children who can operate technology with impressive efficiency, navigating apps and platforms with the confidence of a small CEO. At the same time, those same children can struggle with emotional resilience, delayed gratification, or basic responsibility. This isn't because they lack intelligence or potential, but they haven't consistently been required to develop those skills. And parents are left asking, "What happened?" By the time many parents begin to think seriously about retirement, they discover that the years spent funding childhood expectations have also reduced the resources available to secure their own future.

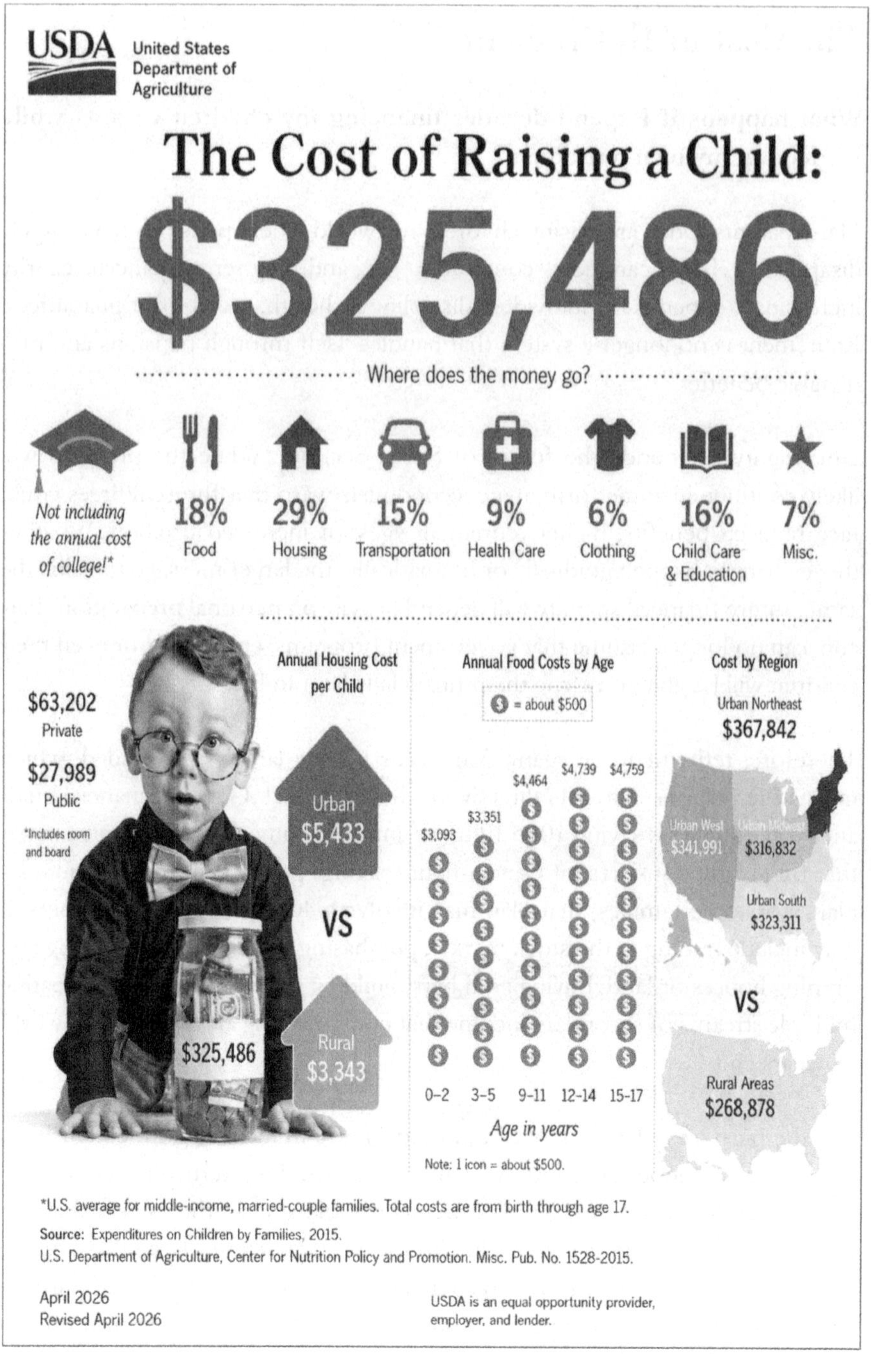
USDA United States Department of Agriculture
The Cost of Raising a Child:
$325,486
Where does the money go?
Not including the annual cost of college!*
18% Food
29% Housing
15% Transportation
9% Health Care
6% Clothing
16% Child Care & Education
7% Misc.
$63,202 Private
$27,989 Public
*Includes room and board
$325,486
Annual Housing Cost per Child
Urban $5,433
VS
Rural $3,343
Annual Food Costs by Age
= about $500
$3,093
$3,351
$4,464
$4,739
$4,759
0–2
3–5
9–11
12–14
15–17
Age in years
Note: 1 icon = about $500.
Cost by Region
Urban Northeast $367,842
Urban West $341,991
Urban Midwest $316,832
Urban South $323,311
VS
Rural Areas $268,878
*U.S. average for middle-income, married-couple families. Total costs are from birth through age 17.
Source: Expenditures on Children by Families, 2015.
U.S. Department of Agriculture, Center for Nutrition Policy and Promotion. Misc. Pub. No. 1528-2015.
April 2026
Revised April 2026
USDA is an equal opportunity provider, employer, and lender.

## The Cost of Retirement

**What happens if I spend decades financing my children's wants while neglecting my own retirement?**

Many parents today are raising children in a world where pensions have largely disappeared, healthcare costs continue to rise, and long-term financial security increasingly depends on individual discipline rather than employer guarantees. Retirement is no longer a system that handles itself through pensions and predictable benefits.

Uncertainty surrounds the future of Social Security. While the program will likely continue in some form, many economists warn that future retirees could face reduced benefits, higher retirement ages, or increased taxation. Whether those changes happen gradually or dramatically, the larger message remains the same: future financial stability will depend heavily on personal preparation. Parents can no longer assume that government programs, employers, or even their children will be able to rescue them financially later in life.

Therefore, retirement for many Americans will be largely self-funded, which means the responsibility sits directly on the individual. General financial guidance often suggests saving 10 to 12 times annual income for retirement, a target that frequently translates into seven-figure savings goals. That reality requires a plan. For some families, that plan may involve a 401(k) or IRA. For others, it may include trading in the stock market, purchasing rental property, buying and flipping houses or land, buying gold bars, building a small business, or creating multiple streams of secondary income that continue long after traditional working years end.

For the purposes of this book, I am modeling retirement investments using a 7% annual compounding rate to demonstrate the long-term impact of redirected spending decisions. Many retirement books are on the market that can help you make the decision of what you want to invest in. Regardless of the specific strategy, the larger principle remains the same: money without purpose or a direction quietly disappears. Money attached to a long-term plan creates options, freedom, and stability. **Every dollar has to have a purpose.** This book helps you understand how you are spending money on your children and how that impacts both your child's independence and your retirement plan.

# Finding Balance

Planning for your retirement while balancing the endless wants of children is not selfish. It is one of the most responsible forms of parenting there is. On one side is the understandable desire to provide, support, protect, and create opportunity for children. On the other side is the responsibility to build a future that does not depend on those same children for financial survival later in life. Both goals are valid, but they draw from the same limited pool of resources. Money does not multiply simply because intentions are good. A retirement plan leaves very little room for casual financial drift or emotional spending disguised as "it's for the kids." Every financial decision connected to children carries a second layer many parents fail to fully calculate. Every extended dependency, every unnecessary rescue, every lifestyle escalation, and every emotionally driven expense also affects the parents' future ability to retire with stability, dignity, and independence. The tradeoffs are rarely visible immediately, but they compound over time.

**According to savings.com, 50% of parents provide regular financial support to adult children with an average monthly amount of $1,474 while the average monthly amount parents contribute to their retirement savings is $673.** And I know you might be saying, but my kid is only six months old or five years old or sixteen years old. Well, the parent giving $1,474 each month to their adult child once had a 6-month-old as well. It is important to understand why kids not only don't fly out of the parents' nest but are also using up their parents' nest egg.

**Forty percent of Americans have already borrowed against or cashed out their 401K.** Every financial decision involves a tradeoff, whether the tradeoff is immediately evident or not. Protecting retirement is not choosing money over children. It is choosing not to become their financial burden later. It is choosing sustainability over short-term approval and long-term independence over immediate emotional comfort. Saying no to a child's additional wants in order to protect retirement is not withholding love. It is modeling restraint, foresight, boundaries, and adult responsibility in a way words alone can never fully teach.

## Rich or Poor - Children Learn About Money

Money enters the parent-child relationship long before a child understands mathematics. Children are learning about money throughout their entire childhood, whether anyone is intentionally teaching or not. They are watching how decisions are made, how requests are handled, and what is considered necessary versus optional. Children absorb financial emotion before they absorb financial literacy. A child watches whether bills create panic at the kitchen table, whether a parent sighs before swiping a debit card, whether "we can't afford that" is said with shame, anger, exhaustion, or calm explanation. A child raised in a home where money is spoken about only during conflict often learns that money itself is dangerous, unpredictable, and emotionally loaded. Another child raised in a home where money is discussed openly, carefully, and without humiliation may grow into adulthood believing financial challenges are problems to solve rather than disasters to fear. If upgrades are constant, they learn that "better" is always expected. If limits are flexible, they learn that boundaries are negotiable. If there are financial gaps, they learn the scarcity and stress of money.

Poverty alone does not automatically create emotional instability. Some financially struggling families maintain extraordinary emotional strength, consistency, humor, and connection despite limited resources. In these homes, children may remember stress, but they also remember resilience, teamwork, and love. The psychological damage often emerges not merely from the lack of money itself but from chaos surrounding the lack of money. When unpaid bills create screaming matches, when eviction threats produce panic, when addiction consumes resources, or when parents emotionally unload adult financial fears onto children, the child may begin living in a constant state of nervous system activation. The body becomes trained to expect instability. Some children in financially unstable homes become hypervigilant adults who obsessively save money because they fear catastrophe. Others become avoidant because money conversations trigger shame and anxiety. Some develop resentment toward parents they believe failed them. Others carry profound guilt for having needs at all. A child who repeatedly hears phrases like "you're too expensive," "we can't survive because of you," or "you always need something" may internalize themselves as a burden. That emotional wound can last decades. Children do not merely experience economic hardship intellectually. They experience it relationally. They study whether their needs are handled with dignity or frustration.

At the same time, children growing up in financially abundant households are not automatically emotionally healthier. Wealth can create its own distortions when boundaries disappear. In some affluent families, children never encounter frustration, limitation, or responsibility because parents attempt to remove every obstacle from the child's life. The child receives a car without contributing toward insurance, an apartment without understanding rent, college tuition without discussion of sacrifice, and spending money without accountability. While this may appear loving on the surface, psychologically it can create profound immaturity. A child who never experiences limitation may struggle to develop resilience because resilience requires contact with difficulty. When parents eliminate all struggle, they also eliminate opportunities for emotional growth. Some financially privileged children become emotionally fragile adults because they mistake comfort for competence. The first financial hardship—a layoff, a late rent payment, debt, or unexpected repair—feels catastrophic because they were never slowly introduced to manageable responsibility. Ironically, children raised with moderate limitations often adapt better to adulthood because they learned early that disappointment is survivable. They learned to wait, save, negotiate, improvise, and recover. Emotional resilience is often built through small frustrations handled consistently over time.

In many families, money becomes more than currency. It represents identity, affection, sacrifice, power, resentment, guilt, fear, or proof of worth. Parents often believe they are simply paying bills, buying shoes, or providing opportunities, but children are studying the emotional climate surrounding every transaction. Children are not born entitled nor are they born with a fear of poverty. They are taught. Financial behavior becomes emotional inheritance.

## Financial Intelligence

Financial intelligence is not simply measured by income or by the ability to afford expensive things. It is reflected in the structure of your freedom and in whether your financial life reduces future pressure or increases it over time. A financially intelligent life is one where money is organized intentionally, where decisions create flexibility instead of obligations, and where long-term stability matters more than short-term appearance. The real signal is not how impressive life looks from the outside. The real signal is whether your choices are building freedom or slowly locking you into commitments that become harder to sustain with every passing year.

Financial intelligence is the difference between carrying large recurring burdens like oversized bills, endless upgrades, constant activities, and long-term debt versus building a life where costs remain manageable and intentional. In that sense, minimalism is not deprivation. It is clarity. It shifts value away from accumulation and toward structure, reducing the number of financial obligations competing for your time, energy, and attention. Fewer obligations create more room for thoughtful decisions, more margin inside a household budget, and more ability to adapt when life changes unexpectedly. Over time, that simplicity compounds into something far more valuable than the emotional high attached to another purchase.

And this is where a critical question starts to matter more than almost any financial strategy you could adopt:

**Does this expense improve life—or require more energy to sustain it?**

That question has a way of cutting through the noise because it forces clarity. Some expenses genuinely improve life by creating meaningful experiences, reducing stress, or adding real value. Others create obligations that demand more work, more time, more energy, and more money just to maintain them. The difference is not always obvious in the moment, but it becomes very clear over time—usually when you're still paying for something on a credit card long after the excitement has disappeared. When spending consistently requires more energy to sustain it, something else has to give. That "something else" is often time—longer hours, increased stress, less flexibility, and fewer moments of actual presence. Ironically, the effort to provide more can sometimes result in being around less, which is not typically the goal when the spending started. It's just the trade that shows up later.

Financial instability does not arrive dramatically. It develops through patterns that seem harmless while they are forming. A slightly higher mortgage. One more travel team. A few more subscriptions. Another camp. Another upgraded vacation. Another year of supporting an adult child who "just needs more time." Each decision can feel reasonable by itself, which is exactly why the pattern becomes difficult to recognize until years have passed. By the time families fully see the financial structure they have built around themselves, it is often emotionally and financially difficult to reverse.

Many parents fear that giving children less materially means giving them less emotionally. In reality, children often crave emotional presence far more than optimized lifestyles. Some of the most meaningful childhood memories involve routines that cost almost nothing: movie nights, neighborhood walks, jokes around dinner tables, road trips with gas station snacks, fishing with grandparents, playing a full game of monopoly, or staying up too late talking in the kitchen. Those moments matter because of emotional atmosphere, not production value.

When consumption slows down, planning becomes easier, and the future becomes less fragile. Retirement savings become realistic. Debt becomes manageable. Stress decreases because fewer financial decisions are being made under pressure. Financial intelligence aligns naturally with this way of living because both prioritize control over impulse and freedom over status. What feels like restraint in the short term often becomes flexibility in the long term.

A key part of financial intelligence is also teaching that planning for the future is not optional. Retirement is not a distant stage of life that magically arrives. It is a financial structure built intentionally over decades through consistency, discipline, and long-term thinking. When parents prioritize long-term stability, they are modeling what children will eventually need to do for themselves.

This book is meant as a financial decision-making guide for balancing the needs and wants of children with the need of retirement savings to help guide parents down a difficult financial road. It is not about extreme rules or unrealistic expectations. It is about awareness, patterns, and the cumulative effect of decisions. In the end, there are two main goals:

1) To give children the ability to function as an adult, and
2) To have enough money saved for retirement.

Let's examine the defining moments of parenthood, chapter by chapter, and uncover the patterns that quietly shape both our children's futures and our own. And maybe, just maybe, the next book you buy will be how to invest the money that is now available to you.

CHAPTER 1

# DESIGNER *Baby*

*If you want your children*
*to turn out well,*
*spend twice as much time*
*with them and half as*
*much money.*

— ABIGAL VAN BUREN

Daniel and Melissa had always believed their story was a fortunate one just not an easy one. After years of fertility treatments, consultations, and IVF cycles that drained both their savings and their patience, Melissa finally became pregnant. When the confirmation came through, it didn't feel like a medical result. It felt like relief. It felt like survival.

"This baby is going to have the best of everything," Melissa said one night, her hand resting on her stomach like she was making a promise. Daniel agreed, at least emotionally. But financially, there was a quiet second conversation happening in his head. He had already seen the numbers leading up to this moment, the cost of just being able to get pregnant, and he knew what "the best of everything" could turn into.

The spending for the baby didn't begin when the baby arrived. It started well before that, and it started in a way that didn't feel like spending at all. Melissa created a designer nursery. Paint, drapes, carpet, lighting, and décor added up to over $4,000. It created a calm, beautiful space that looked like it belonged in a magazine. It also created a room the baby would never remember.

The registry wasn't a list of needs—it was a collection of upgraded decisions. The stroller was a Bugaboo for $1,600, the Restoration Hardware crib that turned into the full-size bed was $2,700 with a matching dresser for $2,265, and each item came with a reason that sounded responsible when explained. That's how this category works. You're not buying things. You're avoiding bad decisions. Safety ratings, materials, longevity for more children that might follow, and design all become part of the justification. Nothing feels excessive in isolation, and that's what makes it easy to move forward without hesitation.

Friends and family adapted quickly to the baby shower. They didn't question the big items; they simply chose from the smaller ones. Blankets, toys, and accessories filled in around purchases that had already been decided.

Then the baby arrived, and with that came a new category of spending that no one really prepares for. It's not hidden, but it just doesn't show up all at once. Hospital bills that don't fully match what insurance "covered" begin to arrive, followed by lactation consultants, formula when breastfeeding doesn't go as planned, and diapers that disappear faster than groceries.

The smaller items begin to stack in ways that don't feel significant at the time. Wipes, creams, bottles, pumps, and replacements for things that didn't work the first time start to rotate in and out of the house. Then the equipment shows up: swings, bouncers, exersaucers, play mats. Each one designed to solve a specific problem or create a moment of relief.

Most of these items are used for a short period of time, and some are barely used at all. None of them feel optional in the moment, because each one is tied to a need that feels immediate. That's the pattern. Nothing feels optional while you're in it.

By the end of the baby's first year, Daniel and Melissa had spent over $28,000. The spending didn't feel excessive, it felt like survival mixed with preparation. They weren't trying to overspend. They were trying to stay ahead of needs that seemed to change every few weeks. But accumulation doesn't announce itself. It builds slowly inside reasonable decisions. Patterns often start here at the beginning. Not dramatically—just gradually.

## Psychological Pattern: Earned Reward Justification

There's a psychological shift that happens after people struggle to become parents, especially in situations like Daniel and Melissa. Infertility treatments, miscarriages, difficult pregnancies, adoption paperwork, NICU stays, and years of uncertainty create an emotional debt that many parents feel entitled to repay with abundance. After enduring so much pain and waiting, restraint feels emotionally inappropriate. The practical voice that once questioned unnecessary spending becomes quieter because the child now represents victory, survival, and gratitude all wrapped into one tiny human being wearing a $94 Ralph Lauren organic cotton sleeper. Parents begin telling themselves that after everything they went through, they are finally going to enjoy this experience fully. Unfortunately, "fully" often turns into financially overspending without anyone realizing when the line was crossed.

The spending rarely begins with extravagance. It starts with understandable upgrades that feel harmless in isolation. A nicer stroller becomes the organic crib mattress, which becomes newborn photography, which becomes a first birthday party requiring balloon arches that look like they were designed by a wedding planner. The emotional logic behind the purchases always feels compassionate and justified. Nobody wants to be the exhausted parent who finally has the child they prayed for only to say, "Actually, we're going to be cautious and budget conscious." That feels emotionally cold, even though financially it may be wise. Pain quietly transforms spending into proof of devotion.

Modern culture reinforces this mindset. Parents are told to cherish every moment, maximize every memory, and never regret giving their children "the best." Social media then amplifies the pressure by rewarding visible acts of abundance with admiration and validation. A modest nursery does not usually go viral, but a custom woodland-themed room with imported wallpaper and a hand-painted mural absolutely might. Parents begin to confuse emotional gratitude with financial excess because the marketplace encourages them to. Every purchase becomes wrapped in emotional language like bonding, memory-making, and intentional parenting. Before long, the child is not just loved deeply; the child is also carrying the weight of an entire emotional recovery process funded one Amazon box at a time.

Parents who recognize this mindset need to understand that gratitude and restraint are not opposites. Loving a child deeply does not require financing an endless stream of upgrades, luxuries, and emotionally driven purchases. One of the healthiest questions a parent can ask is whether the spending is truly benefiting the child or soothing unresolved emotional pain from the journey to parenthood. Children do not measure love through thread counts, imported nursery décor, or extravagant birthday parties nearly as much as adults imagine they do. The emotional security children crave most comes from stability, presence, calmness, and emotionally regulated parents. A financially stressed household filled with expensive things is still a stressed household.

Parents can also begin reframing what "doing it right" actually means. Instead of associating good parenting with maximizing every experience, they can define success as building a healthy family culture that includes boundaries, moderation, gratitude, and financial intelligence. The child who grows up watching emotionally stable financial behavior receives a far greater long-term gift than the child surrounded by constant consumption. Parents who endured difficult roads to parenthood should absolutely celebrate their families. They simply need to remember that celebration does not require permanent financial escalation. Sometimes the healthiest way to honor the struggle is by building lasting security instead of emotionally spending.

## The Quick Math

During their child's first year, Daniel and Melissa spent approximately $28,000 on nursery furniture, decorations, health care, baby gear, clothing, and other ongoing infant expenses. A more conservative approach could have reduced those costs to about $11,400. Please see the example titled "First-Year Baby Budget." If the expenses would have been reduced to $11,400, it would have created a difference of roughly $16,600 in just one year. At first glance, that amount may not seem life-changing, but the long-term impact tells a different story. If the $16,600 savings had been invested for retirement and earned an average annual return of 7%, it would have grown to approximately $64,107 over 20 years. Thoughtful spending does not mean sacrificing a child's well-being; it means recognizing that every dollar spent today is also a dollar that cannot grow for tomorrow. One year of more intentional choices could translate into more than $64,000 in retirement savings, and that's only the beginning. When repeated over many years, these decisions can dramatically shape a family's long-term financial future.

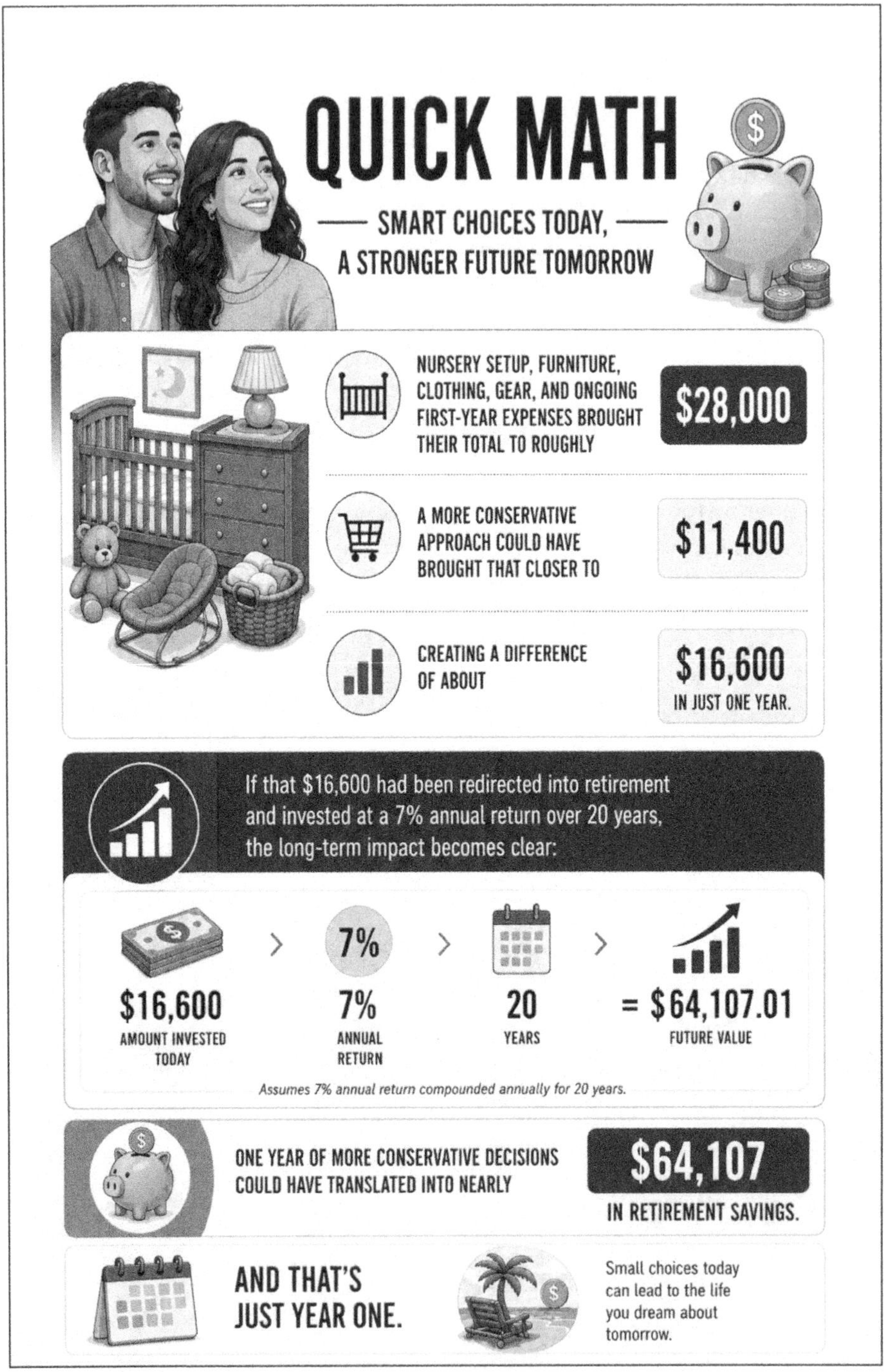
QUICK MATH
SMART CHOICES TODAY, A STRONGER FUTURE TOMORROW
NURSERY SETUP, FURNITURE, CLOTHING, GEAR, AND ONGOING FIRST-YEAR EXPENSES BROUGHT THEIR TOTAL TO ROUGHLY
$28,000
A MORE CONSERVATIVE APPROACH COULD HAVE BROUGHT THAT CLOSER TO
$11,400
CREATING A DIFFERENCE OF ABOUT
$16,600
IN JUST ONE YEAR.
If that $16,600 had been redirected into retirement and invested at a 7% annual return over 20 years, the long-term impact becomes clear:
$16,600
AMOUNT INVESTED TODAY
7%
7%
ANNUAL RETURN
20
YEARS
= $64,107.01
FUTURE VALUE
Assumes 7% annual return compounded annually for 20 years.
ONE YEAR OF MORE CONSERVATIVE DECISIONS COULD HAVE TRANSLATED INTO NEARLY
$64,107
IN RETIREMENT SAVINGS.
AND THAT'S JUST YEAR ONE.
Small choices today can lead to the life you dream about tomorrow.

# FIRST YEAR BABY BUDGET

Plan ahead. Spend intentionally. Build a strong foundation.

| CATEGORY | TYPE | WHAT IT INCLUDES (WITH INDIVIDUAL COSTS) | ONGOING MONTHLY COSTS (12 MONTHS) | | ONE-TIME COSTS (PAID IN FIRST YEAR) | COST (FIRST YEAR) TOTAL |
|---|---|---|---|---|---|---|
| | | | MONTHLY COST | 12 MONTH TOTAL | COST | |
| Feeding | Ongoing (Monthly) | • Formula: $150<br>• Solid food: $30<br>• Bottles: $20 | $200 | $2,400 | – | $2,400 |
| Diapering | Ongoing (Monthly) | • Diapers: $70<br>• Wipes: $30 | $100 | $1,200 | – | $1,200 |
| Clothing | Ongoing (Monthly) | • Baby clothes: $60<br>• Socks: $20<br>• Outerwear: $20 | $100 | $1,200 | – | $1,200 |
| Healthcare | One-time | • Pre-natal visits: $800<br>• Hospital birth & stay: $3,500<br>• Post care (pediatric visits): $500<br>• Other healthcare needs: $200 | – | – | $5,000 | $5,000 |
| Bathing & Grooming | One-time | • Hooded towel: $20<br>• Baby bathtub: $25<br>• Washcloths: $15<br>• Grooming kit: $20<br>• Baby shampoo & wash: $20 | – | – | $100 | $100 |
| Gear | One-time | • Infant car seat: $150<br>• Stroller (basic): $150<br>• Baby carrier: $50<br>• Diaper bag: $50<br>• High chair: $100 | – | – | $500 | $500 |
| Nursery Set Up | One-time | • Crib + changing table: $450<br>• Crib mattress: $150<br>• Bassinet: $150<br>• Bedding (sheets): $50<br>• Rocking chair: $200 | – | – | $1,000 | $1,000 |
| **TOTAL FIRST YEAR BUDGET** | | | **$400** / month | **$4,800** (Over 12 months) | $6,750 | **$11,400** |

**TOTAL FIRST YEAR BUDGET (ONGOING + ONE-TIME)** **$11,400**

**A thoughtful plan today builds a stronger tomorrow.**
Every family is different. Use this plan as a starting point, adjust as needed, and focus on what matters most—your baby's health, your family's happiness, and your future together.

## Recommendations

### Understand Your Health Insurance Before Pregnancy

If both parents receive health insurance through their employers, compare plans carefully before becoming pregnant to determine which policy provides the best overall coverage for prenatal care, labor and delivery, hospitalization, and newborn expenses. In many cases, changing the mother's insurance plan to the father's insurance plan or vice-versa prior to pregnancy can significantly reduce out-of-pocket costs later. Move all family members to the same health plan, so the family deductible is easier to meet. Understand what services are covered, which doctors and hospitals are considered in-network, what deductibles apply, and what percentage of care the insurance company will pay for specific procedures and services. Call the insurance provider directly and ask detailed questions about maternity coverage, pediatric care, emergency services, and anticipated delivery costs for both mother and baby. Under the Affordable Care Act, most insurance plans also cover the cost of one breast pump. Making informed healthcare decisions early can prevent unexpected medical bills and reduce financial stress during an already overwhelming season of life.

### Define "Enough" Before the Baby Arrives

Much of the overspending during the first year of parenthood happens reactively, when exhausted parents are making quick emotional decisions in response to stress, fear, exhaustion, or convenience. Establishing a financial philosophy before the baby arrives creates a framework for decision-making later. Decide early what matters most, what is truly necessary, and where reasonable limits exist. A family that enters parenthood with a defined understanding of "enough" is less likely to be pulled into constant upgrades, impulse purchases, and comparison-based spending. Cost-conscious parenting becomes much easier when decisions are filtered through an established framework rather than made moment by moment under pressure.

## Separate Function from Marketing

The baby industry is exceptionally skilled at convincing parents that convenience products are necessities. Many items marketed as essential are temporary, optional, or designed to solve problems that may never actually occur. Understanding the difference between function and marketing helps families avoid unnecessary upgrades and repetitive spending. Products promising improved sleep, accelerated development, or "must-have" parenting solutions often provide only marginal value while dramatically increasing spending during a short season of life. Not every problem requires a purchase, and not every inconvenience requires a product designed to eliminate it.

## Use Secondhand for Short-Term Items

Many baby products are used for only a few months before children outgrow them entirely. Swings, bouncers, bassinets, exersaucers, infant clothing, and activity centers are often available secondhand in excellent condition for a fraction of retail cost. These are high-turnover items that rarely justify paying full price. Purchasing selectively used items allows families to meet the same practical needs without permanently increasing their spending baseline. Babies do not care whether an item is new; the pressure for everything to be brand-new is often driven more by adult perception and marketing than by necessity. Secondhand clothing is available at garage sales, Facebook Marketplace, online stores like Poshmark or ThredUp, or local stores like Once Upon a Child, Goodwill and Salvation Army.

## Be Intentional About Feeding Costs

Feeding decisions can become one of the largest recurring expenses during infancy. Breastfeeding, when possible, can reduce long-term costs, although it still involves supplies, pumps, storage products, and time. When breastfeeding is not possible or practical, formula becomes a significant monthly expense. At approximately $25–$50 per container, formula can easily total $150–$300 per month during the first year, especially for families using premium or specialty brands. Understanding these costs ahead of time allows parents to budget intentionally instead of reacting emotionally during stressful moments. Awareness creates better financial decision-making even when choices are limited.

## Consider Reusable Options Where Practical

Reusable products are not realistic for every family, but in some situations, they can meaningfully reduce long-term costs. Cloth diapers, reusable wipes, glass bottles, and other reusable baby products may require more effort upfront, yet they can lower recurring monthly expenses over time. Even partial use can create measurable savings. The goal is not perfection or rigid minimalism, but awareness that many recurring purchases marketed as unavoidable may actually have lower-cost alternatives.

## Track First-Year Spending in Real Time

Most parents underestimate how much they spend during the first year because the purchases happen gradually and in small increments. Set a budget for your first-year spending and stick to it. Bottles, clothing, formula, toys, feeding accessories, convenience items, and late-night online purchases accumulate over time. Tracking spending monthly creates visibility and prevents expenses from disappearing unnoticed into the emotional blur of new parenthood. Awareness changes behavior. Once families begin to see patterns repeated in real numbers, financial decisions often become more intentional and less reactive.

The first year doesn't just introduce a child into the household.

It introduces a financial pattern. And once that pattern is established, it rarely stays contained to just one year.

## CHAPTER 2

# PRESCHOOL *Prestige*

*There is no school*
*equal to a decent home*
*and no teacher equal to*
*a virtuous parent.*

— MAHATMA GANDHI

Daphne had two young daughters and a husband named Gary who, in the kindest possible terms, was not built for consistent employment. He was a good person, thoughtful, educated, and well-meaning, but stability had a habit of slipping just out of reach. His PhD looked excellent framed on a wall and sounded impressive in conversation but translated less effectively into steady income. "Not the right fit" became a recurring phrase in their household, and over time it started to mean the same thing as "we need to figure something else out." Daphne figured something else out.

She worked full-time as a lab technician, and unlike framed degrees, her paycheck had a very practical quality. It consistently turned into groceries, utilities, and mortgage payments. She was steady, capable, and deeply committed to giving her daughters a thoughtful, intentional childhood. That commitment shaped her decisions in ways that felt deliberate, not excessive.

Daphne cared about environment, not casually, but in a way that influenced how she saw development itself. She believed what children experienced daily, what they touched, saw, and heard, shaped how they learned and who they became. The tone of a classroom mattered. The pace mattered. The people around them mattered. And she knew exactly what she wanted. A Waldorf preschool.

To Daphne, preschool was not childcare—it was philosophy. It was the beginning of how her children would understand the world, what they would value, and what kind of environment would feel normal. She didn't want fluorescent lighting or laminated charts. She wanted calm spaces, natural materials, and intentional learning. The kind of place where children baked bread, painted with watercolors, and stacked wooden blocks instead of pressing buttons that made noise. She found the school and she loved it. There was just one detail that required a little more thought . . . tuition.

The five-day preschool program was $23,000 per year per child. At that point, the word "preschool" starts to feel like it should come with a graduation ceremony, a small diploma, and possibly a valet parking option for the tricycles. The number didn't feel imaginary—it felt real enough to require justification. And justification is where fear quietly enters modern parenting, because once parents become afraid their child could somehow fall behind or be exposed to something that doesn't feel like their values, almost any price can begin sounding reasonable.

There was a free public preschool available in their district. It had licensed teachers, structured learning, social development, and children who would almost certainly survive snack time without emerging academically ruined. It also had one major disadvantage. The free preschool didn't match Daphne's vision. In her mind, public preschool became emotionally connected to risk. What if the class sizes were larger? What if her children didn't get enough attention? What if the "wrong influences" showed up early? What if the other parents were not like them? Fear-based parenting rarely announces itself dramatically. It often arrives disguised as responsible decision-making.

Free preschool, it turns out, is not always persuasive when compared to philosophy and values. Daphne and Gary made a decision that felt both strategic and slightly heroic. If Daphne worked at the Waldorf school, she could receive a tuition discount. A 40% discount. On paper, this looked like a solution. In practice, it became a system.

Daphne took a position at the school during the day and continued her lab work in the afternoons and evenings. Weekends became catch-up time for everything else including household responsibilities, errands, and whatever energy she could piece together. The schedule worked, at least in the technical sense. The tuition was reduced. The girls were enrolled. Everything aligned with the plan. But plans don't always account for human energy.

Morning at the school turned into afternoon at the lab, which turned into evening at home, and then repeated the next day. At first, it felt manageable. Then it felt tiring. Then it started to feel like something else entirely.

Exhaustion has a way of showing up. It accumulates, much like spending does. A little less energy each day, a little less patience, and a little more time spent recovering instead of engaging.

Her daughters were thriving in their environment. They were learning, creating, and growing exactly as Daphne had hoped. But they were also seeing less of her. Not because she didn't care. Because she was working to support the environment, she believed they needed. This is the part that rarely gets included in the brochure. The cost of something is not always just financial. Sometimes it's time, sometimes it's energy, and sometimes it's presence. Daphne had successfully created the ideal educational environment. But it came with a tradeoff that was harder to measure.

And this is where the logic becomes uncomfortable. If the goal of preschool is development, connection, and foundational learning, then the question becomes what role the parent plays in that equation. A structured environment matters, but so does a present parent. A calm classroom has value. But so does a parent who isn't operating on empty. When those two things begin competing, it's worth asking whether the tradeoff is improving the outcome—or simply shifting where the benefit comes from. This is how prestige enters a family dynamic. Often, not as status, but as alignment with values. And once something feels aligned, it becomes easier to justify—even when the cost extends beyond tuition.

## Psychological Pattern: Fear-Based Parenting

Daphne wasn't really paying only for education. She was paying for reassurance. The tuition purchased smaller classes, enriched programming, and beautifully designed classrooms, but emotionally it also purchased the feeling that she was doing everything possible to protect her children's future. The expensive preschool reduced uncertainty, and uncertainty is one of the hardest emotional experiences for parents to tolerate. The fear was not necessarily rational or measurable, but it felt emotionally convincing. Once that happens, spending stops feeling optional and starts feeling morally responsible.

What made the decision even more psychologically powerful was that the alternative was free. That should have created financial relief, but instead it created emotional tension. Choosing public preschool would have required Daphne to sit with the uncomfortable possibility that her children might still thrive without a prestigious preschool. And if that were true, then maybe the expensive program was not entirely necessary after all. That is a difficult thought for anxious parents because it forces them to separate love from financial escalation. So instead, the expensive choice became easier emotionally, even if it was harder financially.

This is how fear reshapes parenting decisions. Parents stop asking, "Is this valuable?" and start asking, "What happens if I don't do this?" The second question changes everything because now the purchase feels tied to protection, opportunity, and future success. Modern parenting culture feeds this fear constantly by suggesting that childhood is a narrow competitive window where every missed enrichment opportunity carries lifelong consequences. Daphne loved her children deeply, but love mixed with anxiety can become extremely expensive. Fear has a way of turning optional upgrades into emotional necessities.

Fear has become an economic engine in parenting. Parents are constantly warned that one wrong decision could permanently disadvantage their child socially, academically, emotionally, or professionally. If your child is not in enrichment programs by preschool, people wonder whether they are "stimulated enough. Parenting slowly transforms into a continuous attempt to prevent imagined future disasters through spending.

This fear changes how parents evaluate money. Purchases no longer feel optional because they become framed as preventative measures. Travel sports are not expensive hobbies; they are "building discipline and opportunity." A $4,000 summer camp somehow becomes an "investment in confidence and independence." The psychological shift is important because fear eliminates moderation. Parents stop asking whether something is worth the cost and start asking whether failing to buy it could hurt their child later.

The parenting marketplace thrives on this anxiety. Every company markets products and services as essential tools for maximizing childhood outcomes. Parents are told that healthy snacks create smarter brains, elite preschools create future leaders, and coding camps create financial security before the child has mastered basic hygiene. The result is financial exhaustion disguised as responsible parenting. Many parents are not spending extravagantly because they are careless. They are spending because they are terrified of falling behind in a competition nobody fully understands. Fear-based parenting creates households where every opportunity feels urgent and every dollar spent feels morally justified.

Parents caught in fear-based spending need to remember that nearly every industry connected to children profits from parental anxiety. That realization alone can be incredibly freeing. Companies, coaches, schools, camps, and influencers all benefit financially when parents believe every opportunity is urgent and every missed experience carries lifelong consequences. Most children do not need optimization in every category of life. They need supportive relationships, emotional safety, healthy routines, and reasonable opportunities to explore their interests without turning childhood into a résumé-building exercise by fourth grade. Fear makes moderation feel irresponsible, but calm perspective restores balance.

One of the healthiest practices parents can develop is learning to tolerate the discomfort of saying no without immediately assuming harm will follow.

Parents should ask whether decisions are being driven by actual need or by catastrophic thinking about future outcomes. Children benefit enormously from seeing adults make thoughtful financial choices rather than emotionally reactive ones. Sometimes the greatest protection a parent can provide is a financially stable household that is not constantly stretched thin chasing every possible advantage. Security matters more than endless optimization.

## The Quick Math

Gary and Daphne believed they were making the best possible educational choice for their children. The preschool they selected charged $23,000 per child annually, but thanks to a 40% employee discount, their out-of-pocket cost was reduced to $13,800 per child. With two children enrolled, their annual preschool expense reached $27,600. Over two years, they spent a total of $55,200 on early childhood education. Had the same $55,200 been redirected into retirement savings and invested at an average annual return of 7%, it could have grown to approximately $213,728 over 20 years. In other words, more than $200,000 of potential retirement savings was effectively consumed by just two years of preschool tuition. The purpose of this comparison is not to criticize parents who choose private preschool, but to highlight how seemingly short-term decisions can carry long-term financial consequences. Every major expense represents a trade-off between current consumption and future financial security, and understanding those trade-offs allows families to make decisions that align with both their values and their long-term goals.

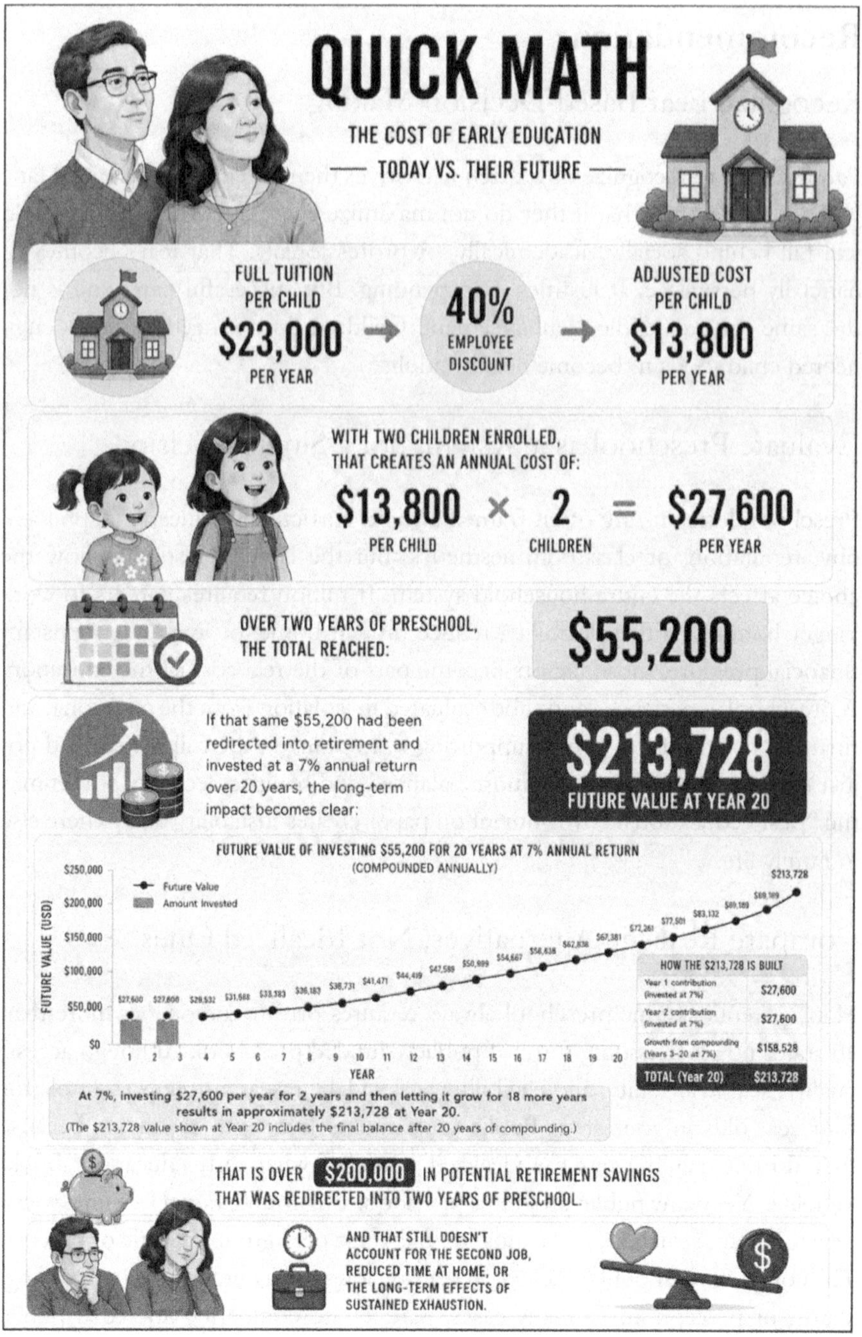
QUICK MATH
THE COST OF EARLY EDUCATION
— TODAY VS. THEIR FUTURE —
FULL TUITION PER CHILD
$23,000
PER YEAR
40%
EMPLOYEE DISCOUNT
ADJUSTED COST PER CHILD
$13,800
PER YEAR
WITH TWO CHILDREN ENROLLED, THAT CREATES AN ANNUAL COST OF:
$13,800 × 2 = $27,600
PER CHILD
CHILDREN
PER YEAR
OVER TWO YEARS OF PRESCHOOL, THE TOTAL REACHED:
$55,200
If that same $55,200 had been redirected into retirement and invested at a 7% annual return over 20 years, the long-term impact becomes clear:
$213,728
FUTURE VALUE AT YEAR 20
FUTURE VALUE OF INVESTING $55,200 FOR 20 YEARS AT 7% ANNUAL RETURN
(COMPOUNDED ANNUALLY)
Future Value
Amount Invested
FUTURE VALUE (USD)
$250,000
$200,000
$150,000
$100,000
$50,000
$0
YEAR
$213,728
HOW THE $213,728 IS BUILT
Year 1 contribution (invested at 7%) $27,600
Year 2 contribution (invested at 7%) $27,600
Growth from compounding (Years 3–20 at 7%) $158,528
TOTAL (Year 20) $213,728
At 7%, investing $27,600 per year for 2 years and then letting it grow for 18 more years results in approximately $213,728 at Year 20.
(The $213,728 value shown at Year 20 includes the final balance after 20 years of compounding.)
THAT IS OVER $200,000 IN POTENTIAL RETIREMENT SAVINGS THAT WAS REDIRECTED INTO TWO YEARS OF PRESCHOOL.
AND THAT STILL DOESN'T ACCOUNT FOR THE SECOND JOB, REDUCED TIME AT HOME, OR THE LONG-TERM EFFECTS OF SUSTAINED EXHAUSTION.

## Recommendations

### Recognize Fear Based Decision Making

Parents need to recognize how often fear drives their parenting decisions. Many parents are terrified that if they do not maximize every opportunity, their child will fall behind socially, academically, or professionally. That fear becomes financially persuasive. It justifies overspending. But successful parenting is not the same thing as endless enhancement. Children do not need perfectly engineered childhoods to become healthy adults.

### Evaluate Preschool as a System, not a Single Decision

Preschool decisions are often framed around curriculum, educational philosophy, reputation, or classroom aesthetics, but the larger question is how the choice affects the entire household system. If tuition requires parents to work longer hours, sacrifice flexibility, reduce time at home, or live under constant financial pressure, those factors become part of the real cost of the education. A preschool experience cannot be evaluated in isolation from the emotional and financial health of the family supporting it. Looking at the full system and not just the school itself creates a more balanced and realistic decision. Sometimes the "best" educational environment on paper creates instability everywhere else in family life.

### Compare Realistic Alternatives, Not Idealized Ones

Many parents assume preschool always requires private tuition, yet more than 40 states now offer some form of publicly funded preschool. Although access, quality, seat availability, and eligibility vary widely, research free preschools for four-year-olds in your state. Public preschool is frequently dismissed because they do not match a family's idealized vision of what early education should look like. Yet many public programs provide strong foundational learning, social development, structure, and exposure to diverse peer groups at little or no cost. The comparison should be based on realistic long-term outcomes, not branding, status, or perception. In many cases, parents are comparing an actual public option against a fantasy version of private education rather than measurable differences in outcomes.

## Account for Energy as a Limited Resource

Financial decisions that require ongoing overwork often reduce a parent's emotional availability at home. That tradeoff is rarely calculated in financial discussions, yet it directly shapes the child's daily experience. A parent working excessive hours to sustain tuition payments may unintentionally lose the very time and emotional presence that children benefit from most. **Energy is a finite resource just like money.** A lower-cost educational option combined with a calmer, more present parent may ultimately provide greater benefit than a more prestigious school attached to chronic stress and exhaustion.

## Avoid Building Identity Around Educational Choices

When educational decisions become deeply tied to personal identity, values, or social image, it becomes much harder to evaluate them objectively. Parents may begin to interpret changes in schooling not as financial adjustments, but as emotional failures or reflections of personal worth. At that point, decisions shift from practical to emotional, and flexibility begins to disappear. Families can become financially trapped inside systems they no longer comfortably afford simply because leaving feels psychologically difficult. Maintaining emotional distance from educational branding allows parents to make clearer long-term decisions as family circumstances evolve.

## Project the Cost Forward Before Committing

One year of tuition rarely remains only one year. Preschool often creates a pathway into private elementary school, then middle school, and then high school. Before committing, families should project the possible long-term financial path rather than evaluating only the immediate cost. What begins as a manageable monthly payment can gradually become a deeply embedded financial structure that is emotionally difficult to leave later. Thinking forward helps parents avoid entering systems that may eventually compete with retirement savings, debt reduction, or overall financial stability.

## Redirect Savings Intentionally

Choosing a lower-cost option only creates long-term value if the savings are used intentionally. Otherwise, the difference simply disappears into everyday spending and lifestyle inflation. Redirecting those funds toward retirement accounts, emergency savings, investments, debt reduction, or future educational needs strengthens long-term financial stability and creates measurable progress over time. The goal is not merely to spend less, but to build more. Small financial decisions made consistently over many years often create far greater security than families initially realize.

CHAPTER 3

# THE CHILDCARE *Conundrum*

*The universe doesn't allow perfection.*

— STEPHEN HAWKING

When our daughter was born, I was twenty-four years old. Three years later, our son arrived. I held an entry level job in IT for EDS, and my husband was a teacher. We had very little money, no nearby grandparents waiting to rescue us with free childcare, a pile of student loan debt, a mortgage at 8% interest, and absolutely no ability to absorb the cost of full-time daycare. At the time, childcare for our two children would have consumed one of our entry level salaries, so we did what many young couples do when they are trying to survive financially. We rearranged our lives around opposite schedules.

I asked my employer if I could work afternoons and they agreed. The sixth floor where my cubicle sat was empty at night. Most of the lights were off except for emergency lighting and a few hallway fluorescents. The blue glow of the computer screen lit my cubicle while the rest of the corporate office felt dark and abandoned. Sitting there alone in a massive building after everyone else had gone home was downright spooky.

Around 7:30 each evening, I would drive home to breastfeed and then return to work until 1:00 am. My husband taught during the day and left by 6:30 am, and we developed a routine that now sounds almost ridiculous in retrospect. We would meet at a gas station that was halfway between our jobs. The children stayed strapped into their seats while we switched drivers in the parking lot like exhausted relay runners handing off a baton. We tried to make it feel normal and cheerful. "We're going to meet Daddy from work," I would tell the kids. One day someone asked my daughter where her daddy worked, and she proudly announced that he worked at a gas station.

I am not telling this story because it was ideal. It was not ideal at all. It was exhausting, stressful, emotionally draining, and financially tight. We were stretching to make our mortgage, trying to build our careers, and functioning on very little sleep. Looking back now, I sometimes question how important those careers actually were compared to the pressure they placed on our family during those years. But at the time, we believed we needed both incomes and both career paths moving forward simultaneously. Our money was still so tight at the time that nothing went to retirement. There was absolutely no extra money. What I understand now is that with children there are rarely ideal solutions. There is only the ongoing process of making life work for your particular family with the resources, energy, and support systems one actually has at the time.

One of the hardest parts of parenting to figure out is childcare. It is not a single decision solved during infancy and then permanently completed. Childcare stretches across years of family life—from newborn care and preschool through summer breaks, teacher workdays, holiday schedules, and endless summers that somehow arrive just as parents are trying to maintain careers and financial stability. Whether a child is two years old in daycare or ten years old heading to full day summer camp, the same question continues to follow parents year after year: **who is watching the children, and at what cost?**

The early childhood years have become one of the most financially demanding periods of family life. Parents are often simultaneously paying for childcare, healthcare, housing, transportation, food, and retirement savings during the exact years when long-term wealth building matters most. According to the Bipartisan Policy Center, families pay an average of $13,128 per child annually for childcare, representing about 10% of dual-income and 35% of single-income household earnings which exceeds in-state public college tuition in 38 states. For many middle-income households who have more than one child, this percentage exceeds the percentage of income spent on housing costs such as rent or a mortgage.

Research shows that over forty one percent of families choose to have one parent at home taking care of the children full time (see chart). This means that fifty nine percent of families either single parents or dual parents use other means of childcare including day care centers, relatives such as grandparents, or in-home nannies. There are no universally perfect systems. There are only different forms of compromise that families make to keep life functioning.

# Who Cares for America's Children Before Kindergarten?

NATIONAL DATA ON CHILD CARE ARRANGEMENTS FOR CHILDREN AGE 5 AND YOUNGER

BASED ON THE MOST RECENT **NCES** DATA (2019)

**59%**

of children age 5 and younger were in at least one weekly nonparental care arrangement.*

(More than 1 in 2 children)

**41%**

of children age 5 and younger were cared for by a parent in all weekly care arrangements.*

(About 2 in 5 children)

**IMPORTANT NOTE**

The percentages below (center-based care, relative care, nonrelative care, multiple arrangements) are among the 59% of children in nonparental care arrangements.

Some children use more than one arrangement, so categories overlap.

## AMONG CHILDREN IN AT LEAST ONE WEEKLY NONPARENTAL CARE ARRANGEMENT (59% OF CHILDREN)

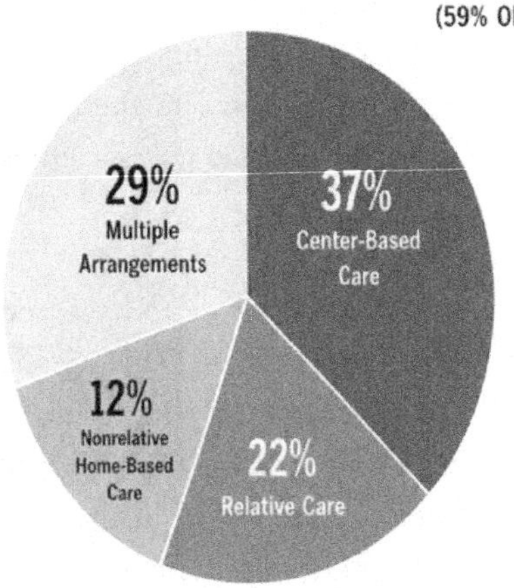


**CENTER-BASED CARE**
(Day care centers, preschools, Head Start, prekindergarten)
62% of children in nonparental care

**RELATIVE CARE**
(Grandparents, siblings, and other relatives)
38% of children in nonparental care

**NONRELATIVE HOME-BASED CARE**
(In-home babysitters, nannies, neighbors, family day care homes)
20% of children in nonparental care

**MULTIPLE ARRANGEMENTS**
(Some children use more than one type of nonparental care)

* *Percentages may not total 100 due to rounding.*

## WHAT THE DATA SHOWS

**PARENTS PROVIDE CARE FOR THE LARGEST SHARE**

About 41% of children are cared for by a parent in all weekly care arrangements.

**CENTER-BASED CARE IS THE MOST COMMON FORM OF NONPARENTAL CARE**

Among children using nonparental care, center-based settings are used more often than relative or nonrelative care.

**FAMILIES USE A MIX OF ARRANGEMENTS**

Many families combine care types to meet their children's needs for cost, schedule, availability, and location.

## SOURCES

National Center for Education Statistics (NCES). *Fast Facts: Child Care Arrangements.* Data from the 2019 National Household Education Surveys Program (NHES).

U.S. Census Bureau. Household Pulse Survey, 2021–2024.

Child Care Aware® of America. *Parents and the High Cost of Child Care*, 2024.

**NOTE:** Children may be in more than one type of arrangement, so percentages overlap.

## The Conundrum

Here lies the true conundrum of childcare. At the exact point in life when adults should be saving the largest amounts of money for retirement—when compound interest has the greatest amount of time to work its magic—is the very same period in which many people are having children. Biology and finance are operating on completely different timelines, and families are caught in the middle trying to satisfy both. The years between roughly ages twenty-five and forty are considered prime wealth-building years, yet they are also the years filled with diapers, daycare, preschool tuition, pediatric copays, summer camps, rising grocery bills, and chronic exhaustion.

The difficult truth is that nearly every childcare option outside of direct parental care is expensive. And even direct parental care can cost one full income as well as many other intangible items. Stepping away from a career often means losing retirement contributions, Social Security credits, promotions, healthcare benefits, and long-term earning power. On the other side sits the dual-income household, where both parents continue working but often at a tremendous cost—emotionally, physically, and financially. The second income can begin to feel partially absorbed by daycare tuition, before-school care, after-school programs, commuting expenses, convenience spending, restaurant meals, and the endless outsourcing required simply to survive the pace of parenting.

What makes this period especially dangerous financially is not merely the expense itself, but the opportunity cost attached to it. A dollar invested at age thirty has decades to compound. A dollar never invested because it was redirected loses not only its original value, but the future growth it could have created. Parents are often not choosing between luxury and discipline. They are choosing between competing necessities while trying to preserve enough energy to make it through the week.

And energy matters more than people admit. Exhausted families spend differently. Fatigue creates convenience spending. Busy parents pay for speed, flexibility, food delivery, subscriptions, easier logistics, and anything that can reduce friction for a household already stretched thin. Childcare itself is not the moral problem. Children are not the problem. The issue is that many families never fully acknowledge the true state of the budget during these years or the long-term financial consequences of operating permanently at the edge of exhaustion.

There also needs to be honesty about what "having it all" often looks like in practice. Two high achieving working parents with young children may appear financially stable from the outside while privately saving very little for retirement after housing, insurance, taxes, and childcare are paid. In some households, retirement contributions shrink year after year because immediate family demands feel more urgent than future financial security. Parents tell themselves they will "catch up later," but later arrives faster than expected. The problem with delaying retirement savings is that compound interest does not generously wait for life to calm down.

This is why families need a realistic framework rather than guilt or perfectionism. Not every household can maximize retirement savings during the childcare years, but every household can remain conscious of the trade-offs being made. Even small, consistent contributions matter. Even maintaining partial retirement contributions matters. Even avoiding unnecessary lifestyle inflation during these years matters. The goal is not to create financially optimized childhoods while emotionally depleted parents collapse under the weight of impossible expectations. The goal is balance—recognizing both the legitimate cost of raising children and the equally legitimate responsibility of protecting your future self from financial instability later in life.

Children eventually grow up. Daycare bills disappear. Summer camps end. Carpools stop. But retirement still arrives. And parents who spent decades investing entirely in everyone else without preserving anything for themselves often discover too late that love alone does not fund aging. Financial responsibility toward children and financial responsibility toward your future are not opposing ideas. They are part of the same long-term family equation.

## The Psychology of Childcare and Guilt

Childcare decisions are rarely just financial decisions. They are emotional decisions wrapped inside financial ones. Parents often carry enormous guilt about absence, work schedules, exhaustion, and the feeling that they are constantly dividing themselves between career responsibilities and family responsibilities. That guilt shapes spending decisions in ways many families do not fully recognize.

Guilt from working long hours may lead to overcompensating and may push families into enrichment programs they cannot comfortably afford. Exhaustion may lead parents toward costly convenience simply because they no longer have the emotional bandwidth to coordinate lower-cost alternatives. None of these decisions are irrational. They are deeply human. But they can create long-term financial pressure while convincing families that the spending is emotionally necessary.

Parenting culture intensifies this pressure by constantly presenting curated images of what "good parenting" supposedly looks like. Parents begin comparing not only themselves, but also their children's experiences. Over time, childcare and summer activities can slowly shift from practical supervision into identity-driven consumption. At the same time, lower-cost childcare solutions often carry emotional discomfort of their own. Parents may feel conflicted relying on grandparents, alternating shifts, or piecing together flexible schedules. Yet many children raised in financially modest but emotionally stable households remember love, consistency, humor, safety, and presence.

There is no universally right answer. Families value different things and operate under different financial realities. Some households prioritize maximizing income and career growth. Others prioritize flexibility, emotional availability, lower stress, or increased time at home during the early childhood years.

# Recommendations

## Cost of Staying Home vs. Continuing to Work

One of the most difficult decisions for young families is whether one parent should remain home with the children or whether both parents should continue working. The calculation is more complicated than simply comparing one salary against daycare costs. Families also need to consider commuting expenses, gas, work clothing, lunches, convenience spending, after-school care, stress-related spending, and the overall exhaustion that often accompanies dual full-time careers with young children.

At the same time, leaving the workforce carries long-term financial consequences that deserve equal attention. A parent stepping away from work may lose retirement contributions, healthcare benefits, career advancement, Social Security earnings, and future salary growth. Reentering the workforce years later can also be financially difficult depending on the profession.

But there are also meaningful gains that are harder to measure financially. A parent at home may reduce household stress, create more flexible routines, lower dependence on convenience spending, simplify scheduling, and increase emotional availability inside the family. Meals may be prepared at home more often. Commuting time disappears. The household may function more calmly and intentionally. Those benefits are intangible, but they are still real. Families should evaluate both the visible financial costs and the less visible emotional and lifestyle effects before deciding what arrangement fits best.

## Ditch the Guilt

Parents should also give themselves permission to let go of the constant guilt surrounding childcare decisions. Modern parenting culture places enormous emotional pressure on families to feel that every choice carries permanent consequences for a child's future. Working parents may feel guilty for spending time away from their children, while stay-at-home parents may feel guilty about lost income, career sacrifices, or financial pressure placed on the household. In reality, most parents are simply doing the best they can with the financial realities, emotional needs, support systems, and opportunities available to them at that stage of life.

Children do not need perfect parents making perfect decisions every day. They need stable, loving, emotionally present adults who are trying to create a healthy family life over time. A parent using daycare is not failing their child. A parent staying home is not wasting their education or ambition. A grandparent helping with childcare is not a sign of weakness. The healthiest childcare decisions are usually the ones made thoughtfully and realistically—not the ones driven by guilt, comparison, or pressure to satisfy outside expectations.

## The Number of Children Changes the Equation

The number of children in a family dramatically changes the childcare calculation. A family with one child may reach a completely different conclusion than a family with four children because childcare costs scale differently than income. For some parents of one child, continuing to work may make clear financial sense because daycare costs remain manageable and the child may benefit from socialization, structure, and interaction with peers.

For larger families, however, childcare expenses can quickly exceed the practical financial benefit of a second income. Multiple daycare enrollments, after-school programs, transportation logistics, and summer care costs may absorb most of one parent's earnings. In those situations, some families conclude that a parent remaining home creates greater long-term stability even if it temporarily reduces household income.

Spacing between children matters as well. Children born closer together may create a shorter but more intense period of high childcare costs, sometimes softened by sibling discounts at daycare centers. Wider spacing can extend the number of years a family remains inside the expensive childcare stage, potentially requiring a much longer interruption to a career or many additional years of dual childcare payments. Families should therefore evaluate childcare decisions not only child by child, but across the full timeline of the family they hope to build.

## Choosing the Childcare That Fits Your Family

Different childcare systems create different types of pressure. Corporate child-care programs and on-site daycare can reduce commuting stress and provide convenience, but they may also increase dependence on remaining employed with a specific company. Grandparents and relatives helping with childcare can dramatically reduce financial strain while strengthening family relationships, although those arrangements sometimes create tension around boundaries, reliability, or parenting differences.

Licensed in-home childcare and family daycare programs may provide a lower-cost and more flexible alternative to larger daycare centers. Smaller environments can feel more personal and emotionally comfortable for some families, particularly for infants or children who struggle in larger groups. Traditional daycare centers remain the most common solution for dual-income households because they provide structure and reliability, but the cost can rival a mortgage payment in many parts of the country, especially for infants or multiple children.

Nannies and au pairs may initially appear extremely expensive, but for larger families they sometimes become financially comparable to daycare while offering greater scheduling flexibility and reducing transportation stress. Families should evaluate not only the direct weekly cost, but also the emotional and logistical effect the arrangement has on the entire household.

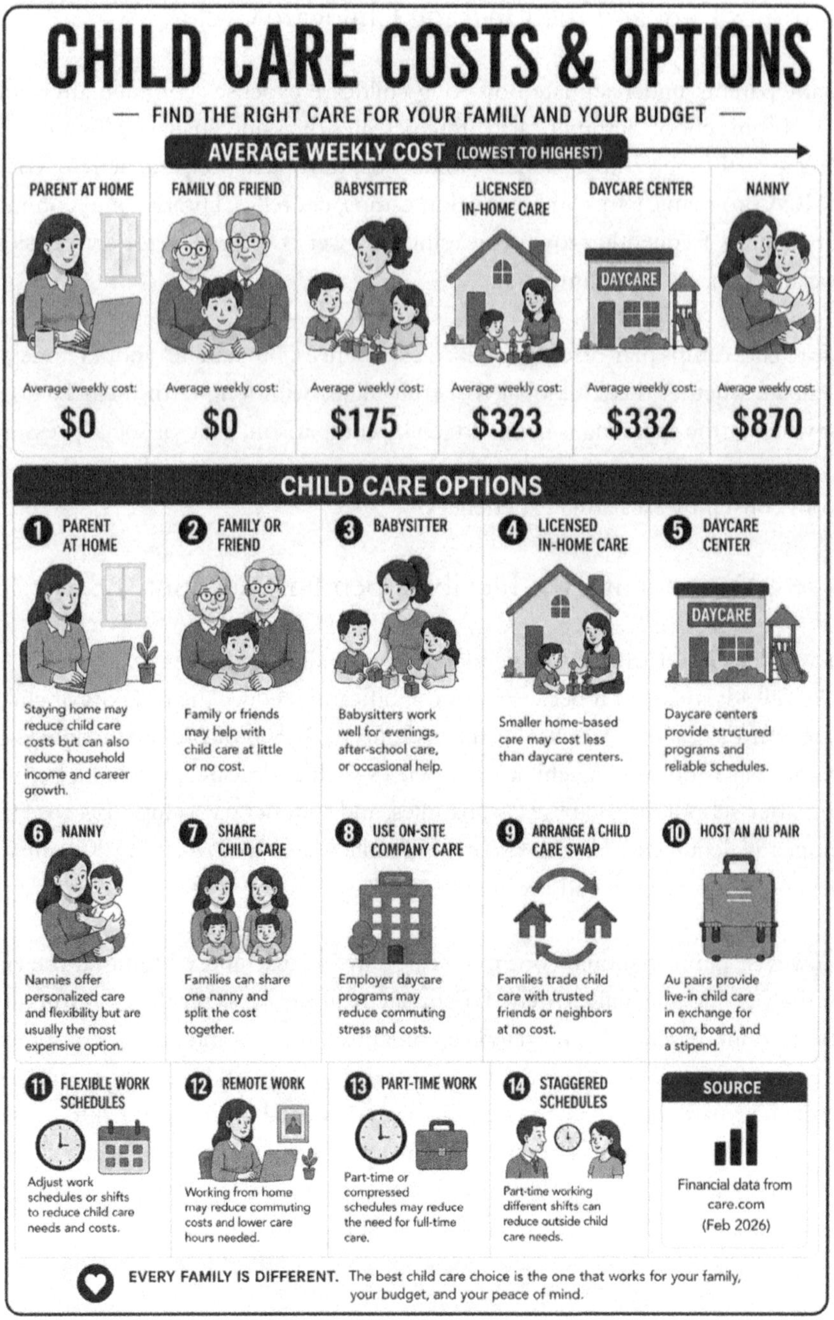
CHILD CARE COSTS & OPTIONS
— FIND THE RIGHT CARE FOR YOUR FAMILY AND YOUR BUDGET —
AVERAGE WEEKLY COST (LOWEST TO HIGHEST)
PARENT AT HOME
Average weekly cost:
$0
FAMILY OR FRIEND
Average weekly cost:
$0
BABYSITTER
Average weekly cost:
$175
LICENSED IN-HOME CARE
Average weekly cost:
$323
DAYCARE CENTER
DAYCARE
Average weekly cost:
$332
NANNY
Average weekly cost:
$870
CHILD CARE OPTIONS
1 PARENT AT HOME
Staying home may reduce child care costs but can also reduce household income and career growth.
2 FAMILY OR FRIEND
Family or friends may help with child care at little or no cost.
3 BABYSITTER
Babysitters work well for evenings, after-school care, or occasional help.
4 LICENSED IN-HOME CARE
Smaller home-based care may cost less than daycare centers.
5 DAYCARE CENTER
DAYCARE
Daycare centers provide structured programs and reliable schedules.
6 NANNY
Nannies offer personalized care and flexibility but are usually the most expensive option.
7 SHARE CHILD CARE
Families can share one nanny and split the cost together.
8 USE ON-SITE COMPANY CARE
Employer daycare programs may reduce commuting stress and costs.
9 ARRANGE A CHILD CARE SWAP
Families trade child care with trusted friends or neighbors at no cost.
10 HOST AN AU PAIR
Au pairs provide live-in child care in exchange for room, board, and a stipend.
11 FLEXIBLE WORK SCHEDULES
Adjust work schedules or shifts to reduce child care needs and costs.
12 REMOTE WORK
Working from home may reduce commuting costs and lower care hours needed.
13 PART-TIME WORK
Part-time or compressed schedules may reduce the need for full-time care.
14 STAGGERED SCHEDULES
Part-time working different shifts can reduce outside child care needs.
SOURCE
Financial data from care.com (Feb 2026)
EVERY FAMILY IS DIFFERENT. The best child care choice is the one that works for your family, your budget, and your peace of mind.

## Summer Care and the Ongoing Childcare Cycle

Many parents underestimate how long childcare expenses continue after children begin school. Summer care often recreates the same financial pressure year after year through camps, supervision needs, transportation, and activity costs. YMCA programs, parks and recreation camps, churches, libraries, and community centers frequently provide meaningful lower-cost options for supervision, socialization, and enrichment.

More elite camps may offer specialized experiences, but families should honestly evaluate whether the additional cost truly aligns with long-term financial goals or whether the spending is being driven by comparison, guilt, or social pressure. Children benefit more from stability, connection, and emotional presence than from constantly escalating experiences.

## Use a Dependent Care Flexible Spending Account (FSA)

If your employer offers a Dependent Care Flexible Spending Account (FSA), take full advantage of it because it can significantly reduce the real cost of childcare. An FSA allows families to set aside up to $7,500 of pre-tax income each year to pay for qualifying childcare expenses such as daycare, preschool, before- and after-school care, babysitters, nannies, and summer day camps. Because the money is deducted before taxes, many families save well over $2,000 annually depending on income and tax bracket.

However, families should contribute carefully because unused funds at the end of the year are generally forfeited. Estimate realistically rather than overfunding the account. Parents also need to keep organized records and submit reimbursement requests properly in order to receive the tax benefit. One important detail many new parents overlook is that the birth of a child qualifies as a "life-changing event," which means parents do not need to wait for annual open enrollment to sign up. In most cases, families only have thirty days after the baby's birth to enroll or adjust contributions, so planning ahead matters.

## Check Whether You Qualify for the Earned Income Tax Credit (EITC)

Many low- to moderate-income working families fail to claim the Earned Income Tax Credit simply because they do not realize they qualify. The EITC is designed to help working households with children by reducing taxes owed and, in many cases, providing a substantial refund. Depending on income level, filing status, and number of children, the credit can range from several hundred dollars to several thousand dollars annually.

For families already struggling with childcare expenses, housing costs, transportation, and rising living expenses, this credit can provide meaningful financial relief. Parents should review eligibility requirements directly through the IRS website or speak with a tax professional to determine whether they qualify.

## Maximize the Child and Dependent Care Tax Credit

Families who pay for childcare so parents can work or attend school should also understand the Child and Dependent Care Tax Credit. This credit allows parents to apply a portion of qualifying childcare expenses toward reducing taxes owed. Families may generally claim up to $3,000 in childcare expenses per child annually, with a maximum of $6,000 per family. Most households ultimately receive approximately 20% of those expenses back as tax savings, which can equal up to $600 for one child or $1,200 for two or more children.

Parents should also understand how this credit interacts with a Dependent Care FSA because the two systems overlap. Families may use both, but FSA contributions reduce the amount of expenses eligible for the tax credit. For example, if parents already used $5,000 through an FSA, only the remaining eligible childcare expenses may be applied toward the Child and Dependent Care Tax Credit. Understanding how these programs work together helps families maximize savings instead of unintentionally leaving money behind.

## Keep a Financial Plan for Retirement

The goal is building a childcare system that is financially sustainable while still maintaining some sort of financial plan for retirement. Do not abandon your retirement plan even if the monthly amounts are small. Consistency counts.

# CHAPTER 4

# TOY *Pendulum*

*You can indulge your child without overindulging them.*

— JEAN ILLSLEY CLARKE

Jim Miller found out the hard way that toys don't just cost money—they multiply, spread, and somehow end up exactly where your foot lands at the worst possible moment. In the middle of the night, Jim was walking barefoot through the house, half awake, heading toward the kitchen for water, when his foot came down on a Lego. He froze, balancing on one leg in the dark, whisper-yelling at no one in particular while trying not to wake the entire house. There are very few moments in parenting that clarify your financial decisions more than stepping on a Lego at 2:00 a.m.

By morning, Jim had reached a small conclusion: there were too many toys in the house. Not a few too many, not slightly over what made sense, but bins, baskets, and piles of toys in multiple rooms that weren't even being used. They were opened, scattered, and abandoned like a system that had lost its purpose somewhere along the way. Most of them had been played with once, maybe twice, before something else took their place. The issue wasn't access—it was excess.

Christmas had just passed, and like most families, they had done what felt reasonable at the time. Jim and his wife Carrie had four kids, and Carrie had set a budget—$500 per child. On paper, it sounded controlled, organized, even responsible. It was also $2,000 spent in a single day, but that part didn't feel as significant when it was divided across four children and wrapped in excitement. That's how spending hides—by feeling smaller than it actually is.

Carrie had a reason for how she approached holidays, and it didn't come from nowhere. Her childhood had been defined by lack, where gifts came from donation drives and were appreciated but not chosen. She didn't remember specific toys as much as she remembered the feeling of not getting what she had hoped for. That feeling didn't disappear as she got older—it shifted direction. And like most unresolved experiences, it showed up in how she parented. The pendulum didn't stop in the middle. It swung all the way to the other side. Her kids would not feel that.

Christmas became something else. Not just a holiday, but a production built around making sure no one felt the absence she once did. There were stacks of gifts under the tree, each child with ten or more presents. Boxes filled the room in a way that looked generous and, for a moment, felt exactly like what Carrie had always imagined it should be. But something else happened during that moment. The pace of the opening of gifts.

Rip. Open. Look. Drop. Repeat.

Each gift lasted a few seconds before the next one replaced it. Every once in a while, something landed—a real reaction, a pause, a moment of excitement—but it didn't hold. It couldn't. There were too many things competing for attention, and attention doesn't expand just because volume increases.

Jim sat there watching it and thought that the amount of effort and money didn't match the experience. 'Why didn't we just get that one thing?'

The cycle didn't stop at Christmas. Two of their children had birthdays within two weeks of the holiday—one just before, one just after. That meant the system didn't reset. What felt like separate events were actually connected, even if no one treated them that way.

At first, birthdays were simple. A few friends, a cake, something manageable that didn't require planning beyond a grocery store trip. But simple doesn't stay simple without intention. Three friends became five, five became ten, and eventually it became a venue. A trampoline park, a water park, a roller rink—each one adding cost, expectation, and a new baseline. Enough became a moving target.

By the end of the year, the spending didn't feel like one decision. It felt like a series of completely separate, reasonable ones. But they weren't separate. They were connected by repetition, and repetition creates a pattern.

The house reflected it. There were toys everywhere, not because the kids loved them, but because there were too many to engage with. They would dump bins out, spread everything across the floor, and then—almost immediately—walk away. Not to play, but to screens. TV, video games, tablets, and kids' iPads that held attention longer than any toy ever could. That was the shift Jim couldn't ignore. The toys weren't solving boredom. They were being replaced.

At first, it seemed like a separate issue—screen time versus toys—but it wasn't. It was part of the same system. When everything is available, nothing has to be worked for, and when nothing has to be worked for, attention shifts to whatever is easiest. Screens are easier. They don't require setup, imagination, or cleanup. They respond instantly, adapt constantly, and never lose novelty in the same way physical items do. Compared to that, a pile of toys—even expensive ones—starts to feel like effort. So, the toys stayed on the floor, and the attention moved elsewhere.

This is where the pattern changes meaning. The issue isn't just the cost of toys. It's what they're training. When children receive large quantities consistently, ownership changes. Items become temporary, replaceable, and less connected to effort. It's not that they don't appreciate things—it's that appreciation doesn't have time to develop. There's always something else, something new.

Once that becomes normal, reducing it doesn't feel like returning to a reasonable level. It feels like taking something away. That's where most families get stuck—not in the initial decision, but in maintaining the pattern after it's already been created. This is where financial intelligence shows up. Not in deciding whether to buy a toy, but in recognizing what repeated decisions are building over time. Every purchase reinforces a pattern, and patterns don't stay contained. They expand into expectations, behavior, and eventually identity.

## Psychological Pattern: Compensatory Parenting

Many parents are not just raising children. They are unconsciously trying to heal their own childhoods while doing it. The mother who remembers not receiving the Christmas present that she wanted may overcompensate by ensuring Christmas is an explosion of toys. What begins as protection slowly evolves into identity-based spending. The purchases are no longer about utility. They are about rewriting emotional history through consumption. The parent is attempting to unconsciously repair their own unmet emotional needs through the child's experience. In these moments, the child is not only receiving gifts. The parent is symbolically giving something to their younger self.

This type of spending feels deeply rational to the parent because the pain behind it is real. Childhood shame and disappointment has a long memory, especially when it involved poverty, exclusion, or social humiliation. Parents who experienced scarcity often develop a near-obsessive desire to remove every obstacle from their child's path, including emotional discomfort. Many children who are financially overprotected never learn how to tolerate disappointment, limitations, or delayed gratification because their parents are still trying to rescue themselves emotionally. The parent may believe they are building confidence while accidentally teaching dependence on material comfort.

Consumer culture exploits this vulnerability. Advertisements are filled with subtle emotional messages suggesting that loving parents provide more, spend more, and upgrade more. Entire industries exist to monetize parental insecurity by framing ordinary childhood experiences as emotionally insufficient unless enhanced with expensive products and curated experiences. Parents then begin measuring success by their child's visible comfort rather than their child's emotional strength or adaptability. The irony is painful. The same parent who desperately wanted their child to avoid insecurity may accidentally create a child who becomes emotionally fragile whenever comfort disappears. Sometimes we are not buying for our children at all. Sometimes we are buying relief for the child we used to be. Parents trapped in corrective parenting patterns should pause and ask themselves an uncomfortable question:

**Am I protecting my child, or am I protecting myself from reliving old pain?**

That distinction matters enormously. Shielding children from every discomfort may temporarily soothe the parent emotionally, but it can unintentionally weaken the child's resilience and perspective. Children do not need manufactured hardship, but they do need opportunities to develop adaptability, patience, gratitude, and emotional endurance. Constantly overcompensating financially may accidentally teach children that discomfort is unacceptable and that identity must always be protected through consumption.

A healthier approach is helping children understand family values without transferring old shame onto them. Parents can openly discuss budgeting, priorities, tradeoffs, and intentional spending in ways that feel empowering rather than fearful. A child who occasionally hears "we're choosing not to spend money on that right now" is not being emotionally damaged. In many cases, they are learning emotional flexibility and patience. Parents who grew up with scarcity can break unhealthy cycles without creating new ones rooted in excess. Healing childhood wounds should happen through emotional growth and self-awareness, not through overspending on your children.

## The Quick Math

With four children, Jim and Melissa simply wanted birthdays and holidays to feel special. Each year, they spent approximately $500 per child on Christmas gifts, totaling $2,000, and another $500 per child on birthday gifts and celebrations, adding an additional $2,000. Combined, their annual spending on toys, gifts, and celebrations reached about $4,000. The financial impact becomes more apparent when examined over time. If that same $4,000 had been invested each year and earned an average annual return of 7%, it would have grown to approximately $164,424 after 20 years. This example is not intended to suggest that families should eliminate birthdays, holidays, or cherished traditions. Rather, it illustrates the opportunity cost of recurring expenses that often feel too small to matter.

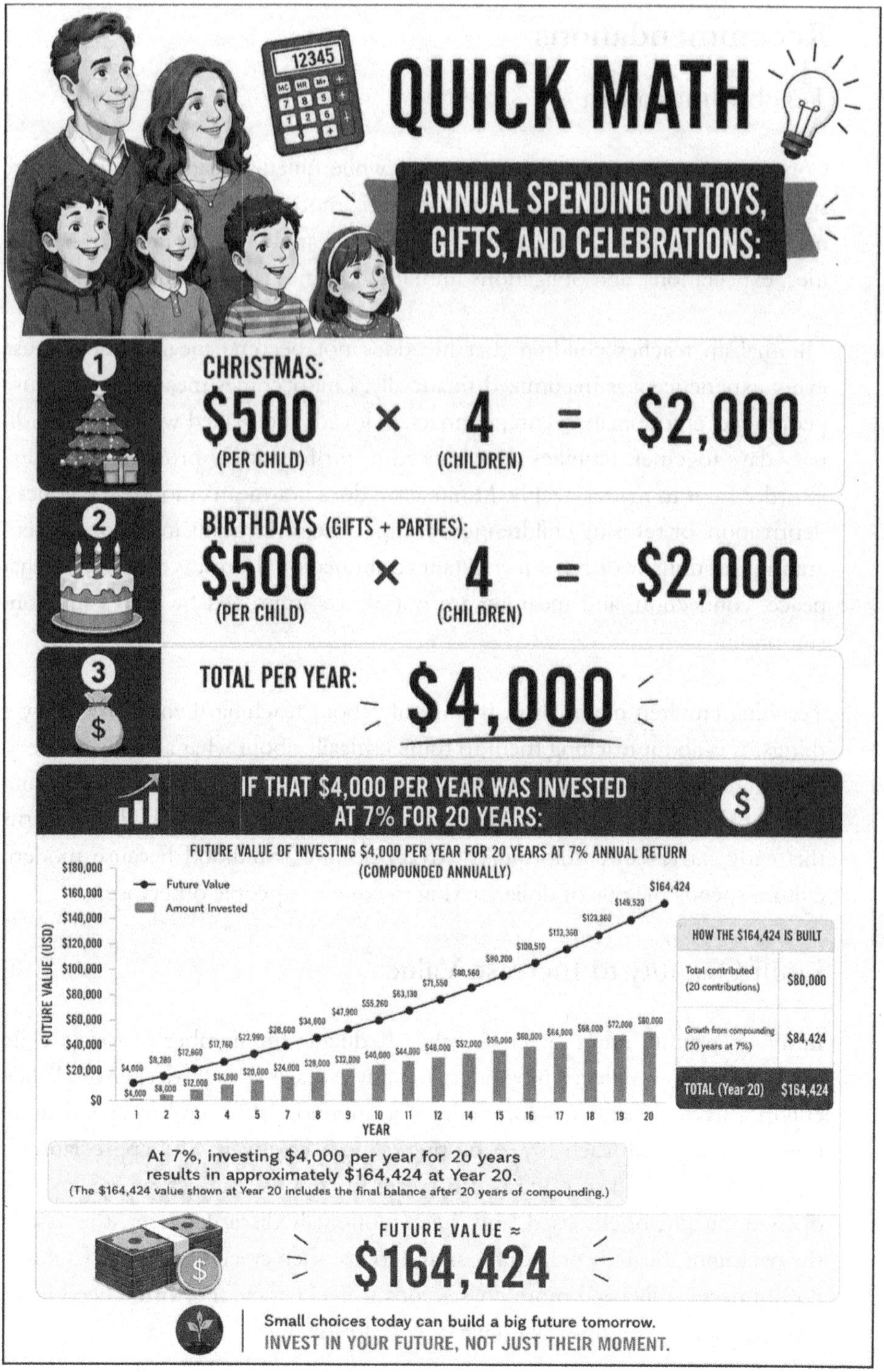

12345
QUICK MATH
ANNUAL SPENDING ON TOYS, GIFTS, AND CELEBRATIONS:
1
CHRISTMAS:
$500 (PER CHILD) × 4 (CHILDREN) = $2,000
2
BIRTHDAYS (GIFTS + PARTIES):
$500 (PER CHILD) × 4 (CHILDREN) = $2,000
3
TOTAL PER YEAR: $4,000
IF THAT $4,000 PER YEAR WAS INVESTED AT 7% FOR 20 YEARS:
FUTURE VALUE OF INVESTING $4,000 PER YEAR FOR 20 YEARS AT 7% ANNUAL RETURN (COMPOUNDED ANNUALLY)
Future Value
Amount Invested
FUTURE VALUE (USD)
$180,000
$160,000
$140,000
$120,000
$100,000
$80,000
$60,000
$40,000
$20,000
$0
$4,000 $8,280 $12,860 $17,760 $22,990 $28,600 $34,600 $47,900 $55,260 $63,130 $71,550 $80,560 $90,200 $100,510 $112,360 $123,360 $149,520 $164,424
$4,000 $8,000 $12,000 $16,000 $20,000 $24,000 $28,000 $32,000 $40,000 $44,000 $48,000 $52,000 $56,000 $60,000 $64,000 $68,000 $72,000 $80,000
1 2 3 4 5 7 8 9 10 11 12 14 15 16 17 18 19 20
YEAR
HOW THE $164,424 IS BUILT
Total contributed (20 contributions) $80,000
Growth from compounding (20 years at 7%) $84,424
TOTAL (Year 20) $164,424
At 7%, investing $4,000 per year for 20 years results in approximately $164,424 at Year 20.
(The $164,424 value shown at Year 20 includes the final balance after 20 years of compounding.)
FUTURE VALUE ≈ $164,424
Small choices today can build a big future tomorrow.
INVEST IN YOUR FUTURE, NOT JUST THEIR MOMENT.

# Recommendations

## Teach Minimalism

Consumerism often promises happiness while quietly creating anxiety. More spending frequently produces more pressure, more comparison, more maintenance, more financial stress, and less freedom. Families accumulate toys, activities, expectations, and obligations until life becomes emotionally crowded.

Minimalism teaches children that life does not become meaningful because every experience was maximized financially. Life becomes meaningful because people feel emotionally secure, connected, loved, and valued while living ordinary days together. Families do not need to professionally produce childhood in order for it to matter deeply. Minimalism does not mean emotional coldness, deprivation, or refusing children joyful experiences. It means intentionally separating emotional worth from constant accumulation. It means recognizing that peace, connection, and meaning are not always improved by increasing consumption.

Teaching children minimalism is not only about teaching them to own fewer things. It is about teaching them to think critically about what actually creates a meaningful life. It is about helping them recognize that identity, confidence, and emotional worth are not dependent on constant acquisition. A child who learns this early carries an extraordinary advantage into adulthood because modern culture spends billions of dollars trying to convince people otherwise.

## Limit Quantity to Increase Value

Limiting quantity often increases value. Reducing the number of toys a child receives does not reduce enjoyment; in many cases, it actually deepens it. When children have fewer items competing for attention, they tend to spend more time engaging with each toy, exploring it more creatively, and appreciating it longer. An overload of options can create the opposite effect, where toys are opened quickly, briefly used, and then emotionally discarded almost as fast as the packaging. Scarcity creates focus and focus often creates gratitude. Children do not necessarily need more possessions to feel happy; they often need more time and space to connect with what they already have.

## Set Both a Budget and a Gift Limit

Setting both a budget and a cap on the number of gifts helps prevent excess from becoming normalized. A financial limit alone still allows overconsumption if the spending is spread across too many inexpensive items. Five or six smaller purchases can create the same clutter and overstimulation as one large purchase. A fixed number of gifts forces prioritization and encourages parents to think more intentionally about what is truly meaningful, useful, or memorable. Over time, children begin to associate celebrations less with volume and more with thoughtfulness, tradition, and connection.

## Control Escalation Early

Escalation needs to be controlled early because birthdays and holidays naturally expand unless someone intentionally contains them. What begins as a few gifts at age three can evolve into overflowing Christmas mornings, expensive themed birthdays, and an unspoken expectation that every year must become larger than the last. Parents often increase spending not because children genuinely need more, but because they fear disappointing them or losing the excitement associated with special occasions. The problem is that when excess becomes the baseline, normal generosity can begin to feel insufficient. Setting reasonable expectations early prevents families from entering an expensive cycle where spending must continually increase simply to maintain the same emotional response.

## Separate Toys from Screen Dependency

If children consistently abandon toys in favor of tablets, phones, gaming systems, or streaming content, the solution is rarely purchasing more toys. In many households, screens have changed children's attention spans and altered how they experience stimulation, novelty, and boredom. Parents may incorrectly assume the child simply "needs something new," when in reality the issue is often overstimulation from digital entertainment. Limiting screen access can restore creativity, independent play, and engagement with existing toys and also reduce unnecessary spending.

## Use Rotation Instead of Accumulation

Rotation is often more effective than accumulation. Children do not need access to every toy they own at all times for those items to remain enjoyable. Rotating toys in and out of storage makes older items feel fresh again and reduces the visual chaos that can overwhelm both children and parents. A simpler environment often increases actual play because children can focus without being surrounded by endless options. Rotation also allows families to recognize which toys are genuinely valued and which are simply taking up space. Instead of continually adding more, families can maximize the usefulness of what they already own.

## Recognize the Pendulum

Parents must recognize the pendulum effect that often drives overspending. Adults who grew up with financial hardship, limited toys, or feelings of deprivation may overcorrect with their own children. The goal should not be to recreate scarcity, but to avoid swinging so far in the opposite direction that children lose perspective on value, patience, and appreciation. Awareness matters because it allows parents to respond thoughtfully instead of emotionally reacting to their own childhood experiences.

Toys don't become expensive because of one holiday.

They become expensive because of repetition. And repetition, left unchecked, turns generosity into expectation—and turns expectation into entitlement that lasts far longer than the toys themselves.

# CHAPTER 5

# CLOTHING, CULTURE AND *Cost*

*Money looks better in the bank than on your feet.*

– SOPHIA AMORUSO

In the Carter household, clothing was never just clothing. It carried meaning in a way that went beyond price or practicality, shaping how people were perceived and where they felt they fit. What someone wore signaled awareness, identity, and whether they understood the environment around them. It wasn't always spoken out loud, but it was always understood.

For Naomi, the pressure came from fear that her children might feel excluded socially if they looked disconnected from the culture around them. For David, it came from something slightly different. David had grown up comfortably middle class, not poor, but in an environment where presentation mattered professionally and socially. He had learned early that people made assumptions quickly based on appearance, confidence, and whether someone seemed culturally aware. In college and later in business, he watched certain people move through rooms more easily because they understood the signals. David didn't obsess over labels personally, but he believed looking sharp communicated competence, belonging, and confidence. To him, it wasn't vanity. It was social fluency.

For their son, Justin, it showed up in sneakers. Justin Carter didn't casually like shoes—he built a collection. His closet had been turned into a wall of shoe boxes stacked from floor to ceiling, each pair placed carefully inside like something meant to be preserved rather than worn. He had over one hundred pairs, and he could tell you the story behind almost all of them, including release dates, collaborations, limited drops, and resale values. To an outsider, it looked excessive. To Justin, it was organized.

In his world, sneakers weren't just something you wore—they were something you understood. They represented music, sports, identity, and status all at once, which made every purchase feel less optional and more necessary. David understood that part more than he admitted out loud. He saw sneakers as a modern version of the same social coding he had experienced professionally for years. There were people who "got it" and people who didn't, and David feared what happened socially when children landed in the second category.

When Justin asked for sneakers, he didn't ask generally. He asked for exact models, specific colorways, and releases that required timing, raffles, or resale purchases that made the original price feel like a suggestion. The language around it always sounded the same. "Mom, these are limited."

That phrase came up often, and it always carried urgency. If you didn't buy them now, they were gone—or worse, they would still be available later at a price that made you wish they weren't. David often found himself helping justify the purchases because he understood the emotional logic underneath them. He told himself sneakers were part hobby, part culture, part self-expression. He also believed confidence mattered socially for boys, and if the right shoes helped Justin feel more secure socially, then maybe the expense was worth it.

Some pairs were a couple hundred dollars. Others climbed into the high hundreds, and a few pushed past a thousand. Each time, the decision felt isolated, manageable, and easy to justify in the moment. It's just one pair. That's how the pattern stays hidden.

But Justin wasn't the only one shaping spending in the household. His younger sister, Grace, had her own version of the same pattern, and it didn't look like a collection. It looked like experiences.

At first, it showed up in Halloween, and it didn't seem like a big deal. When Grace decided she wanted to be Dorothy from The Wizard of Oz, the request didn't feel excessive—it felt specific. She didn't want a version of the costume; she wanted the costume, where the dress matched, the shoes were the right shade of red sequins, and the details mattered in a way that made it feel less like dressing up and more like casting for a role.

That attention to detail didn't stay contained to her. If Grace was Dorothy, then the rest of the family started to fall into place around her, with her mom as the Good Witch, her dad as the Wizard, and Justin—who had not planned on participating at this level—as the Tin Man. Not by choice.

What used to be a simple costume became something coordinated, then something planned, and eventually something expected. There were photos, adjustments, last-minute additions, and more money spent than anyone had originally intended. David actually enjoyed parts of it because he liked seeing his family socially connected and admired. The compliments from neighbors, photos online, and reactions from friends reinforced something emotionally satisfying. The family looked close, current, involved, and successful in a way that felt rewarding without anyone directly saying so. It wasn't one decision—it was a series of small ones layered together until the final result felt complete.

The next year didn't reset back to simple. It started where the last one ended, with costumes that were more detailed, more put together, and, without anyone saying it out loud, more expensive. That's how these patterns establish themselves—not through one big change, but through small upgrades that carry forward.

By middle school, the pattern evolved into something more social. Grace and her best friend began dressing as what they called "twins." They weren't identical in a literal sense, but their outfits were intentionally coordinated. Colors, styles, and even the timing of what they wore were carefully planned so they appeared connected and unified. Their friendship extended beyond clothing. The girls purchased matching "best friends" heart necklaces, each wearing one half of the heart around her neck as a visible symbol of their bond. What began as a simple friendship gradually became another avenue for spending, as maintaining the connection increasingly involved coordinated purchases, accessories, and shared experiences.

That shift changed the frequency of spending. Clothing was no longer tied only to events or seasons—it became part of everyday interaction. If one of them bought something, the other often needed something to match or complement it, and the cycle repeated more often than anyone realized. Naomi saw the social pressure immediately, but David noticed something else. He saw how quickly children formed impressions based on appearance and presentation, and he worried that being disconnected from those social rhythms could isolate Grace socially. He believed confidence was partly built through feeling comfortable in your environment, and looking noticeably out of place felt risky to him.

By high school, the system was fully built, and events like homecoming and prom made it visible in a different way. These weren't single-night decisions—they were multi-step processes that started weeks in advance. Grace didn't just need a dress; she needed the right dress, which is a category that tends to expand the longer you look at it.

That led to shoes, then jewelry, then hair and nail appointments, then makeup, then photos. Each step made the next one feel necessary, and by the time everything was in place, the event itself felt like the shortest part of the process. What mattered wasn't just attending—it was presenting. Because at that point, it wasn't just about being there. It was about how you showed up.

This is where clothing stops being a category and becomes a system. Justin's sneakers followed release cycles, and Grace's events followed social cycles, both of which created movement that never really stopped. Trends shifted, expectations moved, and the spending followed both without ever fully resetting. Nothing felt excessive in isolation.

A pair of shoes.

A costume.

A dress.

Each decision made sense on its own, which is exactly why the total remained invisible. Over time, those decisions layered into a pattern that felt normal, even as it continued to grow. Clothing is harder to control than most categories because it is visible. It shows up immediately in how someone is perceived, and that changes how decisions are made. You don't compare electricity bills. You compare outfits.

Justin's collection created a baseline that needed to be maintained. Once he had a certain number of shoes, keeping that level became expected, not because anyone formally agreed to it, but because it had already been demonstrated. Grace's events followed the same pattern, where each experience built on the last and raised expectations. That's how expectations work. They don't go down on their own.

And once those expectations are in place, decisions become reactive. The question shifts from what makes sense to what is needed to keep up, and that shift is where spending accelerates without anyone fully noticing.

## Psychological Pattern: Social Comparison Drift

Most parents do not wake up one morning intending to overspend on their children. The shift usually happens gradually through repeated exposure to higher spending norms. A child attends a birthday party with luxury gift bags and suddenly simple celebrations feel inadequate. A mother buys expensive sneakers because her son says everyone else has them. A father agrees to elite sports fees because all of his daughter's friends are participating. Parents stretch budgets for phones, prom dresses, senior trips, and birthday parties because they fear what happens socially when their child becomes visibly excluded from the group. The emotional goal is rarely status alone. More often, parents are trying to protect their children from feeling embarrassed, isolated, or different.

This process becomes dangerous because it rarely feels dramatic in real time. Each individual expense appears manageable when viewed alone. The problem is cumulative normalization. Luxury slowly stops looking excessive once everyone nearby participates in it. An $800 prom budget feels outrageous until another parent casually mentions spending twice that amount on dresses, makeup, transportation, and after-party reservations. Parents begin adjusting their own expectations upward without fully realizing it. Budgets rarely explode overnight. They drift through repeated comparison and gradual emotional adaptation.

What makes this emotionally powerful is that many adults still remember their own childhood experiences of feeling financially different. They remember wearing the wrong clothes, missing activities, or feeling embarrassed when they could not participate socially at the same level as peers. Those memories often remain active beneath the surface long into adulthood. When their own children begin approaching similar social situations, the emotional response becomes immediate and protective. Spending money can begin to feel less like indulgence and more like emotional shielding. Parents are not always buying products. Sometimes they are buying temporary relief from the fear that their child might not fit in socially.

Modern culture intensifies this comparison cycle because social media constantly magnifies visible abundance. Parents are no longer comparing themselves only to neighbors or close friends. They are comparing themselves to curated versions of affluent families across entire platforms designed to showcase luxury, convenience, and excess. Ordinary childhood experiences begin to feel insufficient when measured against influencer-style vacations, elaborate birthday installations, designer clothing hauls, skincare routines, and holiday traditions presented as everyday life. Luxury becomes invisible once an entire social circle treats it as standard. The result is financial inflation driven less by survival and more by normalization.

Another hidden danger is that children themselves begin recalibrating what feels "basic." What once felt exciting eventually becomes expected. The first expensive pair of shoes creates excitement. The fifth pair creates a standard. Over time, families can unintentionally train children to associate confidence, belonging, celebration, or self-worth with increasingly expensive purchases. Satisfaction becomes shorter while expectations become larger. Comparison culture moves the emotional finish line farther away every year.

This comparison drift also changes how parents perceive their own financial reality. A family earning a healthy income can suddenly feel financially behind simply because they are surrounded by higher visible spending. Parents start questioning perfectly reasonable decisions. A practical family vacation starts to feel inadequate compared to luxury travel posts online. A reliable first car begins to feel embarrassing compared to classmates driving newer vehicles. Financial anxiety is often fueled not by actual need, but by proximity to visible excess. Humans naturally adapt to the environment around them, which means social circles can dramatically influence spending behavior without families fully noticing the shift.

Many parents also underestimate how quickly comparison culture steals gratitude from both adults and children. A child who constantly consumes images of upgraded lifestyles can lose perspective on what they already have. Instead of excitement over a family beach trip to Florida, attention shifts toward why it was not in Bali. Instead of appreciating a birthday celebration, focus moves toward decorations, gifts, or experiences someone else posted online. Comparison turns abundance into insufficiency remarkably fast because the standard never stops moving. There will always be someone with newer shoes, larger homes, more expensive vacations, or greater access. When identity and belonging become too dependent on external standards, financial pressure becomes endless.

Parents caught in this cycle need to understand that "normal" is often socially manufactured rather than objectively reasonable. Many families participating in expensive lifestyles are also stressed, carrying debt, overextended, or anxious about money behind the scenes. Public appearances rarely reveal private financial reality. One of the healthiest things parents can do is intentionally define family values before outside culture defines them instead. Children benefit enormously from hearing phrases like, "That may work for another family, but it is not a priority for us." Parents who become confident in their own standards are far less vulnerable to lifestyle inflation and comparison-driven spending.

Resisting every social trend does not automatically create isolated children. In many cases, it creates emotionally adaptable children. Children benefit from learning that confidence is not dependent on owning the newest item or participating in every expensive activity. Some discomfort, comparison, and insecurity are normal parts of growing up. A child who occasionally hears "no" without shame often develops stronger internal stability than a child whose environment is constantly adjusted to avoid discomfort. Emotional resilience, humor, kindness, and self-worth ultimately matter far more than perfectly synchronized trend participation.

Financial discipline inside a family also creates something children rarely appreciate until adulthood: freedom. Families that avoid comparison-driven overspending often experience lower stress, fewer financial arguments, more flexibility during emergencies, and greater long-term stability. Children may not fully understand modest decisions in the moment, but many recognize later why their parents protected the family's future instead of chasing every social expectation around them. Sometimes the greatest gift parents can provide is not a lifestyle designed to impress other people. Sometimes it is the stability that comes from living below the pressure of constant comparison.

# The Quick Math

Justin loved collecting sneakers and received about ten pairs annually at an average cost of $400 per pair, bringing his yearly total to approximately $4,000. Grace's clothing expenses, including seasonal wardrobes, accessories, homecoming attire, and other special events, averaged another $2,000 per year. Together, the family's clothing-related spending reached roughly $6,000 annually.

While these purchases may have seemed reasonable when viewed individually, the long-term financial impact tells a different story. If the same $6,000 per year had been invested for six years and then left to grow at an average annual return of 7%, it would have accumulated to approximately $152,268 after 20 years. Of that total, only $36,000 would represent the family's direct spending, while more than $116,000 would come from the power of compound growth. This example is not meant to suggest that children should never receive new clothes, special outfits, or the occasional pair of coveted sneakers. Rather, it demonstrates how recurring lifestyle expenses often become invisible because they are spread across months and years.

# QUICK MATH

## 1 JUSTIN – SNEAKER PURCHASES

About 10 pairs per year

$400 per pair

ANNUAL TOTAL

**$4,000**

+

## 2 GRACE – CLOTHING & EVENTS

- Homecoming, formal events
- Seasonal clothing & accessories
- Approximately $2,000 per year

ANNUAL TOTAL

**$2,000**

**COMBINED HOUSEHOLD CLOTHING-RELATED SPENDING**

AROUND

**$6,000**

ANNUALLY

FOR 6 YEARS = $36,000

Over time, that number becomes more meaningful when viewed as a consistent pattern instead of isolated decisions. If $6,000 per year were redirected into retirement and invested annually at a 7% return over 20 years, the long-term impact becomes clear:

**FUTURE VALUE OF INVESTING $6,000 PER YEAR AT 7% ANNUAL RETURN (COMPOUNDED ANNUALLY)**

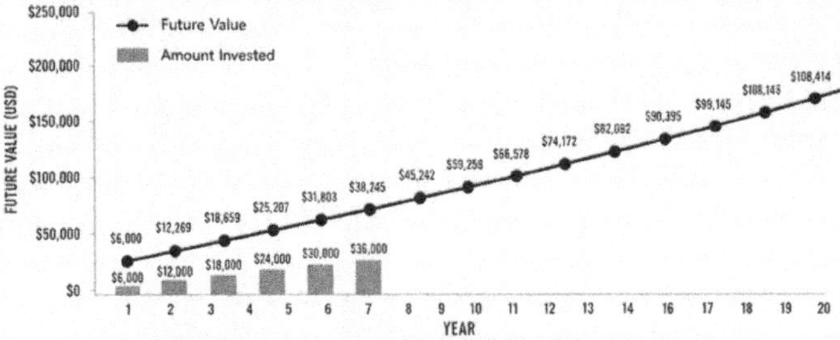


| HOW THE $152,268 IS BUILT | |
|---|---|
| Total contributed (6 contributions) | $36,000 |
| Growth from compounding interest at 7% | $116,268 |
| TOTAL (Year 20) | $152,268 |

At 7%, investing $6,000 per year for 6 years and then letting it grow for 14 more years results in approximately $152,268 at Year 20.
(The $152,268 value shown at Year 20 includes the final balance after 20 years of compuunding.)

FUTURE VALUE ≈

**$152,268+**

in retirement savings from a category that is often overlooked in long-term planning.

# Recommendations

## Set a Yearly Clothing Budget and Stick to It

Instead of responding emotionally to every shopping request, families benefit from establishing a total yearly clothing budget for each child. A structured annual amount creates boundaries and forces prioritization rather than allowing spending to be driven by trends, peer pressure, advertising, or emotional impulse. Without a framework, clothing purchases often happen in small increments that feel harmless individually but become significant when added together over the course of a year. A quick trip to the mall, one pair of limited-edition sneakers, a last-minute online order for a school event, or a seasonal wardrobe refresh can compound into thousands of dollars in annual spending.

A yearly budget also teaches children an important financial principle: resources are finite. When children understand there is a fixed amount available, they begin learning how to make choices, delay purchases, and determine what matters most to them. This creates financial awareness without requiring constant lectures about money. The goal is not deprivation, but intentionality. Families who create structure around spending often experience less financial stress because decisions become guided by a plan rather than emotion.

## Limit Event Escalation Early

Halloween, school dances, themed birthday parties, graduations, prom, homecoming, and other milestone events naturally become more expensive over time unless boundaries are intentionally established. Many parents do not consciously decide to escalate spending; it simply happens gradually through comparison and repetition. The problem is that children quickly adapt to whatever becomes normal inside the household. If every event becomes bigger, more elaborate, or more expensive than the last, families unintentionally create an emotional expectation that celebration must always equal consumption. Keeping events relatively consistent helps prevent the cycle where parents feel pressured to outdo previous years simply to maintain excitement. Often, children remember the experience, the laughter, and the people involved far longer than the amount of money spent.

## Introduce Delay on High-Cost Items

For expensive sneakers, designer clothing, luxury accessories, or trend-driven purchases, implementing a waiting period before buying can dramatically reduce impulsive spending. Many high-cost purchases feel emotionally urgent in the moment because they are tied to status, trends, peer approval, or fear of missing out. A child may feel convinced they "need" a particular item immediately, especially when social media and peer culture amplify the pressure to keep up.

However, time has a way of separating emotional impulse from genuine value. If the item still feels important after several weeks or even a month, it is more likely to hold lasting meaning rather than simply satisfying temporary excitement. Introducing delay also teaches emotional regulation and patience—two skills increasingly weakened by instant online shopping and constant digital advertising. Children who learn to pause before purchasing often become adults who think more carefully about money, debt, and long-term financial goals.

## Use Resale and Secondhand Options

Clothing, especially event-based clothing, is one of the easiest categories in which families can dramatically reduce spending without significantly reducing quality or participation. Formal dresses, sports gear, costumes, winter coats, and trendy items are often worn only a handful of times before being outgrown or forgotten. Purchasing secondhand items or reselling gently used clothing afterward allows families to participate fully in experiences while avoiding the financial waste associated with one-time purchases.

There is also a psychological benefit to normalizing resale culture inside the family. Children begin learning that value is not determined solely by whether something is brand new. In many cases, secondhand purchases are financially smarter, environmentally responsible, and nearly indistinguishable from new items. Resale platforms, consignment shops, community groups, and online marketplaces have made high-quality used clothing far more accessible than in previous generations. Smart financial choices do not reduce dignity or enjoyment; they increase long-term flexibility.

## Normalize Repeating Outfits and Reusing Items

Not every event requires an entirely new outfit. Somewhere along the way, many families absorbed the idea that children should appear in different clothing for every holiday, school function, social event, photograph, or online post. Social media has intensified this pressure by turning ordinary moments into curated visual presentations. Parents often feel judged not only on how their children behave, but on how they are dressed.

Normalizing repeated outfits helps reset expectations and reduces the pressure to continuously upgrade wardrobes. Adults repeat clothing constantly, yet children are often taught the opposite standard from an early age. Reusing dresses, shoes, jackets, accessories, and formalwear teaches practicality and reduces unnecessary consumption. More importantly, it shifts attention away from appearance as the central measure of value. Children do not lose confidence because they repeated a sweater or pair of shoes; they often lose perspective when every event becomes tied to acquiring something new.

## Tie Spending Decisions to Retirement Outcomes

One of the most powerful financial lessons parents can teach is that every spending decision involves a trade-off. Money spent in one area is money unavailable for another purpose, including retirement security, emergency savings, future flexibility, or debt reduction. Helping children understand this connection builds financial awareness without requiring fear or guilt. It reframes purchases not simply as "Can we afford this today?" but also as "What are we giving up later?"

This perspective becomes especially important in households where repeated lifestyle spending erodes long-term financial stability. A pair of sneakers, a designer handbag, or a lavish prom experience may seem isolated in the moment, but repeated over years, those purchases can delay retirement contributions and reduce compound growth significantly. Children who understand these trade-offs early are more likely to become adults capable of balancing enjoyment with long-term planning. Financial intelligence is not about eliminating pleasure; it is about recognizing the long-term impact of repeated short-term decisions. Clothing doesn't become expensive because people like nice things. It becomes expensive because expectations rise. And once they do, they rarely come down.

# CHAPTER 6

# THE SUBSCRIPTION *Childhood*

*Children spell love...*
*T-I-M-E."*

— DR. ANTHONY P. WITHAM

Lisa Reynolds is divorced with two children—a 14-year-old daughter named Ava and a 16-year-old son named Ethan. They live what most people would consider a fairly normal suburban life. Nothing extravagant, nothing extreme, just a working mother trying to balance career demands, parenting, schedules, technology, and the steady stream of expenses that now arrive one subscription at a time.

Lisa is a hospital manager whose days rarely end when her shift technically does. Her ex-husband and co-parent, Mitch, works as a sales executive in technology, a career filled with airport delays, client dinners, and business trips that regularly interfere with scheduled visitation time. Neither of them imagined parenting would eventually feel so logistical, so dependent on calendars, pickups, work calls, and constant adjustments. They both worked hard for the careers they built, and neither wants to walk away from the financial stability, professional identity, and opportunities they spent years trying to reach.

Ava and Cameron spend a surprising amount of time managing their own evenings, reheating leftovers, scrolling through screens, and filling the quiet spaces between their parents' arrivals and departures. Some nights Lisa walks through the front door mentally exhausted from managing problems all day only to find the kids already upstairs wearing headphones, half inside their own digital worlds. Other nights Cameron is gaming online while Ava rotates between TikTok, Netflix, and texting friends, the house technically occupied but emotionally quiet. No one would describe the children as neglected. The bills are paid, the pantry is full, and both parents genuinely love them. But there is an emotional gap that families often try to soften with convenience, entertainment, and technology because those things are easier to provide consistently than time, energy, and presence.

So, when the newest gaming system comes out, or a phone upgrade feels unnecessary but exciting, or another streaming subscription promises entertainment, the purchases become easier to justify. Somewhere along the way, technology stopped feeling like a luxury and started feeling like compensation—a way to keep the house occupied, connected, and emotionally smoother when the parents themselves could not always physically be there.

It started, like most things do now, with a phone. Ava had been asking for a new iPhone for months, and for her birthday she finally got it. Not because she needed it, but because "needed" stopped being the standard a long time ago. The old phone worked fine, but "fine" doesn't survive middle school logic, and within minutes of setting it up she transferred her Candy Crush app and picked up exactly where she left off.

Except now everything was faster, smoother, and just responsive enough to keep her exactly where the app wanted her. Almost immediately, she asked for more gold bars so she could get to the next level. Lisa didn't really think of it as spending because it didn't feel like spending—it felt more like maintenance. A $20 recharge here and there on the credit card, usually once a month and sometimes a little more if she was "so close," felt harmless. It felt controlled, like a small digital allowance for a small digital problem. But the game wasn't built to be finished. It was built to continue.

The game noise used to drive Lisa crazy—the tapping, the sound effects, and the occasional meltdown when she ran out of lives at exactly the wrong moment. Eventually, instead of limiting it, she solved it. "Just use your AirPods," Lisa said, handing her a solution that removed the problem without changing the behavior. The noise disappeared, but the system did not.

To keep things under control, Lisa added structure, or at least what felt like structure. She paid for parental control software on both kids' phones so she could monitor usage, set limits, and remotely shut things off when needed. It gave her a sense of control, like she was still managing the system even if she wasn't home.

Cameron had a different ecosystem entirely, but the pattern was the same. He wasn't asking for gold bars—he was operating inside a fully built system of Fortnite, Call of Duty, and an Xbox Game Pass subscription that ensured there was always something new to play. Like his sister, he wasn't just using a product—he was inside an environment designed to keep him engaged.

To support it all, Lisa upgraded their internet because the original Wi-Fi couldn't handle gaming, streaming, and multiple devices at once. The upgrade made sense in the moment because it reduced complaints and made everything run more smoothly. Then came the equipment, including a gaming chair, a larger TV, a headset, and a room that started to look less like a child's bedroom and more like a private entertainment system. None of it felt excessive while it was happening. It felt like keeping things working.

She told herself it was reasonable because all kids had screens and all kids played games, and this was just what parenting looked like now. Nothing about it felt extreme, and if anything, it felt average. And average is one of the most dangerous benchmarks in modern spending because it rarely gets questioned.

What she didn't notice was that her bills had become a stack of recurring monthly payments that never stopped. There was the phone bill, the parental controls, the game subscriptions, the app purchases, the upgraded internet, and the constant stream of small add-ons that weren't really one-time anymore. Individually, nothing felt dangerous, but together it formed something structured. Structured financial leakage disguised as normal life.

No one stops in the middle of it and asks the obvious question: what are you actually doing? Because nothing looks wrong on the surface, the kids are entertained, the house is quiet, and everything appears to be functioning. That's what makes it difficult to recognize.

But underneath that surface, something very different is being built. Not discipline, not restraint, and not delayed gratification, but a system where wants are immediately serviced and frustration is solved with money. Over time, that changes how problems are approached.

What's happening here isn't just financial—it's neurological. The environments built around games, apps, and subscriptions are designed to deliver immediate rewards with minimal effort. Progress happens quickly, frustration is short-lived, and obstacles can be removed almost instantly with a tap or a small payment. The system is engineered to keep the experience moving forward without interruption. Research consistently shows that high levels of screen time—especially in environments built around instant rewards—are associated with reduced capacity for delayed gratification and impulse control in children. When the brain is repeatedly exposed to immediate outcomes, it begins to expect them as the default, and waiting starts to feel unnecessary.

Candy Crush is a perfect example of how that conditioning happens in real time. Ava wasn't just playing a game—she was interacting with a system designed to remove friction at every possible point. When she ran out of lives, she could wait or pay, and when she got stuck, she could try again or pay. The game never forced the decision. It presented the shortcut. When that pattern is repeated often enough, it doesn't stay inside the game. It begins to influence how problems are approached outside of it, where frustration becomes something to eliminate rather than work through. Progress becomes something that should happen quickly instead of something that takes time.

Delayed gratification teaches a very different lesson, one where effort comes first and reward follows after repetition and persistence. That ability is directly connected to long-term outcomes, including financial stability and goal setting. It requires sitting in discomfort long enough to move through it.

Instant gratification teaches something else entirely. It teaches that obstacles can be removed, waiting can be bypassed, and progress can be accelerated with resources. Over time, those repeated experiences shape expectations about how the world works. Expectations become habits. Because this isn't really about Candy Crush or Fortnite or subscriptions, but rather what gets habitualized or normalized. If every frustration has a payment solution, every limitation has an upgrade, and every pause can be removed with a purchase, then delayed gratification doesn't develop.

## Psychological Pattern: Guilt Compensation

For families like the Reynolds, guilt shows up in the space between work and home, between wanting to be present and simply being exhausted. Many divorced parents carry an emotional pressure that rarely gets discussed. They are trying to balance careers, schedules, custody arrangements, emotional exhaustion, and the constant feeling that they are somehow falling short in multiple directions at once. Other families feel guilty because parenting does not always feel joyful and admitting that feels socially unacceptable.

Lisa feels guilty when work keeps her late at the hospital and she misses another evening at home. Her ex-husband feels guilty when business travel interferes with visitation schedules or important school events. Mark and Lisa love their children, but both are operating inside careers that consume enormous amounts of time and emotional energy. Lisa's hospital management role regularly follows her home mentally even when she is physically there, while Mark's travel schedule means entire stretches of family life happen without him. The kids are safe, fed, connected, and provided for, but they are also alone more often than either parent imagined when they first pictured their family life and co-parenting after divorce. Nobody says it directly, but everyone feels it. Neither parent intentionally uses spending to compensate for absence, but over time the purchases begin serving an emotional purpose far beyond entertainment. Technology becomes an emotional substitute for time, attention, consistency, and presence.

That emotional tension changes how spending decisions get made. The phone upgrade feels easier after missing another school event. The gaming system becomes easier to justify when Cameron spends yet another weekend with Lisa while Mark is away traveling. The subscriptions, AirPods, in-game purchases, and streaming services slowly stop feeling indulgent because they become emotionally connected to comfort, distraction, and compensation. Lisa notices that when the kids are entertained, the house feels calmer, and she feels less guilt. Mark notices that buying something often creates an immediate burst of excitement and connection, especially after being gone. The purchases are not really solving the absence, but for a moment they soften the emotional edges around it. This dynamic becomes particularly dangerous when parents use money as a substitute for emotional connection. Many parents who are exhausted, divorced, guilty, overworked, or emotionally unavailable attempt to compensate through spending.

Children quickly learn that emotions can trigger transactions. Sadness may result in gifts. Boredom may result in shopping or vacation. Achievement may result in expensive rewards disconnected from necessity. In these homes, money stops functioning as a practical tool and begins functioning as emotional regulation. The long-term consequence is significant because the child may never fully develop the ability to self-soothe or tolerate discomfort without consumption. Emotional resilience weakens when every unpleasant feeling is softened through spending. This pattern often follows children into adulthood where they may overspend during stress, accumulate debt attempting to maintain emotional comfort, or expect others to financially stabilize them during periods of difficulty. Parents rarely intend to create emotional fragility. Most are simply trying to create happiness. Yet happiness purchased too frequently often produces dependency instead of strength. The problem is that children begin associating love and attention with material rewards. Parents then feel trapped because the spending becomes part of the emotional structure of the relationship. It is easier to order something online than to sit with guilt and emotional vulnerability.

Retail culture understands this perfectly. Advertisements constantly frame purchases as acts of love, connection, and memory-making. Parents are encouraged to "treat" their children after difficult moments or celebrate ordinary milestones with expensive rewards. The emotional language around consumption makes overspending feel compassionate rather than impulsive. Over time, entire family systems can become organized around emotional spending patterns. Amazon boxes replace conversations, presence, and emotional repair because purchases feel easier, faster, and more socially acceptable than confronting emotional absence directly.

Parents struggling with guilt-based spending need to understand that emotional discomfort cannot be permanently solved through purchases. Gifts may temporarily reduce guilt, but they rarely resolve the deeper emotional issue underneath it. In many cases, the guilt returns quickly, creating a cycle where spending becomes the default coping mechanism whenever emotional discomfort resurfaces. What feels like generosity can slowly become emotional conditioning.

A healthier alternative is learning to replace financial compensation with emotional presence whenever possible. Parents do not need to be perfect, endlessly available, or constantly entertaining to build strong relationships with their children. Simple consistency often matters more than expensive gestures. Honest conversations, routines, undistracted time, and emotional attentiveness create far deeper security than constant purchases ever could. It is okay to do the dishes together, fold laundry together, wash the car together. Parents should also remember that children benefit from seeing adults model emotional accountability rather than emotional spending. Sometimes the most loving thing a parent can say is not "I bought you something," but "I know I've been distracted lately, and I want to spend more time with you."

## The Quick Math

Lisa Reynolds often felt that the digital expenses in her household were too small to matter. A few dollars here for a mobile game, a subscription there for parental controls, gaming memberships, upgraded internet service, and various app purchases seemed harmless when viewed individually. Yet together, those recurring expenses added up to approximately $140 per month, or about $1,680 per year. Importantly, that figure does not include the cost of devices, replacement electronics, upgrades, or other one-time purchases that frequently accompany a technology-centered lifestyle. The long-term financial impact becomes clearer when viewed through the lens of compound growth. If the same $1,680 per year were invested instead for 10 years and then allowed to grow untouched for another 10 years at an average annual return of 7%, it would grow to approximately $45,673 by Year 20. Of that amount, only $16,800 would represent the family's direct contributions, while approximately $28,873 would come from investment growth. This example is not intended to suggest that families should eliminate technology, internet access, or digital entertainment. Rather, it highlights how recurring subscription costs can quietly become permanent line items in a household budget. Because these expenses are often automated and relatively small, they rarely receive the same scrutiny as larger purchases. Over time, however, dozens of seemingly insignificant monthly charges can create a meaningful opportunity cost. The lesson is not that technology is bad, but that recurring expenses deserve the same level of intentional consideration as major purchases, particularly when they compete with long-term goals such as retirement savings and financial independence.

# QUICK MATH

| CANDY CRUSH PURCHASES | PARENTAL CONTROL APPS | GAMING SUBSCRIPTIONS | UPGRADED INTERNET | MISCELLANEOUS APP SPENDING |
|---|---|---|---|---|
| $20 PER MONTH | $15 PER MONTH | $50 PER MONTH | $40 PER MONTH | $15 PER MONTH |

**TOTAL ≈ $140 PER MONTH**

Over the course of a year, that becomes approximately $1,680 in recurring digital lifestyle spending.

**$1,680 PER YEAR**

That number doesn't include devices, upgrades, or larger one-time purchases that tend to show up along the way.

If that $1,680 per year were redirected into retirement and invested consistently at a 7% annual return over 20 years, the long-term impact becomes clear:

**FUTURE VALUE OF INVESTING $1,680 PER YEAR AT 7% ANNUAL RETURN (COMPOUNDED ANNUALLY)**

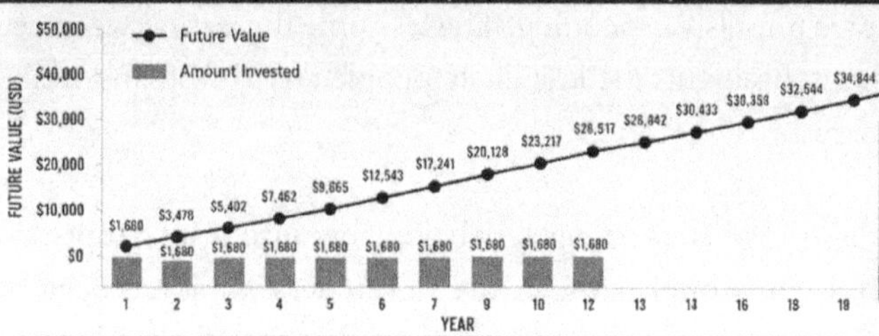


| HOW THE $45,673 IS BUILT | |
|---|---|
| Total contributed (10 contributions) | $16,800 |
| Growth from compounding interest at 7% | $28,873 |
| TOTAL (Year 20) | $45,673 |

At 7%, investing $1,680 per year for 10 years and then letting it grow for 10 more years results in approximately $45,673 at Year 20.
(The $45,673 value shown at Year 20 includes the final balance after 20 years of compounding.)

**FUTURE VALUE ≈**

## $45,673

in retirement savings from a category that is often overlooked in long-term planning.

# Recommendations

## Set a Fixed Monthly Digital Spending Limit Per Child

A fixed monthly digital spending limit creates structure in an area where many families currently have none. App purchases, gaming subscriptions, streaming upgrades, in-game currency, and impulse digital spending often happen in small amounts that feel insignificant individually but quietly accumulate over time. Without a clear limit, spending becomes reactive rather than intentional, driven by boredom, convenience, or emotional pressure instead of thoughtful decision-making.

A defined spending cap also forces prioritization. When children know there is a fixed amount available each month, they begin learning how to evaluate choices and understand trade-offs. Spending money on one game upgrade may mean giving up another purchase later. That process of deciding what matters most is where financial awareness begins. Limits create structure, and structure creates discipline.

## Remove Automatic Payment Access from Apps and Games

Removing automatic payment access restores a layer of friction that modern technology has intentionally eliminated. One-click ordering, saved payment methods, automatic renewals, and instant downloads are designed to bypass reflection and encourage impulsive spending. The less time there is between wanting something and purchasing it, the less likely people are to stop and evaluate whether it is necessary.

Requiring an extra approval step changes behavior because it interrupts automatic consumption. Even a brief pause creates awareness. Children begin recognizing that digital purchases involve real money rather than feeling like invisible rewards inside a screen. Parents also regain visibility into how often spending requests occur and whether those purchases reflect genuine interest or momentary impulse.

## Stop Solving Frustration with Purchases

Many digital purchases are not solving actual needs; they are solving discomfort. A child becomes bored, frustrated, impatient, or disappointed, and money is immediately used to remove the unpleasant feeling. A new app, game upgrade, or subscription temporarily eliminates the tension, but over time children can begin associating frustration with instant consumption rather than learning how to tolerate delay or difficulty.

The ability to sit with discomfort is closely connected to long-term financial discipline and emotional resilience. Children need opportunities to experience boredom, waiting, and limitations without constantly being rescued by purchases. Discomfort is not automatically harmful. In many cases, it is part of normal emotional development and helps build patience, creativity, and self-regulation.

## Audit Subscriptions Every 90 Days

Subscriptions continue largely because they become invisible. Once a streaming service, gaming membership, music platform, or app subscription is placed on autopay, it fades into the background of family finances. Most households do not consciously choose to continue paying for these services every month; they simply never revisit the decision.

Conducting a subscription audit every ninety days forces each service to justify its place in the household again. Families can evaluate whether the service is still being used, whether it still provides value, and whether it aligns with larger financial goals. A regular review prevents digital spending from becoming permanently automatic and helps eliminate recurring expenses that no longer serve a meaningful purpose.

## Track Total Digital Spending Monthly

Most families monitor large expenses such as housing, insurance, and car payments, yet smaller recurring digital costs often go unnoticed. Streaming services, app purchases, gaming upgrades, cloud storage, and delivery memberships are scattered across multiple accounts, making the total difficult to recognize. Because each purchase feels relatively small on its own, the overall impact is easy to underestimate.

Bringing all digital spending into one visible monthly number changes how it is perceived psychologically. Several small subscriptions may not feel excessive individually, but the combined total often tells a different story. Visibility creates awareness, and awareness changes behavior. Once families clearly see how much is leaving the household each month for digital convenience and entertainment, it becomes easier to evaluate whether the spending reflects their actual priorities.

## Eat Dinner Together

One of the simplest and most effective ways to reduce guilt-based spending is to consistently eat dinner together as a family. Shared meals create space for parents to see, hear, and truly listen to their children without needing to purchase anything in order to feel connected. Many parents unconsciously spend money to compensate for time pressure, exhaustion, work schedules, or the emotional fear that they are "not doing enough." Dinner interrupts that cycle. Sitting together regularly creates natural opportunities for conversation, emotional check-ins, humor, storytelling, and daily connection that cannot be replicated through spending. Children who feel emotionally seen and heard often need less material compensation because their primary emotional need—connection—is already being met directly. Family meals also help parents recognize what is actually happening in their children's lives instead of trying to manage relationships through purchases or convenience. The goal is not creating perfect dinners or elaborate meals. The goal is creating consistent moments where family members are emotionally present with one another without consumption becoming the center of the interaction.

## Prioritize Retirement Contributions Before Lifestyle Spending

Every dollar spent on recurring digital convenience is a dollar that is not compounding toward future financial independence. Streaming upgrades, gaming purchases, premium apps, and subscription services may feel minor in isolation, but repeated lifestyle spending competes with retirement savings over time. The issue is rarely one purchase. It is the accumulation of constant small expenses that slowly consume money that could otherwise build long-term security.

Making this trade-off visible changes decision-making. Parents begin asking not only, "Can we afford this?" but also, "What are we giving up later by continuing this pattern?" Retirement contributions are often sacrificed because the consequences feel distant and abstract. Yet the years when families are raising children are also the years when compound interest has the greatest opportunity to work. Long-term security should not be unintentionally exchanged for short-term convenience simply because the individual purchases seem small. It doesn't feel like a system when you're inside it. It just feels like parenting. Until you add it up.

CHAPTER 7

# CLUB AND TRAVEL SPORTS, DANCE AND *Cheer*

*Beware the barrenness of a busy life.*

— SOCRATES

Pete and Rosa were good parents—steady, involved, the kind of people who showed up to everything on time with folding chairs and snacks in labeled bags. They did not think of themselves as emotional people. They thought of themselves as practical people, which is why they were so surprised by how expensive practicality can become.

Ethan, their son, was a good baseball player. A solid pitcher with decent mechanics and enough control to keep coaches interested, but not the kind of athlete scouts reorganize their weekends around. Pete understood this intellectually, although fathers in folding sports chairs have a remarkable ability to confuse a strong inning with a possible professional trajectory. Still, the spending continued because possibility has a way of feeling emotionally larger than probability.

During Ethan's freshman year of high school, one of his travel coaches pulled Pete aside after a tournament and told him Ethan had "a real shot" at playing college baseball if he stayed committed. That single sentence landed like financial gasoline on a fire already burning in Pete's mind. After that conversation, the spending escalated. The private pitching lessons increased. The travel schedule expanded. Pete started talking about exposure tournaments and recruitment calendars as if Ethan's future had shifted from possibility to plan. This is where the scholarship illusion takes hold inside families. A coach mentions exposure. A tournament promises visibility. Someone knows a family whose child "got picked up." Rare success stories stay emotionally alive because hope is persuasive once it attaches itself to your child.

Then came their daughter Madison, who entered competitive cheer and dance, creating an entirely separate financial ecosystem. There were practice uniforms, competition uniforms, warm-up suits, shoes that somehow only worked for one routine, bows, makeup kits, choreography fees, and constant travel weekends. Rosa found herself managing schedules, hair, costumes, and timing like a production coordinator for a traveling performance company.

Madison's world operated on a different type of hope than Ethan's, but it was emotionally similar. Elite squads, national competitions, and university cheer programs created the feeling that constant advancement mattered. Rosa spent hours researching college cheer teams, tryout videos, and scholarship opportunities online. By Madison's senior year, they traveled to multiple university tryouts, paying application fees, hotel costs, travel expenses, and preparation coaching because everyone in the competitive cheer world seemed to know someone whose daughter "made the team."

At some point, Pete and Rosa were no longer simply raising children. They were operating a year-round athletic support system. Every season brought another registration fee, another equipment list, another hotel reservation, and another meal eaten on the road because no one had been home long enough to function like normal people. Individually, each expense looked manageable, which is exactly how the system sustains itself. A uniform here. A tournament there. A travel weekend that felt necessary in the moment. Collectively, it looked like a second mortgage disguised as character development.

The family repeated the phrase parents always use in these moments: "We're giving them opportunities." **Opportunity is one of the most expensive words in the English language because it rarely arrives with a defined limit.** It expands to match whatever parents are emotionally willing to justify.

By high school, the household budget revolved around sports calendars, tournament schedules, dance competitions, practices, and travel weekends. Every month another bill arrived from organizations devoted to helping children "reach their full potential." Pete financed baseball at approximately $7000 per year out of his salary while Rosa financed cheer and dance travel at approximately $6000 per year out of her salary. At that point, the system was no longer being evaluated objectively. It was simply being maintained. The financial math behind these pursuits is often staggering, yet many families never calculate the full number honestly because the spending arrives gradually over years. Tournament fees. Hotel stays. Gas. Flights. Uniforms. Camps. Lessons. Private coaching. Team dues. Meals on the road.

The strange part was that Ethan himself never seemed nearly as emotionally invested as the adults surrounding him. Pete became more emotionally attached to the future version of Ethan than to the teenager sitting in front of him in the present. The recruiting conversations, travel schedules, and private coaching slowly transformed baseball from an activity into an imagined future.

By the time Pete and Rosa finally started questioning whether the spending still made sense, they had already invested years into the system. Their weekends, finances, vacations, and routines revolved around maintaining it. Stepping back no longer felt like making a practical financial decision. It felt like losing everything they had already poured into the dream.

Eventually, the emotional reality arrived all at once. By the end of Ethan's junior year, after years of practices, tournaments, hotel weekends, and endless baseball travel, he abruptly told his parents he was done. He was tired of playing baseball. He wanted to spend time with his friends, work a normal summer job, and experience high school without playing baseball every weekend. Pete reacted as though someone had unplugged a machine he had spent years building. The dream had stayed emotionally alive so long that he no longer realized how much of it belonged to him rather than to Ethan.

In Madison's junior and senior year, she began trying out for university cheerleading squads. But Madison kept getting passed over. One school selected stronger tumblers. Another chose athletes with more advanced stunting backgrounds. At one university, she made it through two rounds before being cut at the end of the final day. Rosa sat in the parking lot afterward trying to sound encouraging while Madison stared out the window in exhausted silence and cried.

The hardest part is that none of this feels reckless while it is happening. It feels loving, supportive, and responsible. That is exactly why achievement projection becomes so persuasive inside otherwise financially careful families. But when the pursuit damages retirement security, long-term stability, or family balance, the financial consequences eventually become shared by the entire household long after the games and competitions have ended.

## Psychological Pattern: Achievement Projection and the Scholarship Illusion

Pete and Rosa were not careless parents. They were loving, responsible people caught inside a system that emotionally rewards possibility while financially punishing realism. Every tournament promised exposure. Every showcase hinted at opportunity. Every coach reinforced the idea that one more camp, one more private lesson, one more elite team, or one more travel season might change everything. Rare success stories stayed emotionally alive because hope is incredibly persuasive once it attaches itself to your child.

Few things are more financially persuasive than the belief that your child might become extraordinary. According to a New York Life 2025 survey, 83% of parents say they believe their child has the ability to play at the college level. And 49% say they're confident their child will get an athletic scholarship. The emotional problem is that possibility and probability are not the same thing. Possibility feels much larger than probability. The real numbers are that out of 100 high school athletes, only about 7 will go on to play college sports at any level.

Of those, roughly 2 will receive any form of athletic scholarship, and most are partial rather than full tuition. The number of athletes who receive a true full-ride equivalent is less than one. Then the numbers narrow again. Of the athletes who do compete in college, only about 1–2% will eventually play professionally.

Families do not emotionally experience statistics when imagining their child's future. They picture scholarships, championships, elite colleges, admiration, and success. Parents naturally want to support talent and ambition because doing so feels loving and responsible. Entire industries profit from keeping those dreams emotionally alive. Coaches, trainers, showcase programs, camps, and recruiting services all reinforce the idea that extraordinary outcomes are achievable with enough commitment and enough spending. This is where the scholarship illusion takes hold. It does not arrive as an obvious lie. It arrives as a possibility that feels realistic enough to justify continued investment.

For Pete, Ethan's baseball ability became emotionally connected to future opportunity and identity. Ethan did not need to be the best player in the country for the dream to remain active. He only needed enough flashes of talent to keep possibility emotionally believable. One strong performance, one compliment from a coach, or one conversation about recruitment could justify months of additional spending. Rosa experienced something similar through Madison's dance and cheer world, where rankings, elite teams, choreography fees, and competition placement constantly reinforced the idea that higher investment might produce higher outcomes.

This is where achievement projection develops inside families. Parents stop feeling like consumers and begin feeling like investors in emotionally imagined futures. The camps, coaching, tournaments, choreography fees, hotel weekends, and year-round schedules become attached to future versions of the child. Maybe Ethan gets recruited. Maybe Madison earns a scholarship. Maybe all the sacrifice eventually "pays off." The imagined future becomes emotionally valuable enough to justify enormous ongoing expense.

The psychological trap becomes even stronger once years of money, time, identity, and emotion have already been invested. By high school, Pete and Rosa's weekends, finances, vacations, and household routines revolved around maintaining the system. At that point, questioning the spending no longer felt practical. It felt emotional. Stepping back felt dangerously close to admitting that the outcome might never justify the sacrifice.

That is what makes sunk cost thinking so powerful. The question shifts from "What makes sense going forward?" to "How do we avoid wasting everything we already spent?" Once that shift happens, families continue spending not because the outcome is becoming more likely, but because stopping feels more painful than continuing.

Parents also underestimate how quickly identity becomes fused with achievement systems. Families begin organizing life around rankings, recruitment, elite teams, scholarships, and advancement. Children may absorb the message that family pride and emotional energy rise and fall alongside performance. Parents rarely intend to create this pressure. Most genuinely believe they are being supportive. But when achievement becomes central to family identity, stepping away from the activity can feel emotionally threatening for everyone involved.

Parents caught in this cycle need to separate genuine support from financially chasing statistically unlikely futures. Children benefit enormously from encouragement and opportunity, but they also benefit from balance, emotional security, and realistic expectations.

## The Quick Math

Pete and Rosa viewed youth sports as an investment in their children's development. Their son Ethan's competitive baseball costs averaged about $7,000 per year, while their daughter Madison's cheer and dance activities added another $6,000 annually, bringing the family's total to approximately $13,000 per year. Over six years, they spent roughly $78,000 on youth activities. If that same $13,000 per year had been invested at a 7% annual return and allowed to grow after the sixth year, it would have grown to approximately $239,785 over 20 years. Of that amount, $78,000 represents the family's direct contributions, while nearly $162,000 comes from compound growth. This example is not meant to discourage sports or extracurricular activities, but to illustrate how quickly recurring activity expenses accumulate, and the substantial opportunity cost they can create. Before committing to increasingly expensive programs, families should consider not only the benefits gained today but also what those same dollars might mean for their future financial security.

# QUICK MATH

## 1 ETHAN – BASEBALL

Ethan's baseball costs averaged around $7,000 per year, including travel dues, private lessons, hotels, food, and equipment.

**$7,000**
**PER YEAR**

+

## 2 MADISON – CHEER & DANCE

Madison's cheer and dance costs averaged about $6,000 per year once competition fees, uniforms, travel, and performance-related expenses were included.

**$6,000**
**PER YEAR**

Together, that created a combined annual cost of approximately: → **$13,000 PER YEAR**

**OVER SIX YEARS, THAT BECOMES:**

**$13,000 × 6 YEARS = $78,000**

If that same $13,000 per year were redirected into retirement and invested consistently at 7% over 20 years (with no additional contributions after Year 6), the long-term impact becomes clear:

**FUTURE VALUE OF INVESTING $13,000 PER YEAR AT 7% ANNUAL RETURN**
**(COMPOUNDED ANNUALLY)**

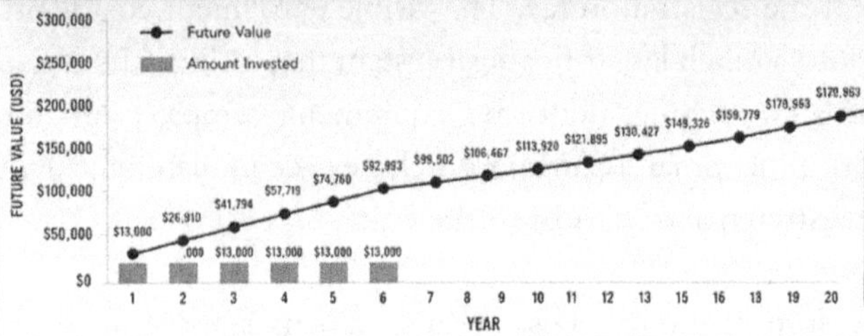


| HOW THE $239,785 IS BUILT | |
|---|---|
| Total contributed (6 contributions) | $78,000 |
| Growth from compounding interest at 7% | $161,785 |
| TOTAL (Year 20) | $239,785 |

At 7%, investing $13,000 per year for 6 years and then letting it grow for 14 more years results in approximately $239,785 at Year 20.
(The $239,785 value shown at Year 20 includes the final balance after 20 years of compounding.)

**FUTURE VALUE ≈**

**$239,785**

in retirement savings from choices made for what matters most today.

# Recommendations

## Set a Total Yearly Sports and Activity Budget

Instead of making emotional financial decisions tournament by tournament or season by season, families benefit from determining in advance what they can realistically afford for sports and extracurricular activities each year. Competitive environments naturally create pressure, excitement, and optimism about future opportunities. Without a defined budget, spending can slowly escalate through emotional momentum rather than intentional planning.

A yearly budget creates boundaries before emotions begin influencing decisions. It also helps parents evaluate opportunities more objectively because every new expense must fit within an existing framework. Financial structure does not reduce support for a child's interests; it simply prevents activities from consuming resources that were intended for long-term family stability.

## Calculate the Full Cost, Not Just Registration Fees

According to NerdWallet 2026, travel sports cost eight to thirteen thousand dollars per child each year. When this number is forecasted over six to ten years, the numbers are large enough to significantly alter retirement outcomes. According to the New York Life 2025 survey, over 25% of parents said they had to pull from their savings to pay for sports costs. Travel sports and competitive activities rarely stop at the registration fee. The visible enrollment cost is often only the entry point into a much larger financial system that includes hotels, gas, restaurant meals, private coaching, uniforms, equipment, camps, tournament fees, and missed work time. Small recurring purchases accumulate quickly, especially when seasons stretch across most of the year.

Many families underestimate the true cost because expenses arrive in separate pieces rather than one large bill. A few hundred dollars for a hotel weekend or private lesson may not feel overwhelming in isolation, but repeated over months or years, the total can become financially significant. Looking at the full annual cost instead of individual expenses creates a more honest understanding of the financial commitment being made.

What many families avoid discussing is that children could often receive many of the same developmental benefits through far less expensive paths. School sports, local leagues, and community programs still provide discipline, structure, teamwork, resilience, friendship, and competition. At a certain point, spending increases dramatically while developmental return increases only marginally. No amount of spending can fully manufacture elite athleticism or extraordinary outcomes at scale.

## Separate Development from Elite-Level Spending

Children can develop discipline, teamwork, confidence, resilience, and structure through sports without participating in the most expensive version of an activity. Explore the possibilities offered with the parks and recreation services and school programs. The emotional trap for many families is assuming that higher spending automatically produces greater developmental value. In reality, many of the most important benefits of sports come simply from consistent participation, healthy coaching, and supportive environments.

Parents should regularly ask whether additional spending is genuinely improving the child's experience or simply escalating involvement in an increasingly expensive system. There is a difference between supporting a child's growth and becoming financially trapped in a culture where every additional expense is presented as necessary for success. Not every child needs private coaching, year-round competition, or national travel to benefit meaningfully from an activity.

## Research Scholarship Probabilities Honestly

Many families emotionally plan around possibilities instead of probabilities. Athletic scholarships and professional advancement receive enormous attention in sports culture, but statistically, they remain extremely rare outcomes.

Yet many families structure spending as though those outcomes are expected rather than statistically rare. That is the disconnect. Parents are making financial decisions based on possibility while the system itself operates on probability. Families involved in expensive activities should periodically ask themselves one uncomfortable but clarifying question:

**If there were no scholarship possibility, would we spend this much?**

That question forces parents to separate genuine enjoyment and developmental value from financially chasing imagined future outcomes.

For many families, the answer reveals whether spending decisions are still grounded in reality or increasingly driven by hope, pressure, and emotional momentum. Activities can absolutely enrich childhood, create memories, and build important life skills. But when financial decisions become dependent on highly unlikely future rewards, families risk sacrificing long-term stability for outcomes that may never materialize.

## Recognize Sunk-Cost Thinking Early

Years of financial and emotional investment can make families feel trapped inside systems that no longer make sense financially. Parents often continue spending because they feel they have already invested too much to stop now. This is known as sunk-cost thinking, where past spending begins controlling present decisions even when continuing no longer aligns with the family's broader goals.

The danger of sunk-cost thinking is that it shifts focus away from the future and toward emotionally protecting past investments. Families may continue expensive commitments not because the activity still provides meaningful value, but because stopping feels like admitting the earlier spending was unnecessary. Recognizing this pattern early allows parents to make decisions based on present reality instead of emotional attachment to prior costs.

## Create Unstructured Family Time

Not every tournament, showcase, travel opportunity, or private lesson is necessary. Competitive activity culture often creates the impression that constant participation is required to remain successful or relevant. Families can begin spending every weekend traveling, reorganizing work schedules, and structuring their entire calendar around one activity.

Defining limits ahead of time helps prevent sports culture from consuming both the family budget and family life. Boundaries protect time, relationships, rest, and financial balance. Children benefit from activities, but they also benefit from unstructured family time, stability, and parents who are not perpetually exhausted or financially stressed by constant competition schedules.

## Evaluate Whether the Child Still Enjoys the Activity

Sometimes parents continue financing activities long after the child's enthusiasm has faded because the family identity has become attached to the sport or competition system. What began as a child's interest can slowly evolve into a family lifestyle involving parental friendships, routines, social status, and future expectations. At that point, it becomes emotionally difficult to distinguish the child's goals from the parents' hopes.

Honest conversations help clarify whether the child still genuinely enjoys the activity or simply feels pressure to continue. Children often struggle to communicate burnout because they fear disappointing their parents after years of investment and sacrifice. Supporting a child's development sometimes means allowing interests to change instead of forcing continuation for the sake of protecting the family's emotional or financial investment.

## Build Family Life Outside the Activity System

When every weekend, conversation, vacation, and relationship revolve around sports or competition, the activity can become the family's primary identity. Over time, families may lose balance without fully realizing it. Siblings, marriages, friendships, and other interests can slowly become secondary to tournament schedules and performance goals.

Maintaining family life outside the activity system creates healthier emotional balance. Children benefit from understanding that they are valued beyond performance, rankings, scholarships, or achievements. Families also need relationships and experiences that exist independently from organized competition. A sport or activity should be part of family life, not the entire definition of it.

## Consider the Financial Cost of the Sport Before Entering It

Parents should think carefully not only about whether a child enjoys a particular sport, but also about the financial ecosystem commonly attached to that activity. Different sports carry dramatically different expectations regarding travel, equipment, coaching, tournaments, camps, uniforms, and year-round participation. Some activities remain relatively affordable at the recreational level but become financially consuming once club teams, elite competition, or travel systems enter the picture. Others, such as hockey, equestrian sports, elite cheer, gymnastics, and travel baseball, often come with high recurring costs almost immediately.

This does not mean children should avoid expensive sports entirely. It means families should enter those systems with full awareness of the long-term financial commitment involved rather than discovering the costs gradually after emotional attachment has already formed. Parents often evaluate sports based on a child's enthusiasm in the present moment without recognizing that certain activities naturally escalate into expensive cultures of travel, private coaching, showcases, and constant advancement. Understanding the financial realities early allows families to create boundaries, protect long-term goals, and make decisions that support both the child's interests and the family's future stability.

Eventually the receipts become retirement sacrifices. The money spent over years could have compounded into long-term stability, financial flexibility, and peace later in life. Instead, many families arrive in middle age financially strained while holding binders full of schedules, medals, trophies, photos, and highlight reels that once symbolized possibility.

# COST OF CLUB AND TRAVEL TEAMS

## UPDATED ANNUAL COST COMPARISON BY SPORT (2026 DOLLARS)

*Original data from TIME Magazine (2017) and updated data from 2024 have been adjusted for inflation to reflect 2026 dollars.*

| SPORT | AVERAGE ANNUAL COST PER CHILD (2026) | MAXIMUM ANNUAL COST PER CHILD (2026) | WHAT DRIVES THE COST |
|---|---|---|---|
| HOCKEY | $8,300 | $22,300 | • Ice time<br>• Equipment<br>• Travel & tournaments<br>• Coaching<br>• League fees |
| EQUESTRIAN | $11,800 | $117,800 | • Horse ownership / leasing<br>• Training & lessons<br>• Boarding & facility fees<br>• Shows & travel |
| LACROSSE | $9,400 | $20,600 | • Club fees<br>• Gear & equipment<br>• Travel & tournaments<br>• Showcases & recruiting |
| BASEBALL / SOFTBALL | $4,800 | $11,700 | • Tournaments & entry fees<br>• Travel & hotels<br>• Equipment & uniforms<br>• Lessons & camps |
| FOOTBALL | $3,300 | $11,200 | • Equipment & pads<br>• Travel & tournaments<br>• Coaching & training<br>• League & registration fees<br>• Camps |
| CHEER / DANCE | $5,200 | $14,400 | • Choreography & coaching<br>• Competitions & travel<br>• Uniforms, shoes, makeup<br>• Camps & technique classes |
| GYMNASTICS | $4,000 | $19,900 | • Gym fees & training<br>• Competition fees<br>• Leotards & equipment<br>• Travel |
| VOLLEYBALL | $3,900 | $12,900 | • Club fees<br>• Travel & tournaments<br>• Gear & uniforms<br>• Coaching & training |
| SOCCER | $1,900 | $7,100 | • Club fees<br>• Uniforms & gear<br>• Travel & tournaments<br>• Training & camps |
| BASKETBALL | $1,500 | $6,700 | • Club / team fees<br>• Travel & tournaments<br>• Shoes & gear<br>• Coaching |

**WHY COSTS ARE HIGHER THAN YOU THINK**

These figures reflect competitive / travel-level participation and include more than just registration. They include equipment, travel, hotels, meals, coaching, camps, uniforms, fees, and other out-of-pocket expenses many families don't anticipate.

**AT THE ELITE TRAVEL LEVEL,** childhood hobbies quietly begin operating like second mortgages.

**RECOMMENDATION:** Think about what sports that you involve your child in and the cost that is generally associated with that sport.

Costs vary by location, level of competition, individual choices, and frequency of travel. These are national average estimates in 2026 dollars.

Sources: TIME Magazine – "The High Price of Youth Sports" (2017)
Aspen Institute Project Play (2024) | Multiple industry reports (2024)
Data has been adjusted to 2026 dollars using 3.0% annual inflation.

# CHAPTER 8

# THE CAR AT *Sixteen*

*A boy who bought his own Toyota is more successful than a boy who shows off his dad's Lamborghini.*

– ANONYMOUS

Abe was a good kid. His parents, Chris and Darla, would joke that he had been raised by wolves—but they had somehow managed to keep him alive. He was not feral in the traditional sense, but if survival depended on loading a dishwasher or finding the on/off switch to the vacuum, the outlook was not promising. His parents had succeeded in raising a kind human being, but the operating manual for basic life skills had clearly been misplaced somewhere along the way.

At sixteen, Abe could not hold a broom correctly. He pushed it around the kitchen like he was fencing with debris, as if the crumbs might attack first and he needed to stay defensive. He had never washed a dish, never washed a car, never mowed a lawn, and had never held any sort of job. He was nice enough, friendly enough, and generally harmless, but the basic mechanics of self-sufficiency were missing in action.

What Abe did possess was a driver's permit earned at fourteen years and nine months and an almost spiritual longing for freedom. He wanted his license and a pick-up truck so badly he could taste it, like independence had a flavor and it was gasoline. He had only snuck his mom's car out one time—which, in his mind, qualified as growth because technically it was not a recurring offense—and he assumed everyone in the household was now emotionally ready to move past that chapter.

When his sixteenth birthday approached, Abe began campaigning for a car with the confidence of someone who had no money, no job, and no practical reason to think this request was reasonable. He spoke about it like it was inevitable, not optional, as if vehicles simply appeared when teenagers reached a certain age. His arguments were passionate, repetitive, and completely disconnected from financial reality, which is a skill many adults also possess.

Chris and Darla were conflicted. A car would genuinely help the family in very real ways, and this is where the story becomes dangerously logical. They both worked full time, which meant if Abe or his brother had anything after school, they either waited until one of them got off work or walked home, a distance that was survivable but unpleasant enough to inspire dramatic storytelling.

A vehicle would allow him to pick up his younger brother from school, run him to soccer practice, grab milk and eggs from the grocery store, and generally function as another driver in a household that often felt logistically stretched. In theory, this was not a luxury purchase—it was a strategic family upgrade. It had efficiency written all over it, at least in the imagination.

That was the hopeful version. The less hopeful version involved handing a machine to a boy who could not clean his bedroom. There is a certain leap of faith required to believe that someone who cannot manage making a bed will suddenly manage speed, space, and judgment.

Abe's grades were mediocre, his work ethic was theoretical, and his parents kept telling themselves that perhaps a car would inspire responsibility. Maybe he would realize cars cost money. Maybe he would understand that money requires a job. Maybe this would be the magical bridge between adolescence and competence, a four-wheeled transformation story. Parents tell themselves about many beautiful things in moments like this. These thoughts are comforting, optimistic, and almost entirely unsupported by historical evidence.

Financially, the plan was shaky from the beginning. They wanted to stay under $5,000 for the vehicle, which already felt like a stretch but also like a victory. It had four tires, an engine, and only a few mysterious sounds, which placed it firmly in the "good enough" category. But the purchase price was only the opening act. There would be insurance, plates, gas, oil changes, maintenance, and repairs. The car was not the expense—it was another subscription service that came with a teenager attached.

On Abe's sixteenth birthday, they parked the used car in the driveway with a giant red bow across the hood, transforming a mildly dented commuter vehicle into what looked like a dealership commercial powered entirely by parental optimism. It was not a pick-up truck, but in that moment, it might as well have been a spaceship.

Abe was ecstatic. He hugged everyone, devoured cake and ice cream at a speed suggesting sugar was now secondary to horsepower, grabbed the keys, and immediately left to pick up his friends. Because naturally the first use of this family-support vehicle was not helping with errands or collecting his younger brother—it was teenage cruising with loud music and absolutely no groceries.

Before he left, his parents reviewed the agreement one more time. Abe would get a Saturday job. Abe would pay for gas. Abe would contribute toward insurance. Abe would cover small maintenance items. It was a beautifully structured plan, spoken aloud with confidence and received with enthusiastic nodding. Abe nodded vigorously. Teenagers are excellent at nodding during free gift ceremonies.

What followed was less an execution of responsibility and more a slow-motion parental sponsorship program. Abe could not seem to find a job, though "could not find" may be too generous a phrase for "did not look with any measurable urgency."

Every other week, he developed a routine that was financially unimpressive but psychologically strategic. He would ask Mom for twenty dollars, then ask Dad for twenty dollars, spacing the requests just far enough apart so each parent believed they were participating in an isolated fuel contribution.

Meanwhile, the car deteriorated into a rolling landfill. Fast food containers slid beneath the seats like they were trying to escape. School papers multiplied in every compartment, achieving a level of organization best described as archaeological layers. The smell of old French fries, gym socks, and stale teenage air settled permanently into the upholstery like a second interior fabric. At some point, the car stopped being a vehicle and became an ecosystem.

The monthly insurance bill of $150 was paid by his parents. The oil change was paid by his parents. The new windshield wipers were paid by his parents. The random maintenance items Abe had enthusiastically agreed would be "his responsibility" became his responsibility only in the sense that he was aware they had occurred.

By the end of the first year, the math looked less like a birthday gift and more like unplanned reoccurring expenses. Because sometimes what feels like teaching independence is really just financing dependency with better transportation. The lesson was happening—it just was not the one they intended.

And underneath all of this was a question that had never been asked. Not whether Abe wanted a car, because that answer had been loud and clear. Not whether the family could make it work, because technically they could. The real question was whether Abe was ready for the responsibility that comes with operating something that requires constant judgment.

Driving is not just a skill. It is a series of decisions made quickly, repeatedly, and often under pressure. It requires restraint when something feels exciting, patience when something feels frustrating, and focus when something feels distracting. These are not driving skills as much as they are emotional skills. Abe was excited, but excitement is not a reliable indicator of readiness. Excitement speeds things up. Maturity slows things down just enough to make better choices. When those two are not balanced, the result is often confidence without control.

It also changes the moment other people get involved. Alone in the car, a teenager is just a driver. Add one friend, and they become a host. Add two or three, and they become an entertainer, a decision-maker, and a participant in a moving social environment that does not always prioritize safety. The car becomes louder. The energy shifts. Nighttime introduces another layer. Decisions become less about what is safest and more about what is happening in the moment. It is not that teens intend to be reckless—it is that they are still learning how to manage competing inputs, and driving is not a forgiving place to practice that.

A simple question becomes surprisingly revealing. Would you feel comfortable if your teen was driving at night, with friends in the car, and you were not there? If the answer includes hesitation, that hesitation is not overthinking—it is information. Another question tends to be even more honest. Would you get in the passenger seat and feel completely relaxed while they drive? Not cautiously optimistic, not monitoring every move, but genuinely at ease. If the answer is no, then the issue is not the car. The issue is readiness, and readiness does not arrive just because a birthday does.

There is also the matter of rules. Most teenagers understand the rules. They can repeat them, agree with them, and even support them in theory. The challenge is not understanding—it is consistency. Do they follow rules when they are inconvenient? Do they respect boundaries when no one is watching? Do they make the same decision when friends are present as they would alone? Because driving is not about knowing the rules. It is about respecting them in real time, repeatedly, without supervision.

And then there is the piece that often gets skipped entirely. The connection between effort and ownership. When something significant arrives without effort, it tends to be treated as something that can also disappear without consequence. Abe never had to save for the car. He never had to experience the quiet discipline that comes from earning something over time. Working to buy your first car builds patience, perspective, and appreciation in ways that cannot be explained—they have to be experienced. When that process is skipped, the object may still function, but the lesson does not.

## Psychological Pattern: Hope-Based Parenting

Abe's parents were not really buying transportation. They were buying a future hopeful version of their son. They imagined the car would unlock responsibility, maturity, discipline, and motivation in ways that had not fully appeared before. Parents often attach emotional transformation to milestone purchases because it feels hopeful and optimistic. The car becomes symbolic, not mechanical. It represents independence, adulthood, and forward movement, even when the underlying habits required for those things are still missing.

This type of parenting is emotionally powerful because parents naturally want evidence that their children are progressing successfully into adulthood. A sixteen-year-old with a license and a car looks independent from the outside. That image creates emotional reassurance for parents who may already worry about maturity, motivation, or readiness. The purchase becomes psychologically comforting because it appears to move the child forward, even if the actual responsibility structure underneath has not changed much at all.

Parents also tend to believe responsibility can be created through privilege rather than demonstrated before it. They hope the pressure of ownership will force growth into existence. Maybe the teenager will suddenly care about money. Maybe they will become organized. Maybe they will clean the car. Maybe they will finally understand effort, maintenance, and accountability. These thoughts feel reasonable because they are hopeful, and hope is one of the strongest emotional forces in parenting. Unfortunately, responsibility rarely appears simply because someone receives access to something expensive.

The car also solves problems for the parents themselves, which makes the decision emotionally easier. Transportation stress decreases. Scheduling becomes simpler. The household becomes more flexible. Parents no longer have to absorb every inconvenience themselves, so the purchase feels practical as well as emotional. This dual benefit makes it harder to recognize when the decision is being driven more by emotional relief than by actual readiness.

Parents caught in this pattern should ask a simple but uncomfortable question:

**Has my child demonstrated responsibility already, or am I hoping this purchase will create it?**

Those are very different situations. Privileges can absolutely help children grow, but only when the emotional and behavioral foundation already exists underneath them. Otherwise, parents often end up financing dependency while telling themselves they are building independence.

## The Quick Math

When Abe turned sixteen, his parents purchased a used truck for approximately $5,000 and covered many of the ongoing costs associated with ownership. Insurance added about $1,800 per year, gasoline subsidies averaged $480 annually, and maintenance expenses totaled roughly $400. In the first year alone, the family's cost reached approximately $7,680. Over the next two years, ongoing expenses for insurance, fuel, and maintenance added another $2,680 annually, bringing the total three-year cost to ap-proximately $13,040.

If the same $13,040 had been invested instead and earned an average annual return of 7%, the contributions would have accumulated to roughly $44,398 after 20 years. In other words, a gift that cost $13,040 during Abe's teenage years carried an opportunity cost of more than $44,000 in future retirement savings. This example is not intended to argue that teenagers should never receive a vehicle. Rather, it illustrates how something that appears to be a short-term convenience can become a long-term financial decision with effects that continue long after the keys have changed hands.

QUICK MATH
12345
MC MR M-
7 8 9
1 2 3
0
Abe is 16 and wants a reliable pickup truck one day. Smart money choices today can drive big dreams tomorrow.
Vehicle purchase = $5,000
Insurance $150 × 12 = $1,800
Gas subsidies $40 × 12 = $480
Oil changes and maintenance = $400
TOTAL YEARLY PARENT COST:
$5,000 + $1,800 + $480 + $400
= $7,680
TOTAL FIRST YEAR COST
OVER 3 YEARS:
$7,680 + $2,680 + $2,680
= $13,040
TOTAL AMOUNT INVESTED
IF THAT SAME MONEY WERE INVESTED INSTEAD:
YEAR 1 INVESTMENT: $7,680 × (1.07)^19 = $27,775
YEAR 2 INVESTMENT: $2,680 × (1.07)^18 = $9,058
YEAR 3 INVESTMENT: $2,680 × (1.07)^17 = $8,466
(7% ANNUAL RETURN, COMPOUNDED ANNUALLY)
TOTAL FUTURE VALUE AFTER 20 YEARS:
$27,775 + $9,058 + $8,466
= $45,299
FUTURE VALUE AFTER 20 YEARS
INVESTING THE $13,040 YOU WOULD HAVE SPENT OVER 3 YEARS CAN GROW TO APPROXIMATELY $45,299 AFTER 20 YEARS AT 7% INTEREST.
FUTURE VALUE OF INVESTING: $7,680 (YEAR 1) + $2,680 (YEAR 2) + $2,680 (YEAR 3)
AT 7% ANNUAL RETURN (COMPOUNDED ANNUALLY)
$50,000
$40,000
$30,000
$20,000
$10,000
$0
FUTURE VALUE (USD)
Future Value (Total Account Value)
Amount Invested (Annual)
$7,680
$10,998
$14,341
$15,345
$16,419
$17,568
$18,798
$20,114
$21,522
$23,028
$24,640
$26,365
$28,211
$28,111
$30,186
$32,299
$34,560
$36,979
$39,568
$42,338
$45,299
$2,680
$2,680
$0
1 2 3 4 5 6 7 8 9 10 11 12 13 15 16
YEAR
HOW THE $45,299 IS BUILT
Total amount invested (Years 1–3) $13,040
Growth from 7% compounding interest for 20 years $32,259
TOTAL FUTURE VALUE (Year 20) $45,299
WHAT LOOKED LIKE A HELPFUL GIFT WAS, IN REALITY, A LONG-TERM FINANCIAL DECISION WITH LASTING IMPACT.

# Recommendations

## Evaluate Emotional Maturity, Not Just Age

Age alone does not determine whether a teenager is ready for the responsibility of driving. Emotional maturity matters just as much, if not more. Parents should look for consistency in behavior rather than promises of future change. A teenager who regularly manages responsibilities without constant reminders, follows through on commitments, and demonstrates good judgment is showing readiness through patterns. A teenager who says, "I'll become responsible once I get a car," is often asking for the reward before the behavior already exists.

Driving is not simply transportation; it is freedom combined with risk. A vehicle places a teenager in situations that require emotional regulation, patience, awareness, and decision-making under pressure. Parents are not evaluating whether their child is perfect. They are evaluating whether the child consistently demonstrates enough responsibility to handle the freedom of driving.

## Use Real-Life Readiness Tests

Parents often know more about their teenager's readiness than they initially admit to themselves. Do you trust your teenager's decision-making at night, around peers, or in stressful situations? These are practical indicators rooted in observed behavior rather than wishful thinking.

If the answer creates hesitation, that hesitation is useful information rather than something to dismiss emotionally. Parents sometimes feel pressured by age expectations, peer comparisons, or cultural norms that suggest driving at sixteen is automatic. But readiness varies significantly from one teenager to another. Delaying expanded driving privileges is not failure; in many cases, it is responsible parenting grounded in reality rather than social pressure.

## Limit Risk Before Expanding Freedom

Freedom should increase gradually as responsibility is demonstrated over time. Teenagers do not need unrestricted driving privileges immediately in order to gain experience and confidence. Restrictions on nighttime driving, passengers, distractions, and distance help reduce risk during the period when new drivers are most vulnerable to poor decisions and accidents.

Structure is not punishment. Gradual increases in freedom allow teenagers to build confidence while also showing that responsibility and privilege are connected. When limits are tied to demonstrated maturity rather than emotion, teenagers learn that freedom is earned through consistent behavior.

## Require Earned Contribution

Children who learn independent earning early frequently develop not only financial confidence but emotional confidence. There is a distinct psychological difference between receiving twenty dollars and earning twenty dollars. Earned money carries identity. The child who earns money through effort often becomes more thoughtful about spending because the money represents time, labor, and capability. They begin understanding trade-offs. They recognize that buying one thing may mean sacrificing another. This understanding creates patience and perspective. More importantly, earning money teaches children they can influence their circumstances. That belief becomes critical during adulthood. A teenager who once mowed lawns, sold handmade crafts, tutored younger children, or found creative ways to earn income often enters adulthood believing solutions exist. They may not panic as quickly during hardship because they have experienced themselves as resourceful. The child who only receives may unconsciously develop passivity. If money has always appeared through another person's effort, they may struggle to imagine themselves generating it independently. This does not mean every child must become entrepreneurial or financially successful early in life. The deeper principle is psychological participation. Children benefit emotionally when they experience themselves as contributors rather than permanent recipients.

The goal is not simply payment. The deeper goal is connection between effort and reward. A teenager who contributes financially begins learning about recurring costs, budgeting, planning, and trade-offs in a practical way. Driving becomes less of an automatic expectation and more of an earned responsibility connected to adulthood.

## Put Rules in Writing and Enforce Them Consistently

Clear expectations reduce repeated arguments and emotional negotiations. Families benefit from putting driving rules in writing, including expectations regarding curfews, passengers, phone use, grades, gas payments, insurance contributions, work responsibilities, and consequences for violations. Written agreements create clarity because everyone understands the expectations ahead of time rather than debating them after problems occur.

Developing a formal contract with a teen driver is especially valuable because written commitments are part of adult life. Adults sign agreements for jobs, apartments, loans, insurance policies, and financial obligations. A driving contract introduces teenagers to the idea that privileges and responsibilities are often connected through documented expectations. Having the teenager review and sign the agreement also reinforces accountability and ownership rather than treating the rules as vague parental opinions.

Consistency matters just as much as the rules themselves. Consequences should be predictable and enforced every time rather than changing based on mood, guilt, or exhaustion.

# HANDING YOUR TEEN THE CAR KEYS– *ARE YOU* CONFIDENT *OR* CONCERNED?

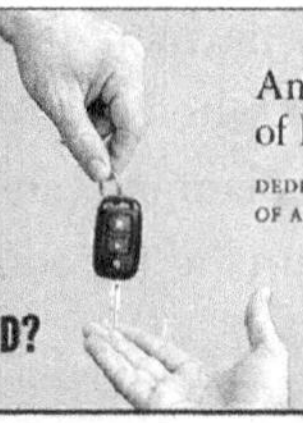

American Academy of Pediatrics
DEDICATED TO THE HEALTH OF ALL CHILDREN

CDC CENTERS FOR DISEASE CONTROL AND PREVENTION

## Parent-Teen Driving Agreement

I, ______________________________, will drive carefully and cautiously and will be courteous to other drivers, bicyclists, and pedestrians at all times.

**I promise that I will obey all the rules of the road.**

- Always wear a seat belt and make all my passengers buckle up
- Obey all traffic lights, stop signs, other street signs, and road markings
- Stay within the speed limit and drive safely
- Never use the car to race or to try to impress others
- Never give rides to hitchhikers

**I promise that I will make sure I can stay focused on driving.**

- Drive with both hands on the wheel
- Never eat, drink, or use a cell phone to talk or text messages while I drive
- Drive only when I am alert and in emotional control
- Call my parents for a ride home if I am impaired in any way that interferes with my ability to drive safely
- Never use earphones to listen to mp3 player or other electronic devices while I drive

**I promise that I will respect laws about drugs and alcohol.**

- Drive only when I am alcohol and drug free
- Never allow any alcohol or illegal drugs in the car
- Be a passenger only with drivers who are alcohol and drug free

**I promise that I will be a responsible driver.**

- Drive only when I have permission to use the car and I will not let anyone else drive the car unless I have permission
- Drive someone else's car only if I have parental permission
- Pay for all traffic citations or parking tickets
- Complete my family responsibilities and maintain good grades at school as listed here: ________
- Contribute to the costs of gasoline, maintenance, and insurance as listed here: ____________

*-Continued-*

VISIT WWW.CDC.GOV/PARENTSARETHEKEY TO GET GOING.

PARENTS ARE THE KEY

American Academy of Pediatrics

DEDICATED TO THE HEALTH OF ALL CHILDREN®

CDC

CENTERS FOR DISEASE CONTROL AND PREVENTION

# PARENT-TEEN DRIVING AGREEMENT

**Additional Promise:** ______________________________

**I agree to the following restrictions, but understand that these restrictions will be modified by my parents as I get more driving experience and demonstrate that I am a responsible driver.**

- For the next _____ months, I will not drive after _______ pm.
- For the next _____ months, I will not transport more than _____ teen passengers (unless I am supervised by a responsible adult).
- For the next _____ months, I won't adjust the stereo, electronic devices, or air conditioning/heater while the car is moving.
- For the next _____ months, I will not drive in bad weather.
- I understand that I am not permitted to drive to off-limit locations or on roads and highways as listed here: ______________________________
- Additional restrictions:

  ______________________________

  ______________________________

  ______________________________

**I agree to follow all the rules and restrictions in this contract. I understand that my parents will impose penalties (see below), including removal of my driving privileges, if I violate the contract. I also understand that my parents will allow me greater driving privileges as I become more experienced and as I demonstrate that I am always a safe and responsible driver.**

**Penalties for contract violations**

- Drove after drinking alcohol or using drugs No driving for _____ months
- Got ticket for speeding or moving violation No driving for _____ months
- Drove after night driving curfew No driving for _____ weeks/months
- Drove too many passengers No driving for _____ weeks/months
- Broke promise about seat belts (self and others) No driving for _____ weeks/months
- Drove on a road or to an area that is off-limits No driving for _____ weeks/months

**Signatures**

Driver: ______________________________ Date: ____________

Parent promise: I also agree to drive safely and to be an excellent role model.

Parent (or guardian): ______________________________ Date: ____________

Parent (or guardian): ______________________________ Date: ____________

*Adapted from the American Academy of Pediatrics "Parent-Teen Driving Agreement"*
(www.aap.org/publiced/BR_TeenDriver.htm)

**VISIT WWW.CDC.GOV/PARENTSARETHEKEY TO GET GOING.**

PARENTS ARE THE KEY

# CHAPTER 9

# VACATION MEMORIES ON A CREDIT *Card*

*Credit buying is much like being drunk. The buzz happens immediately and gives you a lift... The hangover comes the day after.*

– JOYCE BROTHERS

When Daisy and Sam were growing up, family vacations were not curated experiences. They were survival exercises usually in tents held together by mild optimism, and the understanding that no one was getting a refund if it rained. There were no itineraries, no coordinated outfits, and no one using phrases like "core memory" while packing a carry-on.

Vacations were not something you performed—they were something you survived and then talked about later like you had accomplished something. They were simple, imperfect, and somehow still memorable.

The farthest Daisy's parents ever took them was a two-hour ride to Cedar Point for the day, along with a handful of camping trips on Lake Michigan. Everyone slept damp, smelled faintly of campfire for three days, and ate hot dogs and s'mores for almost every meal. There were no matching T-shirts, no "memory package" photos, and no mother planning six months ahead with a Pinterest board titled Magical Family Moments. There was a cooler, maybe bug spray if someone remembered it, and a father angrily trying to hammer tent stakes into dirt that had apparently turned to concrete. In Daisy's adult life, she thought 'how did those count as vacations?'

Daisy didn't make it to Walt Disney World until she was eighteen years old on her senior trip. By then she had listened to enough classmates talk about Disney that she felt like she had been deprived of a constitutional right. She wanted to see what all the fuss was about and, more importantly, confirm that the fuss was justified. She wanted the castle, the rides, the characters, and the version of childhood she assumed she had missed. In her mind, this was not just a trip—it was a correction.

When Daisy and Sam had children of their own, they made a familiar modern declaration. Their kids were going to have experiences, not just trips. These would be the kind of experiences with photos, itineraries, and captions about making memories that sounded meaningful and slightly exhausting at the same time. It felt intentional, thoughtful, and aligned with what good parenting was supposed to look like now and also set a new standard.

Disney was the first major test of that standard. It felt like a milestone, a rite of passage, and a parenting achievement all wrapped into one reservation confirmation email. The kind of trip that says, "We are doing this right," before anyone has even packed a suitcase. Daisy budgeted $5,000 for the trip, which she believed was responsible because it represented 5% of their $100,000 income. She had spreadsheets, categories, and the calm confidence of someone who still believed that budgets would control their spending. Reality, as it turns out, had mouse ears.

By the time flights were booked, airport parking was paid, five hotel nights were reserved, and park tickets were purchased at nearly $200 per person per day, the "carefully budgeted" trip had already started drifting. Then came the purchases no one plans for, but everyone makes, like a $48 safari hat with Mickey ears because apparently one cannot observe plastic safari animals without themed headwear. The $5,000 trip quietly moved toward $8,500. The structure was already shifting, even if no one called it that yet.

And then Disney did what Disney does best. Quick-service meals somehow cost $15 to $20 per person for food that looked suspiciously like it belonged in a middle school cafeteria. Character breakfasts cost significantly more, which meant parents paid premium prices so Mickey could wander by while their child screamed and spilled orange juice. It was less about food and more about the experience, which is how pricing becomes flexible.

Then there were the lines themselves, which Daisy eventually labeled the Triple Disney Line. You stand in one line, then discover it was only the warm-up line, followed by a second line that leads to a third line hidden indoors like a final level of disappointment. By the time you reach the ride, you feel like you have completed a small emotional obstacle course.

The second day they bought the Fast Lane Pass. Disney essentially asks, "Would you like to pay extra to avoid the line you already paid us to stand in?" and exhausted parents say yes because at that point they would pay anything to avoid hearing one more child ask when they are getting on the ride. It is not really a system—it is a test of endurance with optional upgrades. And many families upgrade.

All of this happens in Florida or California heat that feels less like weather and more like a slow-cooking process. Sweat mixed with sunscreen becomes part of the experience, and patience begins to erode somewhere between the third and fourth hidden line. By mid-afternoon, everyone is slightly dehydrated, mildly irritated, and financially committed enough to keep going no matter what. At that point, quitting would feel like wasting money. Still, the kids loved it.

They loved the rides, the characters, the glowing, spinning toys sold every eleven feet, and the Mickey ice cream bars that melt before you finish paying for them. From their perspective, it was magic. From Daisy and Sam's perspective, it was magic with receipts. And those receipts had a way of following them home.

After the trip, Daisy and Sam looked at each other in that dangerous, post-vacation haze and said the sentence that launches a thousand bad financial decisions. This was the best money we ever spent. That sentence should come with a warning label, preferably printed directly on the credit card statement. Because once you say it, something changes. The expectation bar moves.

The kids are no longer comparing Disney to staying home. They are comparing next year to Disney. And once that shift happens, it becomes very difficult to convince anyone that a local park and a sandwich feel equally magical. The baseline has been reset.

So next year they wanted to go back. Or maybe try a cruise. Or maybe Yellowstone in an RV, which sounds simple until you calculate rental fees, gas, campground costs, excursions, groceries, and emergency expenses that somehow resemble a small car payment. Each option felt different, but the pattern remained the same, and continued, year after year.

Each trip built on the last. Another destination, another deposit, another version of "we should do this while they're young," which is the parenting equivalent of a limited time offer that never expires. What felt like intentional family time slowly became an annual expectation with a price tag attached. The system was now in place—not in the trip itself, but in what the pattern becomes.

Daisy became exhausted, not from the vacations themselves, but from figuring out how to pay for them. Every trip came home with souvenirs, stacks of laundry, and a credit card balance that was always slightly higher than expected. There was always something she had forgotten to include. Airports, it turns out, charge aggressively for what they call a carry on. Then came the part no one plans for. The payment phase.

Winter memories showed up on spring statements, and spring memories showed up on summer statements. By the time one trip was finally paid down, Daisy was already planning the next one. It started to feel less like travel and more like a recurring financial cycle.

Somewhere in the middle of all this, Daisy started thinking about her own childhood. Did she love Cedar Point less because it was cheaper, or did it simply feel different because it was simpler? Did camping count less because no one boarded a plane, or had those experiences been just as meaningful in a way that did not require documentation? The question stayed with her longer than expected. It made something feel slightly off. Her children remembered the fun. She remembered the cost. Those two memories were not being stored in the same place, and only one of them came with a monthly statement. That difference mattered more than anyone had said out loud.

Then something else shifted. The kids stopped reacting to trips with surprise and started reacting with expectation. Vacations were no longer special—they were routine. And routine is expensive. "When are we going on vacation?" and "Where are we going?" they would ask.

Social media made it worse. Now childhood was not just compared to last year—it was compared to everyone else. Every scroll showed someone somewhere better, more international, and more impressive. Teenagers backpacking through Europe, posing in Bali, or "finding themselves" in places that required significant parental funding became the new standard. Naturally, Daisy and Sam followed. Europe. Then Asia. Then more spending.

At some point, Daisy noticed something she could not ignore. Her children's passports had more stamps than her own. That realization did not come with anger. It came with confusion. Had they built a spirit for adventure? Or had they built a system of expectation? Because those are not the same thing.

Memories matter, but they are not measured by airfare. Children remember laughing, pillow fights, daring each other to eat hot Takis, running down hotel hallways and moments that feel real. They remember the experience, not the price. Parents, however, are the ones left holding the invoice. And over time, that invoice becomes part of the story too.

## Psychological Pattern: The Scarcity Illusion

One of the most persuasive financial arguments in modern parenting is also one of the simplest: they are only little once. That sentence alone has justified more unnecessary spending than most marketing departments could ever dream of creating themselves. Childhood feels temporary, emotionally fragile, and impossible to recreate once it passes. Parents naturally fear missing moments that someday might matter deeply to their children or themselves. This creates what psychologists often call scarcity thinking around childhood. When something feels scarce, temporary, or fleeting, human beings tend to overvalue experiences connected to it. Financial reasoning becomes emotionally distorted because the spending no longer feels like consumption. It feels like protecting memories before time takes the opportunity away.

Daisy and Sam did not make one reckless financial decision. They made a long series of emotionally understandable ones that slowly built on each other over time. Disney was originally supposed to be a special experience, something magical they could give their children that felt bigger and more memorable than the simpler vacations they remembered from their own childhoods. The first trip genuinely created joy, excitement, closeness, and emotional connection. But once the vacation became emotionally attached to family identity and meaningful memories, the baseline quietly shifted. What began as a carefully planned special event slowly evolved into a recurring lifestyle expectation requiring larger budgets, more planning, and increasingly stressful financial recovery afterward. The problem was never the existence of the trip itself. The problem was allowing emotional experiences to become permanent expectations without ever defining limits.

Psychologically, Daisy was operating inside a deeper emotional framework connected to her own childhood memories. She carried unresolved feelings about experiences she believed she missed growing up. Like many parents, she did not simply want vacations for her children. The trips became symbolic proof that her children were receiving a fuller, richer, more magical childhood than the one she remembered herself having. That emotional framing changed the psychology of spending completely. The vacations no longer felt indulgent. They felt loving, meaningful, and emotionally important. Parents often spend most aggressively not when they are chasing luxury for themselves, but when they believe they are protecting their children from emotional lack.

Modern parenting culture intensifies this psychology constantly. Parents are surrounded by messages about "making memories," "cherishing every stage," and "creating magical childhoods," while social media supplies a nonstop visual comparison system filled with curated family adventures and emotionally edited highlight reels. A local camping trip no longer competes only with other local camping trips. It competes with Disney, Europe, ski resorts, cruises, overwater villas, and teenagers posting sunset photos from destinations their parents are still financially recovering from months later. Ordinary experiences begin feeling emotionally insufficient not because they actually are insufficient, but because the visible standard surrounding childhood keeps escalating

This is one of the central traps of modern parenting culture. Many parents believe they are less materialistic than previous generations because they prioritize experiences over possessions. Families now spend enormous amounts of money curating childhood experiences. The spending feels emotionally elevated because it is framed around connection, bonding, and memory-making rather than objects. Parents convince themselves that experiences are inherently more meaningful and therefore automatically more justified financially.

The emotional danger is that parents slowly begin confusing emotional value with production value. Simpler experiences start feeling emotionally inadequate once children become accustomed to flights, resorts, cruises, expensive attractions, and heavily planned itineraries. Parents then begin chasing the emotional high created by previous experiences, hoping to recreate the same excitement, gratitude, or closeness the family felt before. But emotional highs naturally fade with repetition. What once felt magical gradually becomes routine, and routine requires escalation to maintain the same emotional intensity. That is how special occasions slowly transform into lifestyle maintenance. Families begin financially sustaining emotional expectations they never consciously intended to create.

There is also a deeper emotional layer many parents do not immediately recognize. Trips and experiences often become symbolic reassurance that the family is connected, successful, emotionally healthy, and loving. When Daisy looked at photographs from Disney or Europe, she did not simply see vacations. She saw visible evidence of a happy family creating meaningful memories together. Parents unconsciously start protecting the emotional identity attached to the experiences, not merely the experiences themselves.

The marketplace understands these emotional vulnerabilities extraordinarily well. Vacations become emotional benchmarks for successful parenting. The emotional pressure behind these experiences is enormous because parents fear becoming the family that "never did anything" or failed to provide magical memories while their children were still young enough to appreciate them. Many families are not drowning financially because they are reckless. They are drowning because modern parenting culture transformed childhood into a luxury experience package with recurring monthly costs.

The irony is that children and parents often remember experiences very differently. Daisy remembered the credit card statements, the budgeting adjustments, the low-grade financial anxiety, and the realization that one vacation became several months of financial repair. The children carried the emotional magic. The parents often carried the invoice attached to it. Over time, this imbalance creates emotional exhaustion that families rarely discuss openly because the experiences themselves still produced genuine happiness.

Parents caught in this cycle do not need to eliminate vacations, travel, or meaningful experiences. The issue is not family connection or memory-making itself. The issue is losing the ability to separate emotional connection from financial escalation. Children do not measure love in airfare, hotel categories, luxury resorts, or international passport stamps nearly as much as adults assume they do. In fact, many childhood memories become emotionally permanent precisely because of simplicity, humor, routine, spontaneity, and emotional presence rather than cost. A child who feels safe, relaxed, included, and emotionally connected often remembers ordinary moments with surprising warmth years later.

One of the healthiest mindset shifts parents can make is recognizing that meaningful childhood does not require constant optimization. Families can intentionally reclaim simplicity without feeling like they are depriving their children. A local road trip, camping weekend, board game night, backyard fire pit, movie night, neighborhood walk, or afternoon at the lake can create emotional permanence without requiring financial recovery afterward.

The deepest mistake many modern families make is assuming that memorable childhoods are created primarily through extraordinary experiences. In reality, childhood becomes meaningful because children feel emotionally secure while living ordinary life alongside people who love them. **Simpler experiences are not failed experiences. Unstructured time is not wasted time.** Ordinary routines often create the emotional stability children remember most clearly later in life. Parents do not need to professionally produce childhood in order for it to matter deeply.

Sometimes the richest childhoods are the ones that never became expensive enough to create stress in the first place.

## The Quick Math

Daisy and Sam loved creating memorable family vacations and looked forward to their annual trips each year. Financial planners often suggest keeping travel expenses at or below 5% of household income, which for a family earning $100,000 would equal approximately $5,000 per year. However, their typical vacation cost closer to $8,500 annually, resulting in about $3,500 in spending above their original budget each year. From the time their children were four years old until they turned eighteen, that annual overspending accumulated to approximately $52,500. Importantly, this figure does not represent the family's total vacation spending—it reflects only the amount spent beyond what had originally been planned.

While an extra $3,500 may not feel significant during any single vacation, the long-term opportunity cost can be substantial. If that same $3,500 had been invested at the end of each year for fourteen years and then allowed to continue growing at an average annual return of 7% through year twenty, it would have grown to approximately $112,957. In other words, the family's vacation upgrades, extra experiences, and budget overruns carried a hidden future value of more than $112,000.

This example is not intended to suggest that families should avoid travel or shared experiences. Vacations often create cherished memories and strengthen family relationships. Rather, it illustrates how recurring overspending—even on worthwhile experiences—can quietly reduce future financial flexibility. The lesson is not to eliminate family trips, but to recognize that consistently exceeding a budget has consequences that extend far beyond the current year. Small annual overruns can become six-figure opportunity costs over time, making intentional spending just as important for experiences as it is for material purchases.

# QUICK MATH

| RECOMMENDED TRAVEL BUDGET: | ACTUAL AVERAGE TRIP: | ANNUAL OVERSPENDING: | OVERSPENDING FROM AGE 4 THROUGH 18: |
|---|---|---|---|
| 5% of $100,000 income | | | 15 × $3,500 |
| = $5,000 | = $8,500 | = $3,500 | = $52,500 |

That $52,500 is not total vacation spending.
It is only the amount spent above what was originally planned, which is why it is so easy to ignore.

## IF THAT SAME $3,500 PER YEAR HAD BEEN INVESTED AT 7% OVER THOSE 14 YEARS:

**≈ $112,957**

Future value of investing $3,500 at the end of each year for 14 years at 7%.

That is over $112,000 created from spending that rarely felt excessive in the moment.

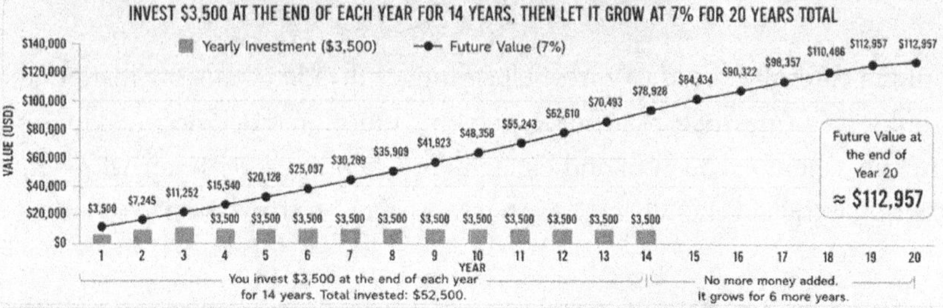


**THE BIG PICTURE:**
Small overspending today can mean huge opportunities missed tomorrow.

# Recommendations

## Set a Fixed Travel Budget

Family travel should fit inside the budget rather than the budget expanding to justify the trip. Establishing a fixed yearly travel limit—such as 5% or less of household income—creates structure before emotions, excitement, and social pressure begin influencing decisions. Without boundaries, vacations can become one of the most financially undisciplined categories in family life because travel spending is often emotionally justified as "making memories."

The problem is not travel itself. Experiences can absolutely enrich family relationships and create meaningful connection. The issue arises when spending expands to match the imagined experience rather than the family's actual financial reality. Financial clarity before booking protects both the trip and the future because it allows families to enjoy travel without carrying stress, guilt, or long-term financial consequences home with them.

## Treat High-Cost Trips Like Strategy, Not Emotion

If families choose expensive destinations such as Disney, large resorts, cruises, or international vacations, the experience should be approached strategically rather than emotionally. High-cost trips naturally encourage overspending through upgrades, convenience purchases, premium experiences, souvenirs, dining packages, and the pressure to "make the most" of the trip. Without structure, the vacation budget can expand dramatically while adding very little additional meaning to the actual experience.

Planning carefully ahead of time helps families decide what truly matters most. Defining priorities before arriving prevents emotional decision-making in the moment, where exhaustion and excitement often override financial judgment. Intentional travel generally creates more satisfaction than reactive spending.

## Alternate Expensive Years with Simpler Ones

Not every year needs to include a major vacation. Families often fall into the pattern of escalating travel expectations where each year must become bigger, farther, or more expensive than the last. Over time, what once felt special becomes emotionally normalized, and increasingly costly trips begin feeling like the standard rather than the exception.

Balancing larger vacations with simpler experiences helps maintain both financial stability and appreciation. Camping trips, regional travel, road trips, cabin stays, national parks, or even thoughtfully planned staycations can create meaningful connection without requiring enormous spending. Simpler years also allow families to recover financially while preventing travel from becoming automatic consumption rather than intentional family time.

## Separate Meaningful from Expensive

Children rarely remember vacations according to price. The danger is that adults sometimes begin confusing expensive with meaningful because modern culture constantly markets travel as performance, status, and lifestyle identity. Social media reinforces the illusion that memorable childhoods require increasingly elaborate experiences. Vacations become larger.

What once feels special quickly becomes normal. Emotional adaptation happens remarkably fast. A child thrilled by a simple trip at age six may barely react to a far more expensive experience at age sixteen because the baseline continually moved upward. Families unintentionally create emotional inflation when every year must outperform the previous one. The goal is not impressive memories. The goal is lasting ones.

## Require Contribution for Major Travel as Children Get Older

As teenagers grow older, requiring some financial contribution toward larger or international trips helps shift travel from expectation to opportunity. A part-time job, savings contribution, or shared expense creates ownership and changes how the experience is perceived. Teenagers who participate financially often appreciate the trip differently because they understand the effort required to make it possible.

Contribution also helps prepare teenagers for adult financial realities. Travel becomes connected to planning, trade-offs, budgeting, and delayed gratification rather than appearing as something that simply materializes through parental sacrifice. The goal is not to make children "pay their own way" entirely, but to help them recognize that meaningful experiences usually require effort, planning, and financial responsibility.

## Ask One Question Before Booking

Before committing to a major vacation, families should ask one difficult but clarifying question: "Are we buying connection, or are we buying optics?" In many cases, the answer reveals the true motivation behind the spending. Some trips are genuinely centered around togetherness, rest, exploration, and family memory-making. Others are driven more by comparison, image, pressure, or the desire to appear successful to others.

That distinction matters because emotionally driven "optics spending" rarely creates lasting satisfaction. Families may spend enormous amounts of money chasing the appearance of happiness or success while simultaneously increasing financial stress at home. Honest reflection before booking helps ensure that travel decisions align with family values rather than outside expectations.

CHAPTER 10

# ALLOWANCE—THE ILLUSION OF EARNED *Money*

*All the perplexities, confusions, and distress in America arise, not from defects in their constitution or confederation, not from want of honor or virtue, so much as from the downright ignorance of the nature of coin, credit, and circulation.*

— JOHN ADAMS (1735–1826), LETTER TO THOMAS JEFFERSON, AUGUST 25, 1787

Dan and Kristal adored their twin girls, Layla and Lola. The twins were the center of everything—birthday parties with matching themes, Christmas mornings with coordinated pajamas, and enough hair accessories scattered around the bathrooms to stock a small beauty supply store. They were, in every sense, girly girls, fully committed to hair, makeup, skincare, shopping bags, bath balms, lip glosses, and the belief that any outing worth attending required a new outfit and a mirror check.

Dan and Kristal loved giving to them, or at least that is what they called it. From the outside it looked sweet, like parents who doted on their daughters and genuinely enjoyed seeing them happy.

The girls had been receiving allowance since they were ten years old. Originally, the plan sounded responsible and well thought out, the kind of thing that makes parents feel like they are building strong habits early. Dan and Kristal decided the money would be tied to chores—clear the dishes after dinner, wipe down the kitchen table, keep the bedroom clean, and make the beds.

For the first month, everyone acted like this was a serious family economy. The chart hung proudly on the refrigerator, the girls occasionally checked boxes, and Dan and Kristal made speeches about responsibility that sounded very convincing at the time. It felt structured, intentional, and briefly impressive. Then, as often happens, real life arrived.

Dan and Kristal got tired of policing whether the beds were actually made or whether "clean room" meant clothes shoved under the bed and the closet door shut quickly before inspection. They got tired of asking, reminding, and repeating themselves, because parenting already felt like a full-time administrative job without adding payroll supervision to the list. So gradually the standards softened, not dramatically, but enough to matter.

The chart remained hanging, but mostly as decoration. Friday simply became allowance day. Ten dollars each, every single week, delivered with consistency that had nothing to do with completed work.

What the girls lacked in chore consistency, they made up for in payday awareness. By Friday afternoon they never forgot, and their internal calendar seemed more reliable than anything hanging on the wall. They would come through the door from school and ask almost immediately, "Do we get our allowance today?" which suggested a level of financial awareness that did not extend to how the money was actually earned. Sometimes, sensing parental hesitation, they would grab a rag and hurriedly wipe some random section of countertop as if evidence of labor had to be manufactured quickly. It was less about completing work and more about creating the appearance of it just in time to justify the transaction.

Everyone understood what was happening, even if no one said it out loud. This was no longer compensation for completed work—it was recurring distribution with occasional household theatrics attached. The system had shifted from earning to receiving.

Children start associating money not with productivity, not with initiative, not with skill, but with routine existence. Do just enough to appear mildly cooperative in the home you already live in, and cash appears. Keep your room from becoming biologically hazardous, and somebody hands you ten dollars like you have provided a specialized service. There is something fundamentally shaky about teaching a child that cleaning up after themselves deserves a wage, because the adult world does not issue checks for not being a slob. The expectation is simply that you maintain your own environment, and the reward is that you get to continue living in it.

Dan and Kristal did not spend much time philosophizing about any of this because ten dollars a week felt harmless. It was small, manageable, and easy to justify as a teaching tool. It felt almost symbolic, like practice money for a future that would eventually become more serious. Until they started noticing where the money was going.

At first it was exactly what parents expect—movies with friends, Starbucks runs, mall food courts, and the occasional smoothie that somehow cost more than a full meal. It was annoying, but it felt normal, like a rite of passage into teenage spending habits. Then Kristal found a vape pen in Layla's backpack. A few weeks later, Dan found a beer tucked into the side pocket of Lola's dance bag. Neither discovery launched a full investigation, but it did raise an uncomfortable question that was difficult to ignore. Who exactly was funding this teenage experimentation? The answer, once considered honestly, was not complicated.

Dan and Kristal were.

Their harmless allowance system had become a recurring subsidy for purchases they neither approved nor controlled. What they thought was teaching "money management" had turned into unrestricted weekly funding with no oversight and no connection to effort.

Although the allowance experience would have been enough financial confusion for one household, Dan and Kristal decided to modernize. When Layla and Lola turned fifteen, their parents added both girls as authorized users on their Bank of America account and handed each of them a credit card. Banks encourage this sort of thing as an early credit-building strategy, and on paper it sounds responsible, forward-thinking, and financially literate.

Children can begin establishing credit history while technically remaining under the umbrella of the parent's account. It feels like preparation, like a head start, like something good parents are supposed to do. In theory, it sounds wonderful.

In practice, there is one obvious problem. A child with no job, no bills, and no monthly statement to pay does not experience a credit card as borrowed money. They experience it as money. That distinction matters more than parents think. Layla and Lola had no earned income, no paycheck, and no understanding of interest or balances. What they had was embossed plastic with their names on it, and psychologically that translated into one very dangerous idea. I can buy things.

Christmas that year provided the perfect demonstration. Dan and Kristal sent the girls to the mall to shop for Christmas presents, thinking they would use their allowance money and buy something small but thoughtful. It sounded sweet in the abstract, like independent daughters choosing meaningful gifts. The twins took the mission seriously. They went to Lululemon and bought Kristal two separate outfits, one from each daughter, at approximately $175 apiece. Then they went to Tommy Bahama and bought Dan two outfits as well, each around $150, creating a shopping experience that was both generous and financially impressive.

Christmas morning was full of enthusiasm.

"Open mine first!" shrieked Lola

"Mom, I got purple because I know you love purple!" Layla smiled with delight.

The girls could barely sit still while Dan and Kristal opened beautifully wrapped, surprisingly expensive gifts that they had, unbeknownst to them, technically purchased themselves. It was thoughtful, generous, and completely disconnected from financial reality.

Kristal finally paused and looked at the twins. "How did you pay for these?"

Layla answered as if the answer were obvious. "The credit card, of course."

Of course.

Kristal smiled, because what else does a mother do when her children have lovingly used her own credit line to surprise her with premium athletic ware. She appreciated the thought, even as she processed the fact that she had financed her own Christmas through two minors who believed they had become holiday philanthropists.

And this is the second major financial distortion. Allowance teaches that cash appears regularly. Credit cards teach that spending appears instantly. Neither one automatically teaches the most important lesson in money, which is that purchasing power is supposed to be connected to labor, limitation, and consequence. Without those three things, spending becomes detached from reality. Children begin to experience money as access rather than effort, which is a very comfortable way to live until the bill arrives.

A debit card loaded with birthday money is one thing. A prepaid account tied to earned deposits is another. But a parental credit card in the hands of a teenager who does not work creates confidence in consumption before any understanding of repayment exists. Debt always feels painless when someone else receives the bill.

And what makes this pattern especially tricky is how easily it carries forward into adulthood. A teenager who learns that money shows up automatically and spending has no immediate consequence does not suddenly reverse course at eighteen. The environment changes, but the behavior often doesn't, and the habits scale up alongside new levels of independence.

Credit limits get higher, purchases get larger, and the illusion of affordability stretches just far enough to feel manageable—until it isn't. What started as ten dollars a week and a shared credit card becomes car payments, rent, and balances that follow them long after the novelty of independence wears off. Because habits don't wait for adulthood to begin; they simply continue with bigger numbers attached.

## Psychological Pattern: Reward without Responsibility

Dan and Kristal did not intentionally decide to raise financially entitled children. What they created happened gradually through convenience, inconsistency, and emotional avoidance. The original allowance system sounded responsible because it gave the appearance of structure and financial education. But once the parents stopped consistently enforcing the chore expectations, the allowance quietly transformed from earned money into automatic money. That distinction matters psychologically because children do not learn from what parents intend. They learn from what the system consistently rewards. Layla and Lola quickly realized the money continued arriving whether effort was attached to it or not. The family stopped operating on earned compensation and started operating on recurring distribution.

The deeper psychological issue was that Dan and Kristal wanted to avoid conflict and exhaustion more than they wanted to enforce consistency. Correcting chores, inspecting bedrooms, arguing about responsibility, and withholding allowance required emotional energy at the exact stage of parenting when many adults already feel depleted. It became easier to hand over ten dollars than to create another argument after work. Over time, convenience replaced intentionality. The parents told themselves the money was symbolic and harmless, but repeated symbolic systems become real systems eventually. The girls began associating money not with work, discipline, or productivity, but with routine existence and parental availability.

The credit card amplified the distortion because it introduced spending power before responsibility had fully formed psychologically. Layla and Lola were not irresponsible in the way adults typically define irresponsibility. They were simply operating inside the financial reality they had experienced their entire lives. Money appeared automatically. Purchases rarely carried visible consequences. Bills existed somewhere in the background handled by adults.

When the girls used the credit card to buy expensive Christmas gifts, the emotional logic made perfect sense to them. They experienced themselves as generous shoppers, not borrowers spending against future debt. Children cannot emotionally understand repayment until they have personally experienced earning, limitation, waiting, and sacrifice connected to money. This pattern enforced that spending is emotionally detached from labor, which creates unrealistic expectations about adulthood later. The girls began associating money not with work, discipline, or productivity, but as an expectation from their parents. In other words, entitlement.

Parents who recognize this dynamic need to reconnect money to visible work, visible limits, and visible tradeoffs. Allowance systems work best when they are tied to optional effort beyond normal household expectations, not basic self-maintenance. Children should regularly experience the relationship between work completed, money earned, money saved, and money spent. That connection creates perspective that automatic access systems cannot provide.

Parents can also correct this pattern by slowing financial access down instead of accelerating it. Debit cards tied to earned balances teach awareness. Saving toward purchases teaches patience. Waiting teaches emotional regulation. Even disappointment has value financially because it teaches children that wanting something and immediately obtaining it are not the same experience. The goal is not raising children who fear money or obsess over it. The goal is raising adults who understand that purchasing power is supposed to be connected to effort, limitation, and consequence. Without those connections, children often grow into adults who feel financially confident long before they are financially capable.

## The Quick Math

Dan and Kristal believed they were teaching their daughters financial responsibility by providing a modest allowance. Each girl received $10 per week, for a combined household allowance of $20 per week. Over the course of a year, that amounted to $1,040, and over the eight years from ages ten through eighteen, the family distributed approximately $8,320 in allowance payments. Viewed in isolation, the amount does not seem excessive. In fact, it feels small, manageable, and easy to justify, which is precisely why recurring expenses like this often go unquestioned.

The long-term financial impact becomes more apparent when the same dollars are viewed through the lens of compound growth. If the $1,040 per year had been invested instead and earned an average annual return of 7%, with contributions made for eight years and then allowed to grow without additional deposits for the following twelve years, it would have accumulated to approximately $24,032 after 20 years. What appears to be a relatively minor household expense today could represent more than $24,000 in future retirement savings tomorrow. This example is not intended to suggest that parents should never provide an allowance. Allowances can be valuable tools for teaching budgeting, saving, and delayed gratification. Rather, it illustrates a broader financial principle: recurring expenditures that seem insignificant in the moment can create meaningful opportunity costs over time. Small amounts given away today may represent substantial financial opportunities lost in the future, making intentionality just as important with small expenses as it is with large ones.

# QUICK MATH

| ALLOWANCE PER WEEK FOR EACH GIRL: | TWO GIRLS: PER WEEK | ANNUAL ALLOWANCE: | ALLOWANCE FROM AGE 10 THROUGH 18 (8 YEARS): |
|---|---|---|---|
|  |  |  |  |
| $10 | $10 + $10 = $20 | $20 × 52 = $1,040 | $1,040 × 8 = $8,320 |
| = $10 | = $20 | = $1,040 | = $8,320 |

That $8,320 is not a catastrophic number on its own.
It feels small, manageable, and easy to justify over time,
which is exactly why systems like this rarely get questioned.

**IF THAT SAME $1,040 PER YEAR HAD BEEN INVESTED INSTEAD, AND ALLOWED TO GROW AT AN AVERAGE RETURN OF 7% FOR 20 YEARS—WITH CONTRIBUTIONS MADE FOR ONLY 8 YEARS (THEN LEFT TO GROW FOR 12 YEARS)—IT WOULD BECOME APPROXIMATELY:**

**≈ $24,032**

That is not just allowance money.

That is retirement money.

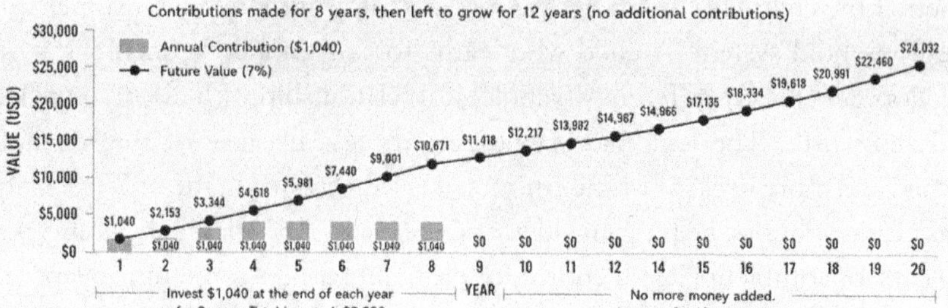


**BAR GRAPH (ANNUAL CONTRIBUTIONS ONLLY)**

$1,040 per year × 8 years = $8,320 total contributed

- Years 1–8: $1,040 each year
- Years 9–20: $0 (no additional contributions)

**LINE GRAPH (FUTURE VALUE WITH 7% COMPOUND GROWTH)**

Formula used: Future Value of Annuity (FVIFA)

$FV = \$1,040 \times [((1.07)^8 - 1) / 0.07] \times (1.07)^{12}$

$= \$1,040 \times 11.1628 \times 2.2539 \approx \$24,032$

## THE BIG PICTURE:

Small amounts given away today can mean significant opportunities lost tomorrow.

# Recommendations

## Stop Paying Children for Basic Responsibilities

Making a bed, clearing dishes, keeping a bedroom clean, and participating in normal household upkeep are not premium services deserving financial reward. They are baseline expectations of living within a shared family environment. When every small responsibility becomes tied to payment, children can begin viewing contribution as optional rather than foundational. The household slowly shifts from a family system built on mutual responsibility to a transactional system where effort only happens when compensation is attached.

Children benefit from understanding that some responsibilities exist simply because they are part of being a functioning member of a household. Adults do not receive bonuses for putting laundry away or taking out their own trash. Basic participation teaches accountability, cooperation, and respect for shared spaces. When parents reserve payment only for work that goes beyond ordinary expectations, money retains its meaning, and responsibility remains connected to character rather than negotiation.

## Replace Standing Allowance with Paid Opportunities

The relationship between parent and child changes dramatically depending on whether the child sees themselves as a contributor or merely a consumer within the household system. A child who learns to earn money in small ways often develops an entirely different psychological relationship with effort, ownership, and self-worth. The lemonade stand matters less because of the ten dollars earned and more because of the emotional wiring created in the process. Cutting grass for neighbors, helping an elderly person carry groceries, babysitting, washing cars, or completing extra chores for payment teaches something deeper than labor. It teaches cause and effect. Effort becomes connected to outcome. The child experiences the pride of solving a problem independently rather than waiting for rescue. That emotional experience is profoundly stabilizing because the child begins to understand they possess capability. Children who repeatedly experience themselves as capable often become adults who face financial hardship with action rather than paralysis. By contrast, children who are conditioned to receive without contributing may slowly begin to associate money with entitlement rather than responsibility. If every desire is fulfilled through parental sacrifice without participation from the child, the parent unintentionally becomes an emotional ATM machine instead of a guide. Gratitude weakens when contribution disappears. Dependence slowly transforms into expectation. Over time, some children stop seeing parental giving as generosity and begin seeing it as obligation.

This distinction matters because automatic allowances can unintentionally normalize income without work. While small allowances may help teach budgeting, children learn much more deeply when they experience the effort required to earn money themselves. Paid opportunities also encourage initiative because children begin recognizing that additional effort can create additional rewards. That mindset mirrors adult financial life far more accurately than passive income provided without contribution.

If parents want to teach children how to earn money, creating optional paid opportunities is often more effective than providing a standing allowance disconnected from effort. Additional work such as washing cars, yard work, organizing storage areas, helping with repairs, or assisting with larger household projects creates a direct relationship between labor and reward. The lesson changes from "money appears automatically" to "money follows effort and contribution."

## Require Visible Labor Tied to Visible Payment

Children should clearly understand why they were paid and what specific work produced the reward. Visible labor tied to visible payment creates a mental connection between effort and income that cannot be replicated through automatic transfers or unexplained spending money. When children physically complete a task and then receive payment afterward, the exchange becomes concrete and understandable.

Invisible systems create confusion because money begins feeling detached from effort. Many children grow up observing digital transactions without fully understanding the labor behind them. Cash payments, direct transfers for completed work, or simple written tracking systems help reinforce the relationship between contribution and compensation. The goal is not giving children money; it is helping them internalize where money comes from and why it exists.

## Do Not Introduce Credit Before Income Exists

Credit should never be introduced as a casual convenience tool. Borrowed money carries responsibility, and children who do not yet have consistent earned income are rarely prepared to manage debt appropriately. If a teenager cannot pay a balance using money they personally earned, they should not have access to borrowed spending. Otherwise, parents unintentionally teach consumption before responsibility and entitlement before accountability.

Many adults struggle financially because they were introduced to credit long before they understood budgeting, delayed gratification, or repayment. Teenagers should first learn how to operate within limits using actual money before gaining access to borrowed money. Credit cards are not simply payment methods; they are financial tools with long-term consequences when misunderstood. Teaching restraint early is far easier than correcting debt habits later.

## Introduce Money Tools in Order

Financial education works best when children move through money systems gradually and sequentially. Cash teaches visibility because children can physically see money leaving their hands. Debit cards and prepaid systems then introduce digital spending while still remaining tied to actual available funds. Children should understand interest rates and be able to calculate actual cost of an item using credit. After children understand balances, limits, saving, credit, and delayed spending and have some form of income outside of their parents, should having a credit card even become part of the conversation.

Skipping developmental steps creates confidence without comprehension. Many teenagers become comfortable swiping cards long before they understand how quickly spending accumulates or what happens when money runs out. Gradual progression allows children to build understanding layer by layer. Financial confidence should grow alongside financial literacy.

## Make Them Fund Their Own Generosity

If children want to buy gifts for friends or family members, that desire should be encouraged. But whenever possible, the money should come from savings or earnings they created themselves. Generosity becomes far more meaningful when it involves personal sacrifice, planning, and trade-offs. A child who spends their own saved money on a birthday present experience giving differently than a child simply handed money by a parent.

This process teaches empathy, intentionality, and appreciation simultaneously. Children begin understanding that generosity is not measured by dollar amount alone, but by willingness to give up something personally valued for the benefit of someone else. When children contribute from their own effort, generosity becomes connected to character rather than convenience.

## Teach One Consistent Rule: Access Follows Responsibility

One of the most important financial and life principles parents can teach is that access follows responsibility. Not age. Not pressure from peers. Not comparison to what "everyone else" has. Responsibility comes first, and access comes second every single time. Whether the issue involves phones, cars, spending money, social freedom, or digital access, the sequence should remain consistent.

Children thrive when expectations feel predictable and stable. When parents consistently connect increased freedom to demonstrated maturity, children begin understanding that privileges are earned through behavior rather than demanded through emotion. This principle also prepares children for adulthood, where greater freedom almost always arrives alongside greater responsibility. The earlier children internalize that connection, the more prepared they are for independent financial and personal decision-making later in life.

# CHAPTER 11

# COST OF HIGH SCHOOL *Failure*

*Children have never been very good at listening to their elders, but they have never failed to imitate them.*

– JAMES BALDWIN

Josh was a really nice kid, and that needs to be established immediately because everyone liked Josh. He was polite in that almost aggressively respectful way that makes adults say, "What a sweet boy," after a five-minute conversation, as if they had just encountered a future mayor. He answered with "yes ma'am" and "no sir," held doors open, smiled at older people, and carried himself with a calm, agreeable presence that made him easy to be around. If you met him in public, you would assume he was exactly the kind of teenager who had his life reasonably together. You would not have guessed that behind that politeness was a complete absence of urgency.

Josh was not the sharpest tool in the shed, but he also was not the dullest. He lived comfortably in that wide middle space where success is entirely possible if the person develops discipline, initiative, and follow-through. Unfortunately, those were not traits that showed up naturally for him, and no one had pushed hard enough for them to develop. He was sweet, kind, and easy to manage, which made everything harder to recognize as a problem. There is something misleading about a pleasant personality, because it masks the absence of progress in a way that feels harmless until it isn't.

Beth and Drew were very nice parents, and they were also very accommodating parents, which is not always the same thing. Their instinct was to help, to smooth things over, and to step in before anything became uncomfortable or difficult. Over time, that instinct turned into a pattern where Josh rarely had to figure anything out on his own. Beth packed his lunch, washed his clothes, and changed his sheets well into high school, while Drew reminded him to pick up his room, sweep, wipe, carry, and generally participate in basic household life one instruction at a time. It did not feel like overhelping or enabling in the moment—it felt like caring.

If Josh was told to do something, he would usually do it, which gave the illusion that things were working. He was not defiant, not argumentative, and not particularly difficult, which made it easy to overlook what was missing. He simply waited to be told what to do, and without that instruction, nothing happened. That was just enough compliance for his parents to mistake obedience for competence. Those are not the same thing, even though they often look similar from a distance.

Freshman year should have been the first flashing warning sign. The school counselor called and explained that Josh was already behind in credits and would need summer school for Algebra and Biology. Beth and Drew paid for summer school and treated it like an inconvenience rather than a signal. It felt manageable, like something that could be corrected with a little extra effort. Plenty of kids stumble freshman year, and plenty of kids catch up, which made it easy to believe Josh would do the same. He did not.

Sophomore year arrived and left behind an even uglier transcript, one that was harder to explain away but still somehow not urgent enough to trigger real intervention. Not only had the summer classes not been properly completed, but Josh now had additional lost credits in Algebra II, Chemistry, and History. History was the baffling one, because Josh genuinely loved it. He read about wars voluntarily, could explain strategies no one had asked about, and knew obscure details that made dinner conversations unexpectedly educational. And yet, despite all of that interest, he failed the class.

This is where Beth and Drew began to learn something they had not fully understood before. Knowledge and grades are not the same thing, and interest does not automatically translate into performance. Grades are often the paperwork of compliance, not curiosity. Josh understood the material in his own way, but he did not complete assignments, follow structure, or meet expectations. The system required behavior, not just awareness.

Josh also failed gym, which requires a very specific level of disengagement. His explanation was that there were too many days he did not feel like getting dressed, which sounds simple until you realize it represents a broader pattern. It takes effort to fail a class centered around participation. Junior year followed with similar results, including failing art because he wanted to draw what he wanted to draw instead of what the assignment required. Josh apparently viewed rubrics as artistic oppression, which is not a position that tends to produce passing grades.

Beth and Drew never hired a tutor, and they told themselves that they did not have the money. That was technically possible, but it was also financially questionable when viewed more closely. Drew was a pack-a-day smoker, which is a measurable amount of money being spent that did not build anything. Beth stopped at Starbucks most mornings, participating in a daily routine that felt small but added up over time. If enough trimming had occurred, tutoring money probably existed, but it never became urgent enough to find it. And that was one of the real issues.

Josh's academics were treated like a developing inconvenience instead of a five-alarm family fire. When something is not treated as urgent, it rarely becomes important, and when it is not important, it does not change. So, life continued in a steady pattern without meaningful action.

Josh turned sixteen, and Beth and Drew told him to get a job, which he did with reasonable consistency. He worked at Subway, then Culver's, then Jimmy John's, building a résumé that was entirely sandwich-based but at least functional. What he did not have was a driver's license, because his parents had decided he would not get one until graduation. This sounded disciplined in theory, but in practice it turned them into uber drivers for a teenager who now needed rides to everything.

When Josh was home, the girlfriend was there, and she quickly became a constant presence. She was sweet enough to make it socially uncomfortable to dislike her, which made it harder to address how often she was there. She sat on couches, raided refrigerators, and participated in long teenage conversations that produced no income and no forward movement.

By senior year, the school delivered the kind of meeting parents dread, the one where optimism is no longer part of the conversation. Even if Josh passed every remaining class, he would not graduate, because he had completed only half the required credits. This was no longer a situation that could be fixed with effort alone. It required time, structure, and a level of urgency that had not previously existed.

The school placed him into a catch-up program beginning in January, with a plan involving a fifth year and additional coursework. Josh kept saying he was doing the work, getting caught up, and making progress, which became a pattern of reassuring language without measurable results. Beth and Drew eventually suggested getting a GED, but Josh refused. He wanted the diploma, or more accurately, he wanted the idea of the diploma without the behaviors required to earn it.

Josh turned twenty, still living in a space between intention and execution, no late graduation and no GED. He briefly announced he wanted to join the military, which for a moment felt like the structure everyone had been hoping for. Discipline, routine, and accountability suddenly seemed possible. But the military requires a diploma or a GED, and Josh had neither, which closed that door.

At some point during this extended stay in Not Quite Adult Land, Josh moved into the partially finished basement. This was described as giving him "his own space," which sounded like progress but functioned more like a separate space where he could be alone with his girlfriend. Now he could exist independently without actually becoming independent, which is a very comfortable place to stay if no one interrupts it.

His girlfriend spent more time there, his friends gathered there, and the faint smell of pot occasionally drifted upstairs, accompanied by a box fan pointed out the basement window like a symbolic attempt at responsibility. Josh paid no rent, bought no groceries, and contributed nothing to utilities. A used car was eventually given to him, but repairs, insurance, and maintenance found their way back to Beth and Drew. The household continued to operate around him.

Eventually, questions began to surface that many parents reach in quiet moments. Where is all of his money going? What is he doing with his time? What is he doing with his life? He works. He has no bills. He lives here, eats here, and drives a subsidized vehicle. And yet he still has the financial profile of someone who forages. And beneath that question sat another one that was harder to answer honestly. When do we get our freedom back?

## Psychological Pattern: Comfortable Dependence

The psychological damage in this chapter did not come from cruelty, neglect, or lack of love. It came from the slow erosion of expectations. Josh grew up inside a household where comfort consistently outranked accountability, and over time, that shaped the way he viewed responsibility itself. Beth and Drew loved their son deeply, but they confused support with protection from discomfort. Every time they stepped in to remind, rescue, smooth over, excuse, drive, subsidize, or delay consequences, they unintentionally taught Josh that life would reorganize itself around his lack of action. The result was not rebellion. It was dependency disguised as niceness. Josh never developed urgency because urgency had never truly been required of him.

There is also an important psychological distinction between compliance and independence. Josh was agreeable, respectful, and emotionally easy to parent, which made the deeper problem harder to detect. Difficult children trigger intervention because their behavior creates immediate stress. Pleasant children can drift for years because their personality softens the alarm system around them. Beth and Drew interpreted Josh's politeness as maturity, but maturity is not measured by tone of voice. It is measured by self-direction, resilience, follow-through, and the ability to function without constant prompting. Josh became psychologically conditioned to wait for external direction because that had always been the structure of his life. Over time, initiative weakens when someone else consistently manages the pressure of daily living.

Another layer of this dynamic was avoidance. Beth and Drew likely experienced growing anxiety about Josh's academic failures, lack of progress, and delayed adulthood, but avoidance became their coping mechanism. Instead of confronting the situation aggressively, they minimized it into manageable pieces: one failed class, one summer school session, one delayed graduation plan, one more year at home. This is psychologically common in families because accepting the full reality of a child's dysfunction can feel emotionally overwhelming. Parents often protect themselves from fear by shrinking the seriousness of the problem. Unfortunately, avoidance does not stop consequences; it only delays them until they become larger, more expensive, and emotionally heavier. By the time Josh was twenty and still dependent, the family was no longer managing a temporary setback. They had normalized stagnation.

The good news is that patterns like this can still be changed, but change requires discomfort from both parents and children. Families often wait for motivation to appear naturally, but motivation frequently follows structure rather than preceding it. Beth and Drew would need to stop functioning as managers of Josh's life and begin functioning as guides with boundaries. That means clear expectations tied to measurable outcomes: employment hours, educational milestones, household contributions, financial participation, deadlines, and consequences if those expectations are not met. Emotional guilt often makes parents hesitate because enforcing boundaries feels harsh after years of accommodation. **Boundaries are not punishment. They are preparation.** Adulthood cannot develop in an environment where parents absorb the weight of responsibility.

Josh would also need to rebuild his identity around competence rather than comfort. Many dependent young adults lose confidence because they know, deep down, they are behind their peers developmentally. That insecurity often creates even more avoidance, procrastination, escapism, gaming, sleeping, substances, or passive living. The solution is not humiliation or constant criticism. The solution is gradual mastery. Small responsibilities completed consistently begin rebuilding self-respect. Paying a bill, keeping a schedule, maintaining a job, completing coursework, buying groceries, contributing rent, or solving problems independently all create psychological momentum. Parents must understand that rescuing an adult child from every struggle may temporarily reduce stress in the home, but long term it often delays the very confidence and independence that child desperately needs. Real love does not remove every obstacle. Sometimes real love requires allowing adulthood to arrive.

## The Quick Math

Beth and Drew wanted to help their adult child get established and remain financially secure. Like many parents, they provided ongoing assistance with living expenses, car expenses, food and housing support, and other financial needs. According to the USDA, the average cost is approximately $17,000 per year to support a child living in your house, whether that child is an adult or not. Temporary support extended into three years, bringing the family's total out-of-pocket cost to roughly $51,000. That figure is the visible cost—the amount that actually left their bank account. What is less obvious is the long-term opportunity cost of those dollars.

If the same $17,000 annual contributions had been invested for three years and then allowed to grow at an average annual return of 7% for the remainder of a 20-year period, the funds would have accumulated to approximately $172,000. This example is not intended to suggest that parents should never help their adult children. Family circumstances vary, and there are times when assistance is both necessary and appropriate. Rather, it highlights an important financial reality: every dollar used to support prolonged dependence is a dollar that is no longer working toward the parents' own financial future. The visible cost is often only the beginning. The larger cost may be the retirement savings, financial flexibility, and long-term security that those funds could have created if invested instead. Every financial decision made today has a future value attached to it, whether that value is realized through spending or through growth.

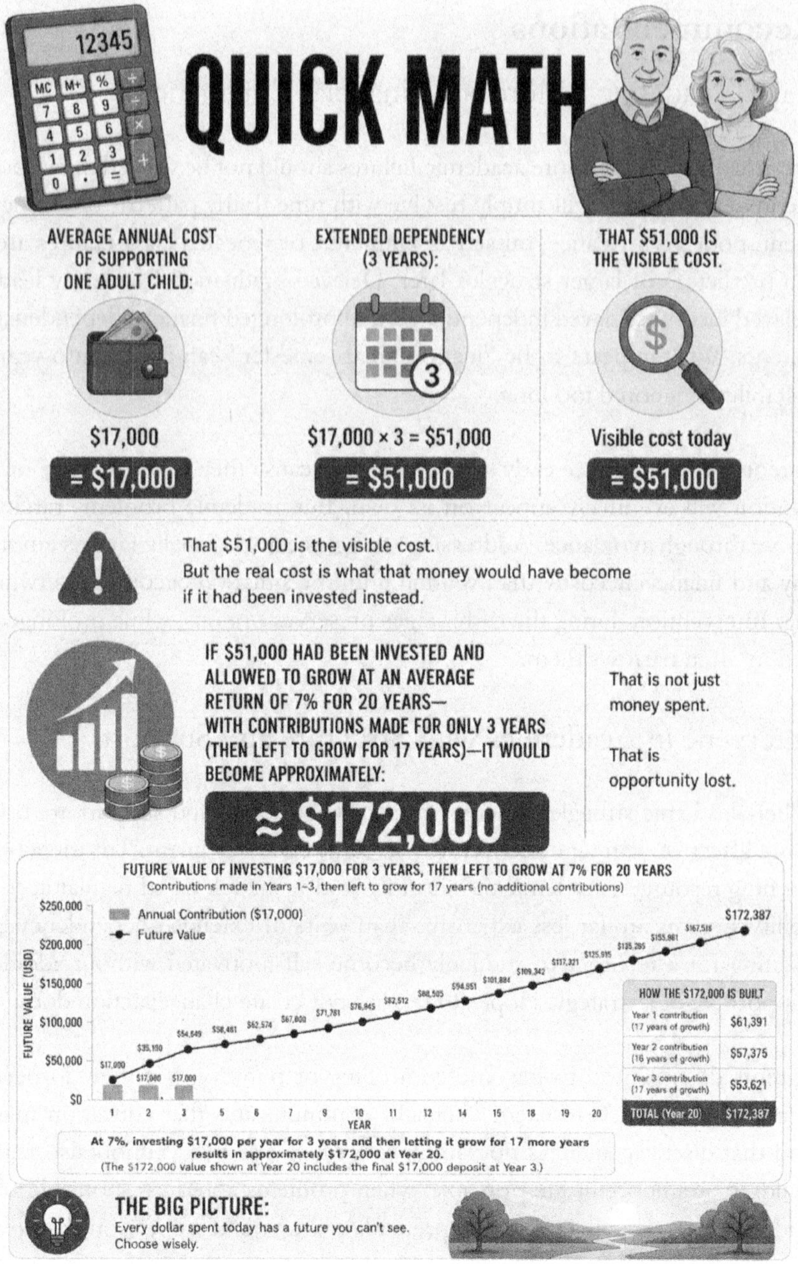
12345
QUICK MATH
AVERAGE ANNUAL COST OF SUPPORTING ONE ADULT CHILD:
$17,000
= $17,000
EXTENDED DEPENDENCY (3 YEARS):
3
$17,000 × 3 = $51,000
= $51,000
THAT $51,000 IS THE VISIBLE COST.
$
Visible cost today
= $51,000
That $51,000 is the visible cost.
But the real cost is what that money would have become if it had been invested instead.
IF $51,000 HAD BEEN INVESTED AND ALLOWED TO GROW AT AN AVERAGE RETURN OF 7% FOR 20 YEARS—
WITH CONTRIBUTIONS MADE FOR ONLY 3 YEARS (THEN LEFT TO GROW FOR 17 YEARS)—IT WOULD BECOME APPROXIMATELY:
≈ $172,000
That is not just money spent.
That is opportunity lost.
FUTURE VALUE OF INVESTING $17,000 FOR 3 YEARS, THEN LEFT TO GROW AT 7% FOR 20 YEARS
Contributions made in Years 1–3, then left to grow for 17 years (no additional contributions)
$250,000
$200,000
$150,000
$100,000
$50,000
$0
FUTURE VALUE (USD)
Annual Contribution ($17,000)
Future Value
$17,000
$35,190
$54,649
$58,481
$62,574
$67,000
$71,781
$76,945
$82,512
$94,951
$101,884
$109,342
$117,321
$125,915
$135,265
$167,518
$172,387
$17,000
$17,000
1 2 3 5 6 7 9 10 11 12 14 15 18 19 20
YEAR
HOW THE $172,000 IS BUILT
Year 1 contribution (17 years of growth) $61,391
Year 2 contribution (16 years of growth) $57,375
Year 3 contribution (17 years of growth) $53,621
TOTAL (Year 20) $172,387
At 7%, investing $17,000 per year for 3 years and then letting it grow for 17 more years results in approximately $172,000 at Year 20.
(The $172,000 value shown at Year 20 includes the final $17,000 deposit at Year 3.)
THE BIG PICTURE:
Every dollar spent today has a future you can't see.
Choose wisely.

# Recommendations

## Early Academic Failure is a Financial Emergency

Freshman and sophomore academic failures should not be viewed as temporary inconveniences that will simply resolve with time. Early patterns of disengagement, poor performance, missed assignments, or repeated class failures are often predictors of larger struggles later. Delayed graduation frequently leads to delayed income, delayed independence, and prolonged financial dependence on parents. What appears to be "just one bad semester" can evolve into years of instability if ignored too long.

Parents often minimize early warning signs because they hope maturity or motivation will eventually appear on its own. But academic problems rarely improve through avoidance. Addressing struggles early is usually far less emotionally and financially costly than waiting until the situation becomes overwhelming. Intervention during the early stages preserves options, while prolonged inaction often narrows them.

## Intervene in Academics with Structure and Support

When academic struggles emerge, immediate structure and support are usually more effective than repeated lectures or vague encouragement. Tutoring, online learning resources, academic monitoring, study schedules, and regular accountability systems are far less expensive than years of extended dependency later. Waiting for a teenager to suddenly become self-motivated without additional support is not a strategy. Hope alone does not create change; action does.

Parents do not need to become controlling or punitive, but they do need to become involved. Consistent oversight communicates that education matters and that disengagement is not simply ignored. Early intervention also teaches children an important life principle: when problems appear, responsible adults address them directly rather than pretending they will disappear on their own.

## Link Education Directly to Financial Outcomes

A diploma, GED, trade certification, or degree is not merely symbolic paperwork. Educational attainment directly influences earning potential, employment stability, and future opportunities. Children often struggle to understand the long-term consequences of academic disengagement because adulthood feels distant and abstract. Parents therefore need to make the connection between education and financial independence early and consistently.

Education directly effects income and unemployment. When parents keep children (even adult children) focused on education, it increases the potential of future employment, wages, and independence. See the weekly wages by educational attainment by the U.S. Bureau of Labor Statistics below.

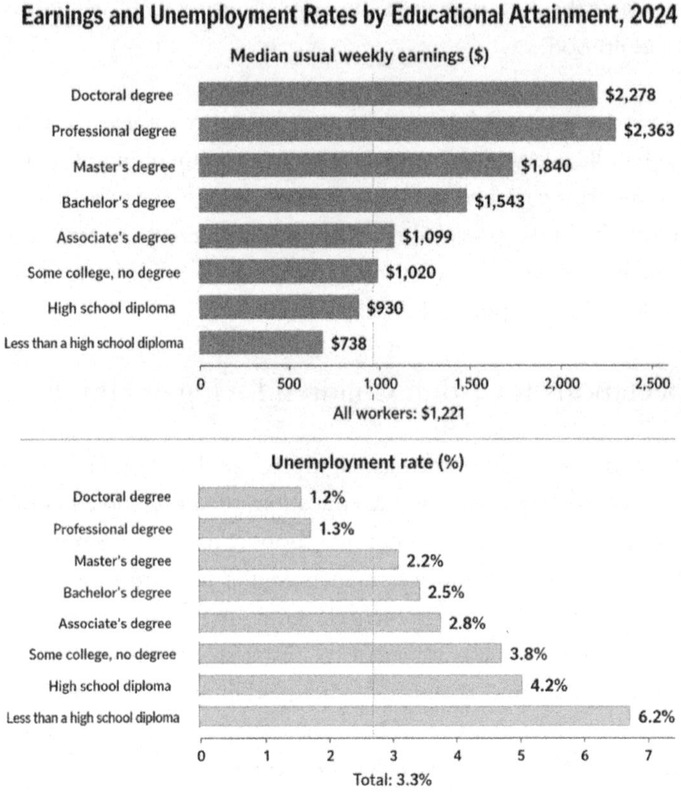


**Note:** Data are for persons age 25 and over.
Earnings are for full-time wage and salary workers.

**Source:** U.S. Bureau of Labor Statistics, Current Population Survey.

Academic drift frequently becomes financial drift later. A teenager who develops habits of avoidance, inconsistency, or low accountability in school often carries those same patterns into employment and adult responsibilities. This does not mean every child must pursue a four-year college degree, but every child does need a realistic pathway toward self-support. Education, training, and skill development are ultimately connected to freedom, stability, and independence.

## Build Life Skills Before Adulthood Arrives

Laundry, cleaning, scheduling appointments, basic cooking, time management, and household contribution should not begin suddenly at nineteen or twenty years old. These are not advanced adult skills; they are baseline responsibilities that should develop gradually throughout childhood and adolescence. Independence is built through repetition over time, not through one dramatic transition into adulthood.

Parents sometimes unintentionally delay skill development because it feels easier or faster to handle everything themselves. But over functioning for children often creates underprepared adults. Children gain confidence when they participate meaningfully in the practical responsibilities of everyday life. Competence grows through practice, and small responsibilities in adolescence become the foundation for larger responsibilities later.

## Set Expectations for Adult Children Living at Home

If an adult child remains at home past eighteen, families benefit from establishing clear expectations regarding work, education, financial contribution, chores, timelines, and long-term goals. Undefined support tends to become permanent support because there is no structure encouraging forward movement. Clarity reduces confusion and helps prevent resentment from building inside the household. Expectations do not need to be harsh or transactional, but they should be measurable and specific. A young adult should understand what is required regarding employment, school progress, household contribution, or savings goals. Parents who communicate expectations clearly are not being unkind; they are preparing their children for the accountability that adult life eventually requires.

## Do Not Confuse Politeness with Preparedness

A respectful and kind child is a wonderful thing, but politeness alone does not prepare someone for independent adulthood. Courtesy may help relationships, but competence is what sustains employment, financial stability, and self-sufficiency. Parents sometimes mistake a child's pleasant personality for readiness because the child is cooperative, affectionate, or socially appropriate. While those qualities matter deeply, they are not substitutes for responsibility.

A young adult ultimately needs the ability to solve problems, manage obligations, tolerate discomfort, and contribute consistently. Therefore, healthy parenting requires attention not only to character development, but also to the practical skills and habits that allow children to function successfully on their own later in life. High school lasts a few years. Adulthood lasts decades. And the habits built in one determine the cost of the other.

# CHAPTER 12

# STADIUM LIGHTS AND *Student* LOANS

*It's not how much money you make, but how much money you keep, how hard it works for you, and how many generations you keep it for.*

– ROBERT KIYOSAKI

Jack missed his glory days not in a quiet, nostalgic way, but in a very active, very expensive, still-living-inside-them kind of way. Friday nights used to mean something, with stadium lights, crowds, and shoulder pads creating the illusion that life was just beginning. It wasn't, of course, but in Jack's mind the movie never fully ended. The feeling stayed active, influencing how he saw opportunity, success, and what might still be possible if things unfolded differently this time. When Jack had children, he did not simply see kids. He saw schedules, uniforms, football games, and another chance to continue a story he had never emotionally retired from.

His wife, Diane, got swept in as well, not because she particularly cared about scoreboards or stat lines, but because youth sports have a way of reorganizing an entire household. Once one child is in an activity, the calendar shifts, weekends disappear, and the family begins operating around practices, fees, and travel. It doesn't feel like a decision so much as a gradual adjustment that becomes permanent. What starts as support slowly becomes structure.

Their son, Luke, was a football kid, and it showed early in the way he moved. He was bigger than the other boys, solid through the shoulders, and naturally comfortable with contact in a way that made coaches notice him immediately. Not because he was exceptional, but because he was reliable, coachable, and easy to trust, which carries more weight in youth sports than most parents realize. That combination creates opportunity, even if it doesn't guarantee outcome.

Like most expensive journeys, it didn't begin with a major commitment. It started with "just one camp," then "just this season," followed by "he's really got something if we keep him in it." Each step felt small, reasonable, and justified in isolation. No single decision felt excessive, and that is exactly how the pattern takes hold. By the time anyone pauses to evaluate it, the structure is already built.

By middle school, Luke was in off-season training programs, speed and agility camps, and position-specific coaching sessions. Then came weight training programs designed for teenagers who were still growing into their bodies but were already being treated like finished athletes. The language shifted subtly from participation to preparation, from playing to pursuing. It stopped looking like sports and started looking like an investment in something described only as "the next level."

Jack liked that part—the idea of the next level. He had been a decent high school athlete, nothing legendary, nothing that followed him into adulthood in any measurable way, but just enough that the memory stayed active. It lived in the background, influencing what felt possible, what felt unfinished, and what might still be achieved through someone else. That is how past identity becomes present motivation.

Luke's calendar filled completely. Practices during the week, camps on weekends, seven-on-seven tournaments in other states, weight training sessions, and film study that sounded strategic but mostly involved teenagers watching other teenagers. Diane handled the logistics, the driving, the scheduling, and the constant coordination. Jack handled the belief. By the time Luke reached high school, Jack and Diane had spent years in a system where effort was assumed to eventually convert into recruitment. It felt like a pipeline, like progress was being made even when results were unclear. The assumption was simple: if you keep investing, something will eventually come back. It doesn't always.

Luke was still solid, still respected, still the kind of player who contributes meaningfully without becoming the reason anyone attends a game. That is a difficult category in American sports culture, because "solid" is praised in theory but rarely rewarded in reality. It sits in the middle, acknowledged but not elevated. Then came the conversation they had been circling for years without fully acknowledging . . . college. Luke had options, just not the kind that came with headlines or scholarship announcements or anything that changed the financial equation. He had an offer from a Division III private school where he could absolutely continue playing football and remain part of the structure that had defined most of his adolescence. But no athletic scholarship was offered.

At the same time, Luke was an excellent student. He carried a 4.2 GPA, strong academically, and the kind of student who opens doors that don't require shoulder pads or highlight reels. He had academic scholarship options that materially reduced tuition and changed what a family would actually pay.

Jack saw the spreadsheet that Diane and Luke had put together. For just tuition, the private school was $32,000 per year while the academic scholarship paid 100% of tuition. Diane saw Jack's face and knew where this conversation was headed. The college with the academic scholarship was financially sensible in a way that did not require explanation. But it didn't come with football. And football, for Jack, had become more than a sport—it had become continuity, identity, and a story still in motion. The decision narrowed itself into two realities. Play college football at a Division III private school and pay full tuition using loans. Or attend a college with a scholarship for tuition and step away from football. And that is where emotion overpowered math.

Jack told Luke that football had opened doors for him, that the experience mattered, that the relationships, discipline, and memories would stay with him forever. He talked about brotherhood, commitment, and "finishing what you started," which sounded noble enough that nobody wanted to immediately challenge it. The problem was not that football had value. The problem was that the value being described was emotional while the cost was painfully financial. Luke enrolled at the Division III private school where he could continue playing football. Because the Division III school did not offer athletic scholarships, the tuition gap was closed with student loans . . . lots of them.

Luke signed paperwork at eighteen that translated into years of future payments, most of which he barely understood because teenagers rarely feel the weight of debt in real time. Debt at eighteen feels abstract, almost fictional, especially when adults around you frame the decision as an "opportunity." Jack encouraged him forward because he saw the experience first and the repayment second.

The irony was that Luke had already earned something more valuable than football had given him: academic opportunity. His grades had created options that could have reduced debt substantially and positioned him for financial freedom earlier in life. But the emotional gravity of sports pulled harder than the spreadsheet. It often does in families. Parents will spend enormous amounts of money chasing athletic continuation while ignoring the reality waiting on the other side of graduation - even if the future student loan debt belongs to their child.

## Psychological Pattern: Unfinished Identity Parenting

Jack and Diane were not making financial decisions from a place of recklessness or irresponsibility. They were making them from a place of emotional attachment that had slowly replaced objectivity over time. Football had become far more than a sport in their household. It shaped weekends, dictated travel schedules, filled photo albums, created friendships for not only the child, but also the parents. Football provided a steady source of pride, excitement, and identity for the entire family. By the time Luke reached college age, football no longer felt like one activity among many. It felt woven into the emotional structure of their lives. Walking away from the sport did not emotionally register as simply choosing a different educational path. It felt like losing a future the family had spent years building together.

For Jack specifically, the emotional attachment ran much deeper because Luke's football career had become psychologically connected to unresolved parts of his own identity. Jack's athletic experience had never fully emotionally ended after his own playing years were over. Like many former athletes, some of his strongest memories of confidence, recognition, excitement, belonging, and personal significance were tied to sports. Football represented a stage of life where he felt admired, capable, energetic, and filled with possibility. Adulthood eventually became more predictable—mortgage payments, work schedules, routines, responsibilities, and the repetition that often defines middle age. But football still gave him emotional access to the version of himself he missed most. Watching Luke compete was not simply about supporting his son. It allowed Jack to reconnect with a younger version of himself that still carried emotional meaning.

This is where parental identity extension often begins. Parents do not always realize when support slowly becomes emotional continuation. A father who once played football may genuinely believe he is simply encouraging discipline, teamwork, opportunity, and ambition in his son. On the surface, the behavior looks loving and devoted because it often is loving and devoted. But underneath the encouragement, the child's success gradually begins carrying emotional meaning for the parent as well. Luke's touchdowns, recruitment conversations, scholarships, and athletic recognition likely felt deeply personal to Jack in ways that extended beyond ordinary parental pride. Every achievement validated not only Luke's future, but also Jack's connection to his own unfinished story.

Parents sometimes unconsciously experience their children as extensions of their own unrealized ambitions, regrets, or unresolved identities. The child becomes connected not only to the future, but also to the emotional past of the parent. This dynamic becomes especially powerful when a parent once built identity around achievement, talent, status, recognition, or unrealized potential. The former athlete who never made it professionally may struggle emotionally when the child loses interest in sports because the activity represents far more than a hobby. It represents youth, identity, validation, belonging, admiration, and the possibility of completing something emotionally unfinished.

The same psychological pattern can appear academically, artistically, socially, or professionally. A parent who once dreamed of becoming a musician may push a child intensely toward performance opportunities. A parent who regrets career limitations may pressure children toward prestige-driven educational paths. Parents often believe they are helping children maximize opportunity while unconsciously asking them to carry emotional meaning connected to the adult's unresolved past.

What makes this dynamic so difficult to recognize is that it usually develops inside genuinely loving families. Jack loved Luke deeply. He likely believed he was giving his son opportunities he never fully had himself. Modern parenting culture also rewards this level of investment because highly involved parents are often praised as sacrificial, devoted, and committed. Elite camps, private coaching, recruiting showcases, personal trainers, equipment upgrades, travel teams, and specialized programs all become framed as noble investments in the child's future. Very few people stop to ask whether the child truly wants the same dream with the same intensity as the parent. Emotional projection is wrapped in bonding, encouragement, pride, and love.

Another difficult truth about achievement projection parenting is that children often absorb emotional pressure even when parents never directly verbalize it. Luke may have genuinely loved football, but children are highly sensitive to parental identity, pride, disappointment, and expectation.

When parents become emotionally invested in a specific outcome, children often internalize the belief that continuing the path protects the emotional stability of the family itself. Conversations gradually revolve around rankings, recruitment, scholarships, advancement, performance, and future opportunity. Love remains present, but it becomes increasingly tangled with achievement and identity. The child can begin feeling responsible not only for personal success, but also for protecting the emotional dreams of the parent. Parents caught in this dynamic need to ask themselves a painful but necessary question:

**Does the dream belong to me or my child?**

The answer often reveals whether the dream truly belongs to the child or partly belongs to the parent's unresolved identity. Healthy parenting requires allowing children to develop separate ambitions, preferences, identities, and definitions of success without carrying the emotional burden of completing someone else's unfinished story. Children deserve freedom from inherited expectations disguised as support. Sometimes the most loving thing a parent can do is allow a child to become fully themselves instead of becoming an emotional continuation of someone else's unrealized life.

Luke may have loved football, but his strongest long-term opportunity may ultimately have been academic rather than athletic. There is nothing wrong with sports, ambition, discipline, teamwork, competition, or dreaming big. The problem begins when parental nostalgia, unresolved identity, emotional projection, and fear begin influencing financial decisions more heavily than objective reality. Stadium lights eventually turn off. Athletic careers usually end far earlier than families expect. But financial consequences often remain for decades. In this case, even though, the emotional dream belonged to the parent, the long-term financial burden belonged to the child.

## The Quick Math

Four years of tuition at a private Division III school totals approximately $128,000, while an academic scholarship option could reduce that cost to zero. The immediate difference is $128,000, but the true cost extends beyond the tuition bill. It reflects a decision to prioritize identity and participation in a particular athletic experience over a lower-cost educational pathway.

The financial impact becomes even more significant when considering opportunity cost. If the same $128,000 were invested instead of spent on tuition and allowed to grow at an average annual return of 7%, it could accumulate to approximately $418,900 over a 20-year period. Through the power of compound growth, each year's tuition payment represents not only money spent but also future wealth that is no longer available for retirement, financial security, or other long-term goals.

This example is not intended to discourage participation in college athletics. Rather, it highlights the importance of understanding the full financial implications of major educational decisions. The choice is not simply between one college and another—it is also a choice between spending and investing, between present identity and future financial flexibility.

# QUICK MATH

## THE COST OF CHOOSING IDENTITY
## —— OVER OUTCOME ——

**DIVISION III PRIVATE COLLEGE (FOOTBALL PARTICIPATION):**

$32,000 × 4 YEARS

**= $128,000**

**ACADEMIC SCHOLARSHIP OPTION:**

$0 × 4 YEARS

**= $0**

**TOTAL DIFFERENCE:**

$128,000 – $0

**= $128,000**

**THAT $128,000 IS NOT JUST TUITION.**

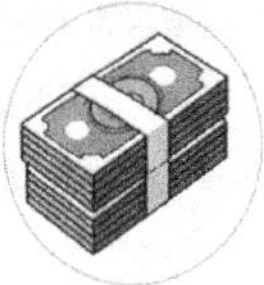

It's the cost of choosing identity over outcome.

That $128,000 is not just tuition.
It is the cost of choosing identity over outcome,
and the cost does not stop when the check is written.

**IF THAT SAME $128,000 HAD BEEN INVESTED INSTEAD AND ALLOWED TO GROW AT AN AVERAGE RETURN OF 7% FOR 20 YEARS, IT WOULD BECOME APPROXIMATELY:**

**≈ $418,900**

That is not just money spent.

That is opportunity lost.

**FUTURE VALUE OF INVESTING $32,000 FOR 4 YEARS, THEN LEFT TO GROW AT 7% FOR 20 YEARS**

Contributions made in Years 1–4, then left to grow for 16 years (no additional contributions)

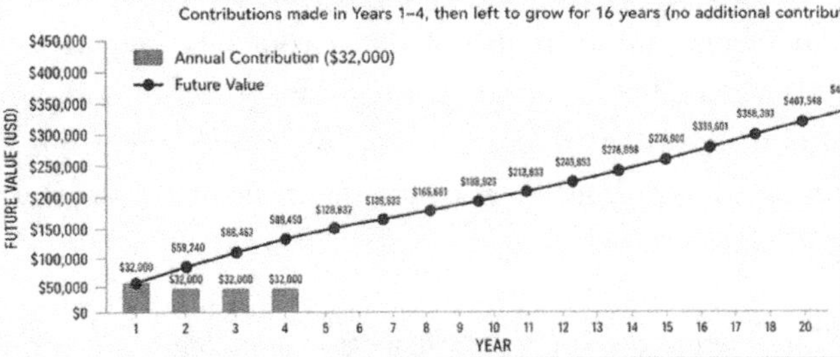


| HOW THE $418,900 IS BUILT | |
|---|---|
| Year 1 contribution (19 years of growth) | $115,587 |
| Year 2 contribution (18 years of growth) | $108,025 |
| Year 3 contribution (17 years of growth) | $100,958 |
| Year 4 contribution (16 years of growth) | $94,353 |
| TOTAL (YEAR 20) | $418,923 |

**At 7%, investing $32,000 per year for 4 years and then letting it grow for 16 more years results in approximately $418,900 at Year 20.**

(The $418,923 value shown at Year 20 includes the final $32,000 deposit at Year 4.)

## THE BIG PICTURE:

That is not just college money.
That is retirement money.

# THE COST OF COLLEGE

**PLAN TODAY. SAVE TOMORROW. GRADUATE DEBT-FREE.**

## AVERAGE COSTS (2026)

Per Year

| Type of School | Tuition & Fees | Room & Board | Total / Year |
|---|---|---|---|
| In-State Public | $14,190 | $15,210 | $29,400 |
| Out-of-State Public | $37,620 | $15,210 | $52,830 |
| Private University | $53,430 | $18,250 | $71,680 |
| Community College | $4,390 | $11,680 | $16,070 |

Source: College Board, Trends in College Pricing 2026
(Rounded to nearest $10)

## THE TRUE COST OF COLLEGE

- Tuition & Fees
- Room & Board
- Books & Supplies
- Transportation
- Personal Expenses
- Technology

**Plan for it all.**

## 4 SMART WAYS TO SAVE NOW

**START EARLY**

Even small amounts grow significantly over time.

**USE TAX-ADVANTAGED ACCOUNTS**

529 Plans offer tax-free growth for qualified education expenses.

**LOOK FOR FREE MONEY**

Apply for scholarships, grants and financial aid every year.

**PAY AS YOU GO**

Save as you earn. Avoid borrowing whenever possible.

## REDUCE COLLEGE COSTS

- Attend community college for the first 1–2 years.
- Choose in-state public schools.
- Live at home while attending school.
- Take AP or CLEP exams to earn college credit.
- Graduate on time—extra semesters cost more.
- Work part-time or intern to reduce borrowing.
- Apply to be a Resident Assistant for free living expenses.
- Choose a career path with strong earning potential.

## THE GOAL

Graduate with a degree, not debt.

## HOW MUCH COULD 4 YEARS COST?

| Type of School | Total 4-Year Cost (Tuition, Room & Board) |
|---|---|
| In-State Public | $117,600 |
| Out-of-State Public | $211,320 |
| Private University | $286,720 |
| Community College | $64,280 |

## PLAN YOUR SAVINGS GOAL

Example: Saving $300/month at 7% return

| Years | Total Saved |
|---|---|
| 5 years | $22,900 |
| 10 years | $48,500 |
| 15 years | $81,700 |
| 18 years | $113,900 |

Every dollar saved today is a dollar your child won't have to borrow tomorrow.

## THE COST OF BORROWING

Borrowing $30,000 at 6.5% interest for 10 years means paying back over $39,000.

**Debt today can limit your freedom tomorrow.**

## TALK ABOUT MONEY

Make college costs and expectations part of family conversations early. A plan today creates options tomorrow.

**INVEST IN THEIR FUTURE. PROTECT THEIR FREEDOM.**

Smart planning today. More opportunities tomorrow.

## Recommendations

### Separate the Child's Future from the Parent's Unfinished Identity

Parents sometimes unknowingly continue their own unfinished dreams through their children. A father who misses football, a mother who regrets abandoning dance, or parents who still emotionally identify with their own athletic past can begin making decisions based as much on personal nostalgia as on the child's actual long-term interests. Nostalgia is powerful because it reconnects adults to feelings of youth, purpose, identity, and significance. But nostalgia is not a retirement plan, and emotional attachment should not override financial reality.

### Prioritize Education Over Identity

A stable adult life has more long-term value than extending a sports identity for a few additional years. Parents and teenagers sometimes become so emotionally invested in continuing athletic participation that they lose perspective on the larger purpose of education itself. A debt-free degree, trade certification, apprenticeship, or strong academic foundation often creates far more lasting opportunity than preserving an athletic role into early adulthood.

The goal should be building an independent and financially stable future, not preserving a high school identity indefinitely. Sports can remain meaningful without becoming the central organizing principle of adulthood. Parents who prioritize education over emotional attachment to athletics help their children transition more successfully into adult life beyond competition.

### Teach Children to Calculate Opportunity Cost Early

Teenagers often agree to large student loans because debt feels abstract at eighteen years old. Monthly payments, interest accumulation, delayed home ownership, delayed retirement savings, and long-term financial stress are difficult for young people to fully imagine because the consequences exist so far in the future. Parents therefore need to translate borrowing into concrete, understandable numbers.

Every borrowed dollar carries a future cost attached to it. Showing teenagers what repayment actually looks like over ten or twenty years helps them understand that financial decisions made at eighteen can shape adulthood for decades. Opportunity cost matters because money directed toward debt repayment is money unavailable for investing, saving, buying a house, or future retirement. Financial literacy requires helping children see not only what debt provides immediately, but also what it delays later.

## Allow Children to Grieve the Ending of Sports Without Rescuing the Identity

Many parents fear their child will lose confidence, direction, or identity if sports end after high school or college. Because of that fear, families sometimes continue making financially destructive decisions simply to preserve athletic participation a little longer. But adulthood is filled with transitions and learning how to move beyond one stage of identity is part of healthy emotional development.

Children need support as they grieve the ending of an important chapter, but they do not need rescue from reality. A former athlete can become a successful professional, entrepreneur, teacher, coach, parent, artist, or leader. The uniform was never supposed to become the entire personality. Healthy families teach children that identity expands throughout life rather than remaining permanently attached to one role or achievement.

Real success is not preserving a fantasy at all costs. Real success is entering adulthood with stability, opportunity, and manageable financial obligations. Families who make grounded decisions may temporarily feel less impressive socially, but they often gain something far more valuable: freedom from unnecessary debt tied to nostalgia, pressure, and emotionally driven expectations.

## Evaluate Career and Educational Opportunities

Parents should compare outcomes honestly and objectively. If academic scholarships, stronger educational programs, lower-cost schools, or trade certifications provide greater long-term financial stability, those options deserve serious consideration. A dream should not require financial blindness in order to survive. Supporting children also means protecting them from entering adulthood burdened by avoidable financial damage created through emotional decision-making.

According to the U.S. Bureau of Labor Statistics' Occupational Employment and Wage Statistics (2025), evaluating career and educational opportunities after high school reveals a wide range of earning potential across different paths. Skilled trades such as construction laborers, carpenters, electricians, plumbers, and first-line supervisors offer median annual wages ranging from $47,230 to $79,770, often requiring vocational training or apprenticeships rather than a four-year degree. For those pursuing professional and business careers, which typically require a college education, average weekly earnings reach approximately $1,655 per week, or roughly $86,000 annually, compared to the national median of $1,204 per week, or about $62,600 per year for all workers. Ultimately, both trade and professional career paths offer competitive wages, and the best choice depends on an individual's interests, strengths, and financial goals rather than a single educational route.

Sometimes the healthiest decision for after high school is the one that appears less glamorous in the moment. Choosing the affordable school, accepting academic scholarships, or pursuing a trade is not failure. In many cases, it reflects maturity, perspective, and long-term thinking.

# CHAPTER 13

# THE COLLEGE *Experience*

*The greatest gifts you can give your children are the roots of responsibility and the wings of independence."*

– DENIS WAITLEY

Janice graduated from Brown University in 1994, and she still talked about it like it was part of who she was. Her memories of Brown weren't just academic—they were social, emotional, and deeply embedded in how she defined that period of her life. She pledged Delta Sigma Theta, and her sorority became part of her experience. She remembered girls showing up to orchestra concerts with carefully curated bouquets, as if applause alone wasn't enough. She remembered friendships that carried you through breakups, stress, and moments that felt bigger than they probably were. Brown had not just been a school; it had been an identity wrapped in brick buildings and late-night conversations.

Those memories had texture. Nights out, nights in, days spent with her Sorors. Cups of hot chocolate held between cold hands, late-night study sessions where exhaustion somehow became bonding, and fall trips to pumpkin patches that required far more coordination than necessary. There were picnics in the spring, community events and fundraisers, and the freedom of being young with very few real responsibilities. It all felt important at the time, and over the years, that feeling had only grown stronger.

After graduation, Janice built a career in public relations at General Motors. Somewhere between press releases and corporate travel, she met Ethan, and together they built a stable, comfortable life. They did what responsible adults do—they planned, they saved, and they made decisions that seemed logical at the time. Their lives moved forward in a predictable, steady way.

Janice waited until she was thirty-four to have Amy, which made the experience feel more intentional. Amy was a good kid; the kind of daughter teachers use as an example when other students start slipping. She liked working with children, babysat constantly, and declared early—very early—that she wanted to be a teacher. It wasn't a phase or a suggestion; it was a statement she repeated often enough that it became part of how everyone saw her.

Janice was thrilled. This was perfect—stable, meaningful, and respectable, the kind of career people praise in theory and underpay in reality. It felt aligned with everything she believed about purpose and contribution. And without much hesitation, Janice and Ethan made a decision that felt natural.

Amy would go to Brown.

Not just to college—specifically to Brown. The same campus, the same traditions, and the same formative experience that had shaped Janice's early adulthood. She even hoped her daughter would join Delta Sigma Theta, the sorority Janice considered a lifelong sisterhood and remained actively involved with through regular events and alumni activities. For Janice, this was never just about earning a degree. It was about preserving a legacy, reliving a cherished chapter of her own life, and passing that experience on to the next generation.

When Janice had attended Brown, tuition had been about $17,000 a year. It was expensive, but it lived in that manageable category of "we'll figure it out," supported by loans, effort, and a general sense of optimism. It felt like a stretch, not a transformation. Now, for Amy, Brown was sitting at roughly $71,000 a year.

But Janice barely hesitated. That's what good parents do, or at least that's how it felt in the moment. You absorb the shock privately, then replace it with phrases like "it's an investment in her future." The number becomes secondary to the narrative.

There was also the detail that Brown's teaching path was not a simple four-year commitment. It required five years—four for the undergraduate degree and an additional year for a master's plus certification. Five years in one place, five years of tuition, five years of reinforcing a single decision that had already been made emotionally before it was evaluated financially. But they could make it work. They always made it work. Because it wasn't really about cost, it was about the experience.

Meanwhile, Amy had also gotten into the University of Michigan, a strong program with a respected education track and a campus filled with familiar faces. It was a place where she could still build friendships, still develop professionally, and still move toward the same career outcome. The difference was not opportunity—it was framing and tuition.

At Michigan, in-state tuition was about $18,000 per year, a number that felt dramatically different when compared side by side. It didn't require long-term financial strategy or quiet sacrifices that no one discussed openly. It felt manageable in a way Brown did not. But Michigan didn't come with the same story. It didn't come with the framed memory, the emotional continuity, or the sense that something meaningful was being recreated across generations. And that is where the real tension lived—not in prestige versus practicality, but in identity versus outcome. The decision hovered there. Not loudly. Not dramatically. Just enough that it became harder to evaluate clearly.

Amy went to Brown.

## Psychological Pattern: Nostalgic Identity Projection

One of the most powerful psychological forces in parenting is the desire to recreate meaningful life experiences through children. In this pattern, parents are not simply helping children make educational decisions. They are unconsciously trying to preserve a part of their own emotional identity. For Janice, Brown University represented far more than academics. It symbolized friendship, belonging, youth, achievement, and emotional security during an important stage of life. Over time, the school became psychologically tied to how she understood herself and the memories she valued most. What began as a college experience gradually transformed into a deeply personal emotional landmark.

This pattern becomes especially influential because nostalgia changes the way people evaluate the past. Human beings naturally remember emotionally significant periods of life with warmth and selective emphasis. For Janice, the emotional highlights remained vivid while the financial stress, uncertainty, and ordinary difficulties faded into the background. Her memories were real, but they had been emotionally refined over decades. When parents idealize a past experience, they often begin believing that recreating the same environment will recreate the same emotional outcome for their children. The institution itself starts to feel psychologically connected to happiness, purpose, legacy, and identity rather than simply education.

Parents caught in nostalgic identity projection often struggle to separate what was meaningful for them from what is financially reasonable for the child standing in front of them. Amy wanted to become a teacher, a profession known more for stability and purpose than high income. From a practical perspective, the University of Michigan offered a respected education program at a dramatically lower cost. The likely career outcome would have been similar without requiring the same level of financial sacrifice. But Brown carried emotional continuity. Janice was not evaluating the schools equally because one represented a treasured part of her own life story. In many families, decisions like these appear to be about opportunity on the surface, while underneath they are deeply connected to parental identity and emotional memory.

The emotional danger of identity projection is that children can become extensions of adult ego. A child's experiences are no longer evaluated solely on whether the child enjoys them, but also on whether the experiences communicate something impressive about the family. Overspending becomes easier because it no longer feels selfish. Parents are not technically buying things for themselves, which helps disguise how deeply personal the validation actually is.

Another characteristic of this pattern is the way emotions reshape financial reasoning. Once parents become emotionally attached to a symbolic decision, they begin framing the expense in ways that feel morally or emotionally justified. Statements like "it's an investment in her future" help reduce discomfort about the actual numbers involved. The financial burden becomes psychologically connected to love, sacrifice, and good parenting. Parents rarely want to admit that emotions may be influencing expensive decisions, so the brain naturally builds narratives that make the choice feel responsible and necessary.

Generational continuity also plays an important role in this psychological pattern. Janice did not simply want Amy to attend Brown. She wanted her daughter to experience a familiar emotional world that felt connected to family identity and tradition. The same school and even the same sorority created a sense of continuity between mother and daughter that felt comforting and meaningful. Parents often experience subtle anxiety as children grow into independent adults with identities that may differ from their own. Recreating familiar experiences can temporarily reduce that discomfort because it preserves a sense of emotional connection. The challenge is that children are not designed to fulfill emotional narratives from their parents' pasts. Healthy parenting requires allowing children to build lives that reflect their own personalities, goals, and realities rather than inherited emotional blueprints.

The difficult truth about nostalgic identity projection is that meaningful experiences cannot simply be transferred from one generation to another through repetition. Amy could attend Brown and still have a completely different emotional experience than Janice did because the world, the economy, and the pressures surrounding young adulthood had changed dramatically. Nostalgia can make familiar choices feel safer and wiser than they actually are. But financial decisions rooted primarily in emotional memory can create long-term strain when they are disconnected from realistic outcomes or affordability. Loving children well sometimes means resisting the temptation to recreate the past through them. It means recognizing that a child's future does not need to mirror a parent's most treasured memories in order to become meaningful, successful, and emotionally rich.

## The Quick Math

Choosing an expensive college experience over a lower-cost alternative can have financial consequences that extend far beyond tuition. In this example, Amy's decision to attend Brown University for five years at a cost of approximately $355,000 is compared to attending the University of Michigan for four years at approximately $72,000. The difference between the two educational paths is $283,000. While families often focus on the prestige, experience, and opportunities associated with a particular school, the true financial impact lies not only in what is spent, but also in what that money could have become if invested elsewhere.

If the $283,000 difference had been invested and earned an average annual return of 7%, it could grow to approximately $890,000 over a 20-year period. Through the power of compound interest, each tuition payment represents more than an educational expense—it represents future wealth that will no longer be available for retirement, financial independence, healthcare costs, or future generations. The opportunity cost of the decision grows larger with time, as investment gains begin earning gains of their own.

This comparison does not suggest that one college choice is inherently right or wrong. Rather, it illustrates the importance of understanding the trade-offs involved in major financial decisions. Parents and students should consider not only the immediate educational benefits but also the long-term financial implications. In many cases, what appears to be a college decision is also a retirement decision, a wealth-building decision, and a family legacy decision.

12345
QUICK MATH
THE COST OF CHOOSING ONE EXPERIENCE OVER ANOTHER
AMY'S TUITION AT BROWN:
$71,000 × 5 YEARS
= $355,000
UNIVERSITY OF MICHIGAN OPTION:
$18,000 × 4 YEARS
= $72,000
TOTAL DIFFERENCE:
$355,000 – $72,000
= $283,000
THAT $283,000 IS NOT JUST A TUITION GAP.
It's the cost of choosing one experience over another.
It is the cost of choosing one experience over another, and the real impact is not just what was spent, but what that money no longer had the chance to become.
IF THAT SAME $283,000 HAD BEEN INVESTED INSTEAD AND ALLOWED TO GROW AT AN AVERAGE RETURN OF 7% FOR 20 YEARS, IT WOULD BECOME APPROXIMATELY:
≈ $890,000
That is not just money spent.
That is opportunity lost.
FUTURE VALUE OF INVESTING THE $283,000 DIFFERENCE
Contributions made in Years 1–4, then left to grow for 16 years (no additional contributions)
Average return: 7%
Annual Contribution ($53,000)
Future Value
FUTURE VALUE (USD)
YEAR
HOW THE $889,880 IS BUILT
Year 1 contribution (19 years of growth) $191,454
Year 2 contribution (18 years of growth) $178,929
Year 3 contribution (17 years of growth) $167,224
Year 4 contribution (16 years of growth) $156,284
Year 5 contribution (15 years of growth) $195,989
TOTAL (YEAR 20) $889,880
At 7%, investing $53,000 per year for 4 years and then letting it grow for 16 more years results in approximately $889,880 at Year 20.
(The $889,880 value shown at Year 20 includes the final $71,000 deposit at Year 5.)
THE BIG PICTURE:
That is not just college money.
That is retirement money.
Sources: College Board; Brown University; University of Michigan; Federal Reserve (Average Long-Term Return).
All values rounded.

# Recommendations

## Separate Identity from Financial Decision-Making

Many parents measure themselves through the visible outcomes of their children's lives. What begins as a desire to help children thrive can gradually turn childhood into a reflection of parental identity. A child's accomplishments become emotional evidence that the parent did something right, creating pressure to optimize every opportunity and engineer the "best" possible future. In the process, parenting can shift from guidance to performance, leaving parents exhausted and children carrying expectations that were never entirely their own.

One of the healthiest shifts a parent can make is recognizing that children do not exist to validate the parent's identity. Parenting outcomes are never fully controllable because children are independent individuals with their own personalities, preferences, strengths, and aspirations. Emotional attachment should be acknowledged honestly, but it should not override financial reality. A school may feel deeply meaningful while still being financially unwise. Separating emotion from evaluation allows families to make decisions based on long-term stability rather than personal symbolism, remembering that successful parenting is measured by raising a capable, healthy, and independent adult.

## Always Compare Full Costs Side by Side Before Choosing

Families should evaluate costs clearly and objectively before emotional preferences begin dominating the conversation. Tuition, housing, fees, transportation, books, and projected borrowing amounts should be placed side by side in visible numbers before discussions about campus culture, prestige, or emotional attachment take over. Financial clarity changes decision-making because it forces families to confront the actual scale of the commitment being made.

Many parents and students make decisions based on emotion first and then attempt to rationalize the numbers afterward. That sequence often leads to financial blind spots and underestimated debt. When families begin with transparent cost comparisons, they create a healthier framework for evaluating whether the educational experience truly justifies the long-term financial impact.

## Include Total Program Length, Not Just Undergraduate Years

Many careers require additional schooling, certifications, licensing programs, internships, or graduate degrees beyond a traditional four-year undergraduate program. Families often underestimate the true financial commitment because they evaluate only the first phase of education rather than the entire pathway required to enter the profession successfully.

A teaching degree, medical field, law program, counseling certification, or other specialized profession may require years beyond the initial bachelor's degree. Looking only at undergraduate costs can create a dangerously incomplete picture of future debt and delayed financial independence. Families should calculate the entire educational timeline, including the years in which the student may still be financially dependent while continuing advanced training or credentialing.

## Ask What This Decision Costs in Future Flexibility

Families should evaluate not only whether a college choice is affordable today, but also what it limits tomorrow. Large educational expenses affect retirement savings, debt levels, emergency funds, housing opportunities, career flexibility, and long-term financial independence. Every major financial decision removes options from the future, even when the consequences are not immediately visible.

Opportunity cost matters because money directed toward tuition and debt repayment cannot simultaneously build wealth elsewhere. A more expensive college may delay home ownership, postpone retirement investing, or increase financial stress during the early adult years. Families often focus intensely on gaining a particular educational experience while failing to fully consider the freedoms being sacrificed later in exchange for it.

## Recognize When "Experience" Becomes Justification

Campus life, friendships, traditions, athletics, social experiences, and independence absolutely hold value. College is not purely an economic transaction. However, families sometimes begin using the word "experience" to justify spending levels that no longer make financial sense. Emotional excitement about dorm life, football culture, prestige, or the atmosphere of a particular university can slowly overshadow practical financial evaluation.

Experiences should be weighed thoughtfully, not automatically treated as worth any cost. Parents and students should ask whether the emotional benefits of a more expensive option truly justify years of additional financial burden afterward. Meaningful memories can absolutely matter, but long-term financial stress also shapes quality of life long after graduation.

## Do Not Equate Prestige with Outcome

In many professions, career outcomes are not dramatically different across institutions, particularly when students are motivated, capable, and willing to work hard regardless of where they attend school. Families often assume that paying significantly more automatically produces better opportunities, stronger careers, or greater long-term success. Paying more does not always produce more. Especially in fields such as education, business, communications, or many public-sector professions, long-term outcomes may depend more on work ethic, networking, internships, and practical experience than on the prestige of the institution itself. Families should evaluate return on investment honestly rather than assuming higher cost automatically guarantees greater success.

## Frame the Decision as a Household Financial Choice

College decisions do not affect only the student. They shape the financial trajectory of the entire household. Parents may delay retirement contributions, increase debt, postpone paying off mortgages, or sacrifice long-term stability in order to finance educational choices. Because of that, college should be framed as a family financial decision rather than solely an emotional milestone for the child.

Aligning the decision with long-term family goals creates healthier and more realistic conversations. Families are not simply purchasing memories or preserving identity; they are financing futures. The goal should be helping children enter adulthood with opportunity and stability while also protecting the financial well-being of the parents who will eventually need security and independence later in life. Janice thought she was giving Amy the same experience she had. In reality, she was deciding how much that experience was worth—and how much of the future she was willing to trade to recreate it.

# CHAPTER 14

# WEDDINGS AND THE COST OF *Love*

*If you want children to keep their feet on the ground, put some responsibility on their shoulders."*

– ABIGAIL VAN BUREN

Raj and Priya Patel believed in education the way some families believe in inheritance. Education was the inheritance. They had spent most of their adult lives pouring money, time, pressure, and sacrifice into making sure their three daughters had opportunities they never had growing up. Their daughters attended excellent schools, graduated with advanced degrees, and built careers that sounded impressive at family gatherings where introductions often felt suspiciously similar to LinkedIn summaries. Vamika became a physician, Aditi became a dentist, and Aadhya became an attorney. Raj liked saying all three professions in a row because it sounded successful, stable, and expensive all at once. And it was.

The Patels had spent decades moving money around like people trying to stop leaks in a sinking boat. Tuition payments, apartments, graduate school expenses, exam prep courses, flights home, cars reliable enough for clinical rotations and internships—it never seemed to end. Priya once joked that she could identify each daughter's educational phase by the level of financial panic attached to it. Medical school had the "silent staring at retirement statements" phase. Dental school introduced the "maybe we work five more years" phase. Law school brought them into what Raj called "retirement optimism denial." The jokes worked because everyone understood there was truth underneath them.

Still, Raj never complained much because he loved his daughters deeply. There was something profoundly emotional for him about watching three little girls grow into accomplished women. He remembered braiding hair badly when Priya worked late, sitting through dance recitals that lasted longer than most international flights, helping with science fair projects he did not understand, and carrying sleeping daughters from the car after late-night events. Somewhere along the way, providing for them had become psychologically attached to love itself. Every tuition payment, every sacrifice, every delayed retirement contribution felt like evidence that he had done his job well as a father. Their success became one of the great emotional achievements of his life.

For Raj especially, these weddings represented something emotional and difficult to explain. He had spent his entire adult life protecting, guiding, and providing for his daughters. Paying for the weddings felt like one final act of fatherhood before fully stepping aside into a different phase of life. The ceremonies symbolized not only marriage, but the emotional completion of decades spent raising children he adored.

By the time the girls were financially independent adults, Raj imagined life might finally slow down. For the first time in decades, he allowed himself to think about retirement without immediately calculating educational expenses in his head. Maybe there would be more travel. Maybe mornings without alarm clocks.

Maybe fewer conversations involving interest rates and tuition balances. Then the weddings started.

The Patels had always imagined traditional Desi weddings for their daughters. Not small weddings. Not efficient weddings. Big weddings. Multi-day celebrations with music, dancing, ceremonies, outfit changes, coordinated family colors, jewelry that required insurance riders, and guest lists large enough to resemble political fundraisers. In their social circle, weddings were not simply celebrations. They were presentations of family identity, generosity, success, hospitality, and cultural loyalty. People evaluated everything—the food, decor, clothing, venues, music, flowers, and guest count—while pretending they were simply there to celebrate love.

Priya had attended weddings where the groom rode in on a white horse. Raj still remembered a wedding where the dessert display looked like a luxury shopping mall had collided with a bakery. There were ice sculptures, imported flowers, synchronized dancers, and enough gold embroidery to temporarily blind guests seated too close to the stage. Somewhere along the line, weddings had stopped resembling family celebrations and started resembling corporate product launches with emotional speeches.

"You cannot do small," Priya told Raj one evening while reviewing venue pricing online. "People will think something is wrong."

Raj stared at the numbers. "What if something is wrong?" he asked softly.

The problem was that years earlier they had tried to prepare responsibly. They had saved fifty thousand dollars for each daughter's wedding, which once sounded enormous. But wedding inflation had apparently entered its own economic category. Catering costs rose with every additional ceremony. Floral arrangements looked less like decorations and more like botanical investments. Meanwhile, Raj had started doing math late at night in his office. The kind of math people do when they already know the answer but continue checking anyway because denial briefly feels comforting. Venue costs. Catering. Hotels. Entertainment. Transportation. Decor. Raj found himself irrationally annoyed by phrases like "simple elegance" because simple elegance somehow still cost forty thousand dollars.

Then Vamika became engaged to Austin. Austin was white. Very white. His ideal wedding involved approximately forty people, an outdoor ceremony, and "good barbecue afterward." When Priya explained the concept of a four-day wedding schedule, Austin looked like someone had just been informed he would also need to complete military training before the reception.

To his credit, Austin tried hard. He attended family dinners, practiced Hindi phrases, and smiled politely through conversations about ceremonies he barely understood. But one evening he asked Vamika, "Do you even want this?" The question stayed with her longer than she expected. Vamika was not entirely sure.

She loved parts of the culture deeply. She loved the music, the dancing, the clothes, the energy, and the feeling of family gathering together. But she also understood that the wedding carried emotional meaning for her parents far beyond the event itself.

Then came Aditi's engagement, and unlike Vamika, Aditi wanted everything. Every ceremony. Every tradition. Every event. She had Pinterest boards organized with the precision of Swiss watch.

The strangest part was that none of the daughters actually needed financial help. Vamika and Austin earned enough money to comfortably pay for their own wedding. Aditi's dental practice was thriving. Aadhya billed clients at hourly rates that made Raj briefly reconsider every career decision he had ever made. The daughters were financially successful adults. Yet Raj and Priya still felt responsible for funding the weddings because culturally, paying symbolized love, sacrifice, generosity, and successful parenting even though they knew their daughters could afford to pay.

Raj suggested one evening to Priya. "Maybe we scale back."

Priya looked horrified. "People will talk," she said.

And there it was. The sentence beneath almost every oversized family expense. People will talk. Nobody ever identified exactly who these people were, but apparently, they possessed extraordinary influence over financial decision-making across multiple continents and generations.

But underneath all of it was something deeply emotional for Raj as a father. He did not simply want impressive weddings. He wanted his daughters to feel cherished. He wanted them to remember walking into rooms filled with people who loved them. He wanted them to feel celebrated publicly, culturally, emotionally. Somewhere in his mind, reducing the weddings started feeling dangerously close to reducing the love itself, even though logically he knew those things were not the same. This is what makes emotional spending so powerful. Financial decisions slowly stop feeling financial at all.

By the time Aadhya became engaged, Raj felt emotionally exhausted every time wedding planning discussions started. But Aadhya surprised everyone. "What if we just did something smaller?" she asked carefully during dinner one night. Priya nearly dropped the serving spoon.

"Smaller?" she repeated.

Aadhya nodded. "I don't know if I need all of it."

Silence settled over the table. Raj felt immediate relief mixed with guilt for feeling relieved. What Aadhya recognized before anyone else was that the weddings had stopped being entirely about the daughters. They had become emotionally attached to family image, obligation, tradition, sacrifice, identity, and fear of judgment. The scale of the event no longer reflected the actual needs of the couples. It reflected decades of accumulated expectation. Later that evening, after everyone left, Raj admitted something to Priya while sitting at the kitchen table surrounded by venue brochures and budget estimates. "I think I kept believing this was part of being a good father," he said.

Priya looked at him carefully."And maybe it was," she replied softly. "But maybe it doesn't have to cost everything."

## Psychological Pattern: Love, Obligation, and Consumer Identity

One of the most emotionally powerful financial patterns in families occurs when love, identity, and spending gradually become emotionally intertwined. In this pattern, parents are not overspending because they are shallow, irresponsible, or obsessed with appearances. They are spending because financial decisions slowly become connected to devotion, sacrifice, generosity, cultural identity, and the desire to make children feel deeply loved. For Raj and Priya, the weddings represented far more than celebrations. The events symbolized successful parenting, cultural continuity, family reputation, hospitality, and emotional abundance. Over time, the weddings stopped feeling like optional expenses and started feeling like emotional responsibilities. Once spending becomes psychologically attached to love and identity, reducing the event can begin to feel emotionally similar to reducing care itself.

Part of Raj and Priya's pattern is that they had spent decades prioritizing their daughters' futures above their own comfort. They paid for excellent schools, graduate degrees, apartments, transportation, tutoring, exam preparation, and every opportunity they could reasonably provide because giving had gradually become one of the primary ways, they expressed love. Raj especially connected financial provision with fatherhood itself. Their success validated decades of pressure, work, sacrifice, and delayed gratification. By the time weddings arrived, continuing to spend heavily felt psychologically consistent with the role he had carried for decades. The financial support was no longer just practical. It had become symbolic love.

There was also a powerful emotional fear operating underneath the spending. In many families, parents unconsciously begin associating extravagance with emotional adequacy. A smaller wedding can start to feel emotionally uncomfortable not because the love is smaller, but because parents fear the child may feel less valued, less celebrated, or somehow less important. Emotional reasoning replaces financial reasoning. The logic becomes: if this moment matters deeply, then the spending should reflect that depth emotionally. That is how love slowly becomes measured through visible abundance rather than emotional presence, consistency, or long-term stability.

Another important layer was cultural visibility and social evaluation. Weddings in Raj and Priya's community were not simply private family celebrations. They were highly visible social events communicating generosity, success, hospitality, loyalty to tradition, and family standing. Phrases like "people will talk" carry enormous emotional power because human beings naturally fear judgment and exclusion from the communities shaping their identity. Raj and Priya were not only planning weddings for their daughters; they were navigating decades of cultural expectation layered on top of genuine parental love. Overspending often occurs when emotional devotion and public pressure become psychologically intertwined.

This dynamic becomes even more complicated because comparison rarely happens directly. No one announces that a wedding must cost hundreds of thousands of dollars. Instead, expectations rise gradually through repeated exposure to larger venues, luxury receptions, multi-day celebrations, and increasingly elaborate events until extravagance begins to feel normal. A family that originally planned a moderate wedding may suddenly feel uncomfortable hosting something noticeably smaller than recent weddings within their social circle. Social comparison changes perception quickly. Once enough people around you participate in luxury consistently, excess stops feeling excessive.

What made the situation especially difficult was that the daughters no longer needed financial rescue. They were highly successful adults fully capable of funding their own weddings comfortably. Yet Raj and Priya still felt emotionally responsible because caregiving identities do not disappear automatically once children become financially independent. Parents who spend decades sacrificing for children often struggle emotionally when the provider role begins changing. Continuing to give feels familiar, purposeful, and emotionally reassuring. **Stepping back can feel strangely empty, almost as if reducing financial involvement reduces parental importance.** Many parents whose primary love language is giving experience discomfort when they can no longer express devotion through financial sacrifice at the same level. In reality, love does not disappear simply because support changes form, but emotionally that transition can feel surprisingly difficult for many families.

Children also absorb these patterns more deeply than parents often realize. When emotional milestones consistently involve escalating spending, children can unconsciously begin associating love, celebration, and belonging with financial output. The emotional baseline rises over time. What once felt extraordinary eventually starts feeling expected. Families rarely intend to create this pattern, but emotional reinforcement is powerful. If the largest expressions of love consistently arrive through expensive gestures, gifts, or events, financial intensity slowly becomes connected to emotional significance inside the family system. This does not mean generosity is harmful. It simply means families benefit from making sure emotional intimacy is not becoming financially dependent.

The difficult truth about love-based obligation spending is that love and financial overextension are not the same thing. Weddings last days. Retirement lasts decades. The danger begins when emotional expression becomes financially unsustainable, and parents sacrifice their own future stability in order to perform love publicly. Children benefit far more from emotional security, wisdom, consistency, communication, and long-term family stability than from extravagant spending designed primarily to satisfy fear, obligation, comparison, or cultural pressure.

Healthy families eventually learn that generosity and boundaries can exist together. Traditions can be honored without becoming financially destructive. Weddings can remain beautiful, meaningful, emotional, and culturally rich without requiring parents to compromise retirement security or carry overwhelming financial stress into later life.

## The Quick Math

As their daughters approached marriage, Raj and Priya hoped to honor family traditions with large, culturally significant weddings. They had saved $50,000 for each daughter, or $150,000 total, but with estimated wedding costs of approximately $150,000 per event, the total expense could reach $450,000. This creates a potential shortfall of $300,000, even before considering the many additional costs that often accompany large celebrations.

The issue is whether the financial sacrifice aligns with long-term family goals. If the original saved $150,000 were invested instead of spent, it could grow to approximately $295,072 in ten years at a 7% annual return. That growth represents more than an additional $145,000 created through compounding alone. Those dollars could strengthen retirement security, provide greater financial flexibility later in life, or become part of a family's legacy. Every dollar spent on a wedding is also a dollar that loses the opportunity to continue compounding, making the true cost far greater than the event itself.

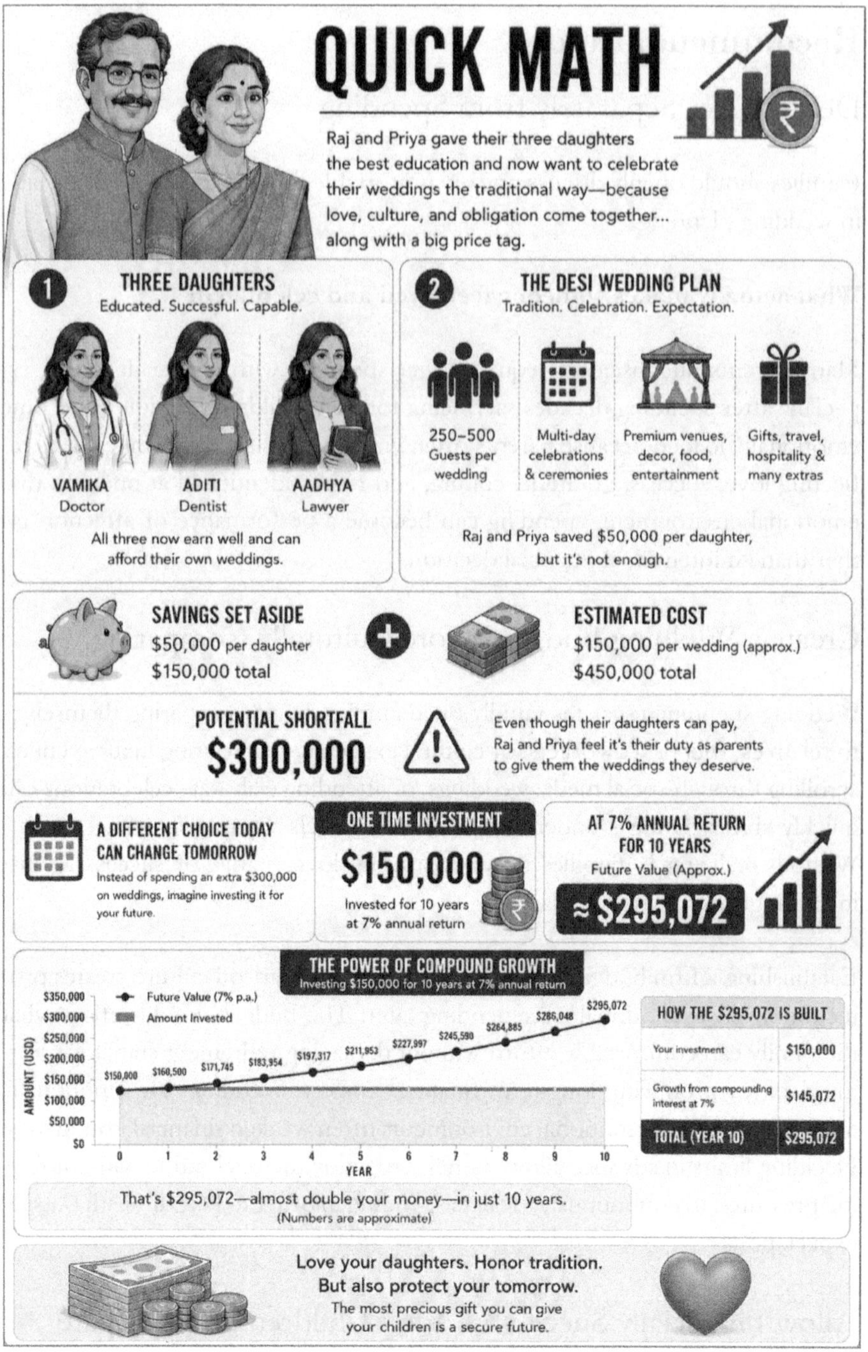
QUICK MATH
Raj and Priya gave their three daughters the best education and now want to celebrate their weddings the traditional way—because love, culture, and obligation come together... along with a big price tag.
1
THREE DAUGHTERS
Educated. Successful. Capable.
VAMIKA
Doctor
ADITI
Dentist
AADHYA
Lawyer
All three now earn well and can afford their own weddings.
2
THE DESI WEDDING PLAN
Tradition. Celebration. Expectation.
250–500 Guests per wedding
Multi-day celebrations & ceremonies
Premium venues, decor, food, entertainment
Gifts, travel, hospitality & many extras
Raj and Priya saved $50,000 per daughter, but it's not enough.
SAVINGS SET ASIDE
$50,000 per daughter
$150,000 total
ESTIMATED COST
$150,000 per wedding (approx.)
$450,000 total
POTENTIAL SHORTFALL
$300,000
Even though their daughters can pay, Raj and Priya feel it's their duty as parents to give them the weddings they deserve.
A DIFFERENT CHOICE TODAY CAN CHANGE TOMORROW
Instead of spending an extra $300,000 on weddings, imagine investing it for your future.
ONE TIME INVESTMENT
$150,000
Invested for 10 years at 7% annual return
AT 7% ANNUAL RETURN FOR 10 YEARS
Future Value (Approx.)
≈ $295,072
THE POWER OF COMPOUND GROWTH
Investing $150,000 for 10 years at 7% annual return
Future Value (7% p.a.)
Amount Invested
AMOUNT (USD)
$350,000
$300,000
$250,000
$200,000
$150,000
$100,000
$50,000
$0
$150,000
$160,500
$171,745
$183,954
$197,317
$211,953
$227,997
$245,590
$264,885
$286,048
$295,072
0 1 2 3 4 5 6 7 8 9 10
YEAR
HOW THE $295,072 IS BUILT
Your investment $150,000
Growth from compounding interest at 7% $145,072
TOTAL (YEAR 10) $295,072
That's $295,072—almost double your money—in just 10 years.
(Numbers are approximate)
Love your daughters. Honor tradition.
But also protect your tomorrow.
The most precious gift you can give your children is a secure future.

# Recommendations

## Define Love Separately from Spending

Families should openly discuss one uncomfortable but important question early in wedding planning:

**What actually makes someone feel loved and celebrated?**

Many parents unconsciously equate larger spending with deeper devotion, especially after spending decades sacrificing for their children. Weddings become emotionally loaded because parents often view them as symbolic milestones reflecting love, success, gratitude, culture, and family identity all at once. In that emotional environment, spending can become a performance of affection rather than an intentional financial decision.

## Create a Wedding Budget Before Culturally Comparing

Wedding spending escalates rapidly once families begin comparing themselves to relatives, friends, coworkers, or cultural expectations. Touring luxury venues, scrolling through social media weddings, or attending elaborate celebrations can quickly shift a family's understanding of what feels "normal" or "necessary." Without realizing it, families begin measuring love, status, or success against increasingly expensive standards.

Establishing a firm budget before entering that comparison culture creates protection against emotional overspending later. The budget should reflect what the family can comfortably afford without damaging retirement stability, creating debt, or producing long-term financial anxiety. Weddings are emotionally intense events, and emotional environments often weaken financial boundaries. Deciding limits in advance allows families to enjoy the celebration without feeling pressured to continuously escalate spending in order to keep up with outside expectations.

## Allow Financially Successful Adult Children to Participate

Adult children contributing financially to their own weddings is not evidence of failed parenting. In many cases, shared financial responsibility creates healthier communication, more realistic decision-making, and greater emotional balance.

Parents can still provide meaningful support without assuming total financial responsibility for every aspect of the event.

Financial partnership also changes priorities. Couples who contribute their own money often become more intentional about what truly matters to them rather than automatically reproducing expensive cultural expectations or social traditions. Shared responsibility can reduce emotional pressure on parents while helping adult children transition into marriage with greater awareness of budgeting, compromise, and financial planning. Support does not always require complete financial sacrifice.

## Discuss Traditions Honestly Instead of Automatically

Not every family tradition carries the same emotional meaning for every generation. Some children may deeply value large cultural ceremonies, religious traditions, or extended family celebrations, while others may prefer smaller gatherings, blended ceremonies, destination weddings, or entirely different approaches. Problems often arise when families assume traditions must be reproduced without discussing their actual emotional significance or financial cost.

Open conversations create clarity. Families benefit from asking, "Which traditions matter most to us emotionally?" rather than assuming every expectation must be fulfilled equally regardless of expense. Honest discussions also help distinguish between traditions rooted in genuine meaning and traditions maintained primarily through social pressure or fear of judgment. Traditions should strengthen families emotionally, not destabilize them financially.

## Protect Retirement Intentionally

Parents who spent decades funding education, childcare, activities, and emotional support often feel tempted to make one final large sacrifice during weddings. The wedding can emotionally feel like the culmination of years of parenting, and many parents fear disappointing their children during such an important milestone. But retirement deserves protection too. Parents eventually need financial stability, healthcare resources, housing security, and independence later in life. One helpful question is:

**Will we still feel comfortable with this spending ten years from now if it delays retirement or creates financial stress?**

Emotional moments pass quickly, but financial consequences often remain much longer. Parents who compromise their own future stability for a single event may later experience resentment, anxiety, or regret that overshadows the memory of the celebration itself. Healthy generosity still requires boundaries.

## Remember That Children Usually Want Presence More Than Presentation

Many parents believe their children will remember extravagant decor, luxury venues, elaborate floral arrangements, or large guest counts most clearly. In reality, people usually remember emotional atmosphere far more than financial presentation. They remember feeling supported, welcomed, celebrated, connected, and emotionally present with the people they love most.

People remember how a wedding felt emotionally long after they forget the centerpieces, chair coverings, or elaborate details. Separating emotional love from financial performance allows families to make healthier decisions without feeling emotionally deprived. Love does not become more authentic simply because the floral budget increases.

CHAPTER 15

# THE HOUSE THAT *Mom* BOUGHT

*It is not what you do for your children, but what you have taught them to do for themselves that will make them successful human beings.*

– ANN LANDERS

Linda worked, saved, and sacrificed in ways that felt normal at the time and only became visible later. When her son Jake said he wanted to become a teacher, she didn't hesitate because helping him felt like the obvious thing a good mother would do. Four years of tuition, books, and living expenses added up to an education that cost more than her first house. Jake graduated, got a teaching job, and everyone clapped like the story was over, as if the hardest part had already passed. It hadn't.

Jake was now thirty, with a degree, a career as a teacher, and the kind of confidence that comes from never having fully failed financially. He had always landed on his feet, but not always by himself, and that distinction mattered more than anyone had acknowledged. He was renting a small one-bedroom apartment alone, a setup that only looked sustainable because Linda was still helping behind the scenes. On paper, the obvious solution was a two-bedroom apartment with a roommate who could split rent and utilities, but Jake had no interest in sharing space, schedules, nor responsibility with another person. His preference for privacy became a financial liability that someone else was helping absorb.

When the rent climbed to $1,200 a month, what had already been fragile started to sink faster. Jake seemed to be getting more underwater, and Linda found herself covering small gaps that slowly became routine. What looked like temporary help gradually became part of the structure that kept his lifestyle functioning. She didn't call it support anymore because it felt too normal to question. It simply became what she did.

So, when Jake announced that he wanted to buy a house, it sounded like progress. It sounded like adulthood finally arriving in a clean, respectable package, the kind that reassures parents that things are moving forward. His justification was simple enough to sound responsible: the mortgage would probably be less than rent. Linda thought, "With what money for a down payment? With what credit?" but instead she stepped in, because stepping in was her role.

She co-signed, but not just in the technical sense of signing paperwork. She co-signed in the real sense of absorbing risk, because Jake's credit wasn't strong enough, his savings weren't enough, and his financial habits were not built for a thirty-year commitment. She helped with the down payment, closing costs, and "just this once" shortfalls when things got tight. Every contribution was framed as temporary, which made it easier to justify and harder to stop.

At first, it didn't feel dangerous. It felt responsible, like love with paperwork attached, the kind of thing good parents do when their children are trying to move forward. Linda told herself it was just until things stabilized, just until he got on his feet, just until life smoothed out. But when you remove the consequences of ownership, you don't create stability—you create distance from responsibility. Jake had the house, but he never fully felt the weight of it.

The urgency wasn't there because the pressure never fully reached him. The moment where someone says, "If I don't figure this out, I lose everything," never arrived, because there was always a buffer. That buffer absorbed stress, softened consequences, and prevented small problems from becoming defining moments. Over time, the absence of pressure became its own pattern. And that pattern had a name . . . Linda.

Jake also had a new TV, a gaming system, and weekend spending habits that didn't match someone struggling to stay afloat. Nothing extreme, nothing dramatic, just enough steady spending that the important things kept falling short. Groceries turned into takeout, bills turned into "I'll get it next month," and Amazon boxes appeared with regularity. When Linda visited, she noticed the food deliveries, the casual purchases, and the faint smell of marijuana drifting through the living room. Each time, the same thought surfaced, even if she didn't say it out loud. How are you struggling and still spending like this?

Slowly, without anyone announcing it, the system shifted. Not legally, but practically, Jake didn't think of it as dependence and Linda didn't think of it as enabling. It just became the way things worked, a pattern so familiar it stopped feeling like a decision. If money got tight, there was a solution, and if a payment felt stressful, there was a call. If life didn't line up, someone else adjusted for it. That someone was Linda.

Meanwhile, Linda was sixty-two, and retirement was no longer a distant concept she could ignore. It was supposed to be close enough to plan around, something she could see coming instead of something she kept delaying. But her money wasn't fully hers, because every month a portion of it still flowed into Jake's life.

This is where co-signing becomes misunderstood, because it is not just paperwork. Co-signing is shared liability without shared control. You don't get to manage the decisions, but you remain fully exposed to the outcomes. If payments are missed, your credit feels it, and if the budget collapses, your retirement absorbs it. You are, in effect, underwriting an adult life you no longer direct.

So why isn't Jake stepping up? Because he doesn't have to. Jake isn't irresponsible in a dramatic way. He is simply operating within the system he was given, one where help shows up, consequences are softened, and someone else fills the gap. So, he prioritizes wants first and needs eventually, because historically that has worked.

Linda, on the other hand, is stuck in a loop where she tells herself it's temporary, even as the pattern continues unchanged. And here's the truth she's avoiding. Every dollar she gives him is a dollar she's taking from her future.

This is how people get here—not through one big mistake, but through a series of small, loving decisions that never had an end date. Co-signing just this once, helping until he gets on his feet, covering gaps because he's trying—each time felt reasonable in isolation. At no point did anyone stop and ask the most important question. When does this stop? Because without that question, there is no exit. Just continuation.

Jake doesn't change because nothing requires him to. His bills get paid, his lifestyle continues, and his safety net remains active and reliable. Meanwhile, Linda is asking herself a different question now, one that is harder and far more honest. What am I doing? This situation isn't just about Jake anymore. It's about her quality of life. At some point, helping becomes hurting—not just for the parent, but for the child. Jake isn't learning to carry his own weight. He's learning that someone else will. Until that changes, nothing changes.

## Psychological Pattern: The Dependency Buffer

Linda's situation reflects a powerful psychological pattern that appears in many families without anyone intentionally creating it. Parents often confuse reducing discomfort with helping growth, especially when the child appears functional on the surface. Jake had a degree, a job, and eventually a house, which allowed the relationship to look healthy from the outside. But underneath that appearance was a system where consequences rarely landed fully on him because someone else kept absorbing the impact. Linda did not think of herself as enabling dependence because the support was always framed as temporary, loving, and reasonable. That is what makes this dynamic so psychologically dangerous. It rarely arrives looking reckless. It arrives disguised as support during transitional periods that never end.

Parents often struggle to recognize when helping crosses into buffering adulthood itself. Every time Linda covered a shortfall, co-signed a risk, or softened a financial consequence, she unintentionally interrupted the pressure that normally forces growth and adaptation. Human beings often mature financially because consequences become uncomfortable enough to require change. Roommates are tolerated because rent becomes too high. Budgets are created because accounts hit zero. Spending habits improve because there is no rescue waiting in the background. Jake never fully experienced that pressure because Linda absorbed too much of it before it reached him. Love became a financial shock absorber.

This dynamic is especially common among parents who see themselves as protectors, fixers, or stabilizers within the family. Linda's identity became emotionally tied to being needed. Helping Jake did not only solve his problems; it reinforced her role as the reliable parent who always shows up. That emotional role can become addictive in subtle ways because being needed creates purpose, connection, and emotional reassurance. Parents sometimes fear that stepping back financially will damage the relationship or make them appear uncaring. In reality, what they often fear most is watching their child struggle without intervening. Unfortunately, protecting children from all struggles can also protect them from growth.

There is also a psychological phenomenon called learned dependence that develops in these systems. Jake is not irresponsible in a dramatic or malicious way. He has simply adapted to an environment where shortfalls repeatedly disappear before becoming crises. Over time, people stop feeling urgency when experience teaches them someone else will stabilize the situation eventually. That is why Jake could simultaneously struggle financially while continuing food deliveries, recreational spending, and casual purchases. The brain prioritizes differently when survival pressure never fully arrives. Responsibility becomes emotionally optional when consequences remain consistently diluted by outside support.

Parents caught in this cycle need to understand that boundaries are not abandonment. Allowing adult children to fully experience the weight of their own financial decisions is not cruelty; it is part of adulthood. Linda's money was no longer just helping Jake survive difficult moments. It was quietly delaying her own retirement, peace, and long-term security. One of the hardest realizations for loving parents is understanding that rescuing an adult child repeatedly may feel compassionate in the short term while creating weakness and dependence long term. Healthy support has structure, limits, timelines, and expectations. Without those things, helping slowly transforms into sustaining a system where nobody fully changes because nobody fully has to.

## The Quick Math

Linda wanted to help her adult son, Jake, achieve the dream of homeownership. To ease the financial pressure, she contributed approximately $800 per month toward his mortgage, shortfalls, and other expenses. While the monthly amount may have seemed manageable, it added up to $9,600 per year and a total of $96,000 over ten years.

Had Linda invested $800 per month and earned an average annual return of 7%, those contributions could have grown to approximately $353,732 over twenty years. More than $257,000 of that amount would come from investment growth rather than her original contributions. This example illustrates how financial support for adult children often carries a much larger opportunity cost than parents realize. Every dollar given away today is a dollar that can no longer compound for retirement, making the true cost far greater than the check that was written.

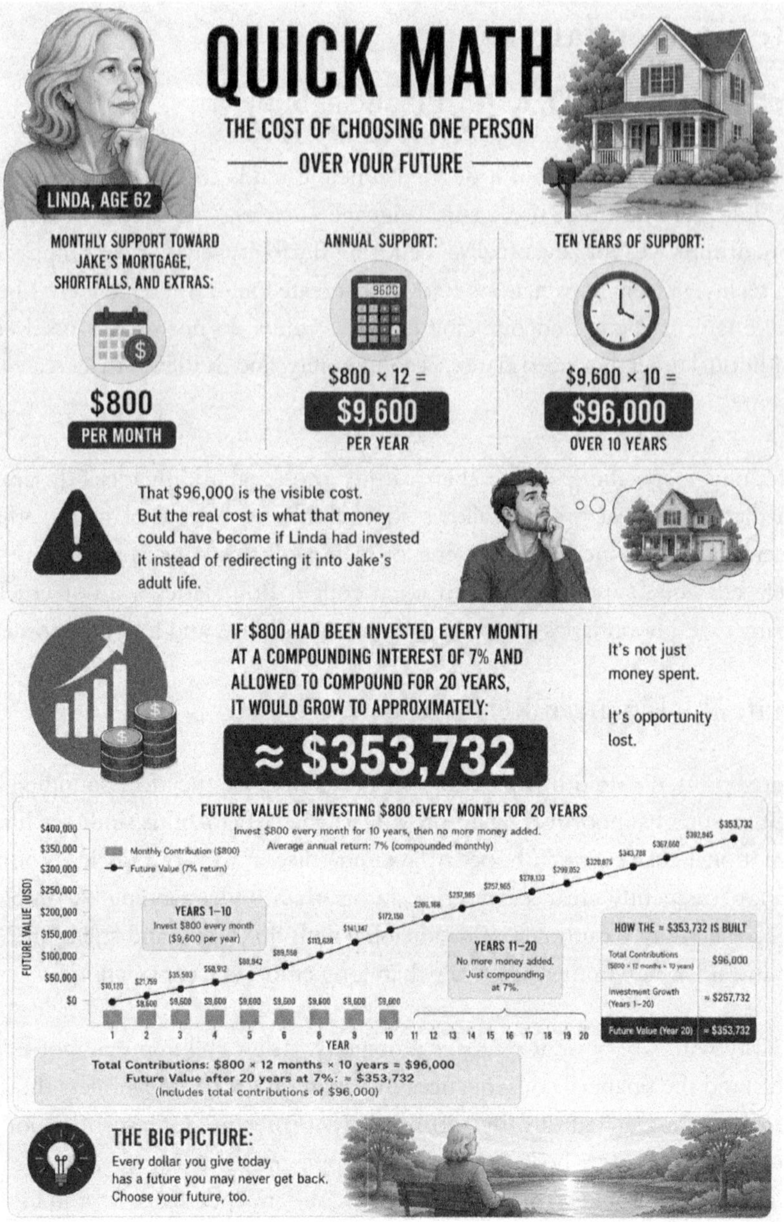
QUICK MATH
THE COST OF CHOOSING ONE PERSON
OVER YOUR FUTURE
LINDA, AGE 62
MONTHLY SUPPORT TOWARD JAKE'S MORTGAGE, SHORTFALLS, AND EXTRAS:
$800
PER MONTH
ANNUAL SUPPORT:
9600
$800 × 12 =
$9,600
PER YEAR
TEN YEARS OF SUPPORT:
$9,600 × 10 =
$96,000
OVER 10 YEARS
That $96,000 is the visible cost.
But the real cost is what that money could have become if Linda had invested it instead of redirecting it into Jake's adult life.
IF $800 HAD BEEN INVESTED EVERY MONTH AT A COMPOUNDING INTEREST OF 7% AND ALLOWED TO COMPOUND FOR 20 YEARS, IT WOULD GROW TO APPROXIMATELY:
≈ $353,732
It's not just money spent.
It's opportunity lost.
FUTURE VALUE OF INVESTING $800 EVERY MONTH FOR 20 YEARS
Invest $800 every month for 10 years, then no more money added.
Average annual return: 7% (compounded monthly)
Monthly Contribution ($800)
Future Value (7% return)
FUTURE VALUE (USD)
$400,000
$350,000
$300,000
$250,000
$200,000
$150,000
$100,000
$50,000
$0
YEARS 1–10
Invest $800 every month
($9,600 per year)
YEARS 11–20
No more money added.
Just compounding at 7%.
$353,732
YEAR
HOW THE ≈ $353,732 IS BUILT
Total Contributions ($800 × 12 months × 10 years) $96,000
Investment Growth (Years 1–20) ≈ $257,732
Future Value (Year 20) ≈ $353,732
Total Contributions: $800 × 12 months × 10 years = $96,000
Future Value after 20 years at 7%: ≈ $353,732
(Includes total contributions of $96,000)
THE BIG PICTURE:
Every dollar you give today
has a future you may never get back.
Choose your future, too.

# Recommendations

## Set a Clear End Date for Financial Support

Financial support without a defined timeline tends to become permanent by default. Parents often use vague language such as "for a little while," "until things improve," or "eventually," believing flexibility feels more compassionate. In reality, unclear expectations frequently create long-term dependency because there is no structure encouraging change. Adults do not usually need endless additional time; they need clarity, accountability, and deadlines that create movement.

Defining a specific end date changes the emotional and financial dynamic immediately. A clear timeline allows adult children to begin planning, adjusting spending habits, increasing income, or making difficult decisions they may have delayed while support remained open-ended. Boundaries are not cruelty. In many cases, boundaries create urgency, responsibility, and forward momentum.

## State the Financial Reality Clearly

Parents often soften financial conversations because they fear sounding harsh, selfish, or unsupportive. They provide vague explanations, indirect hints, or emotional cushioning in hopes of avoiding discomfort. But unclear communication frequently creates confusion rather than understanding. A simple sentence such as, "I cannot continue helping with this house and still retire," communicates reality more effectively than long emotional explanations.

Clarity works because it removes ambiguity. Adult children may not fully understand the financial consequences their parents are carrying unless those consequences are stated directly and honestly. Protecting retirement is not abandonment. Parents who spent decades supporting children also deserve long-term financial stability, healthcare security, and independence later in life. Honest communication allows adult relationships to operate from reality rather than avoidance.

## Stop Covering the Gap

As long as financial shortfalls are repeatedly filled externally, behavior inside the system often remains unchanged. If parents continuously absorb missed payments, overspending, poor budgeting, or avoidable financial decisions, there is little pressure forcing adjustment. Human behavior typically changes most when consequences become visible and unavoidable.

This does not mean parents should become cold or indifferent. It means they must recognize that repeatedly rescuing financial situations can unintentionally delay growth. Responsibility develops when adults experience the direct connection between choices and outcomes. If every financial problem is softened immediately by parental intervention, the urgency required for behavioral change often never fully develops.

## Separate Your Finances from Their Spending Behavior

Many parents become emotionally consumed by monitoring how their adult children spend money. They have access to their accounts, they analyze purchases, criticize decisions, offer repeated advice, and attempt to control behavior indirectly through frustration or supervision. But monitoring another adult's spending habits rarely changes the underlying system. What changes the system is adjusting financial boundaries.

Parents cannot fully control how adult children manage money, but they can control whether their own finances continue absorbing the consequences. Separating finances from another adult's spending behavior restores clarity and accountability. Emotional energy spent policing decisions is often less effective than calmly redefining what support will and will not continue.

## Require Full Ownership of Obligations

If an adult child has a mortgage, rent payment, car loan, or other major financial obligation, they need to experience the responsibility attached to it fully. Urgency develops through ownership, not through repeated advice or parental worry. Adults tend to take obligations more seriously when the consequences belong directly to them rather than being shared or absorbed by parents behind the scenes.

This is especially important because adulthood requires learning how to tolerate financial pressure, make adjustments, and solve problems independently. Ownership creates maturity because it forces adults to evaluate priorities, increase income, reduce spending, or make difficult but necessary changes.

## Recognize When Helping Becomes Enabling

The emotional relationship between giving and taking inside a family is complex because generosity itself is not harmful. Many parents sacrifice deeply for their children in healthy and beautiful ways. The issue is not giving. The issue is whether giving is paired with growth. Healthy parental support gradually moves a child toward greater independence. Unhealthy support prolongs dependence because the parent unconsciously needs the child to remain reliant. In some families, financial dependence becomes emotionally intertwined with identity. The parent feels valuable because they are needed. The child avoids adulthood because dependence feels safer than responsibility.

Over time, resentment develops on both sides. The parent begins feeling used, exhausted, and unappreciated. The child feels controlled, judged, or emotionally indebted. Financial support that once felt loving slowly becomes emotionally suffocating. This is especially common when money is repeatedly provided without expectations for accountability, work ethic, or contribution. A thirty-year-old who has never paid a bill may still emotionally function like an adolescent because responsibility was continuously postponed. Yet the deeper issue is often relational rather than financial. Families sometimes fear the emotional distance that independence creates. Money becomes the cord that keeps everyone psychologically attached. Unfortunately, dependence maintained through money rarely produces closeness. It more often produces guilt, anger, obligation, and silent hostility.

Support becomes enabling when it removes the pressure necessary for independence to develop. Parents often continue helping because they fear their child will struggle, fail, or experience discomfort. But discomfort is frequently what motivates growth, adaptation, and responsibility. Endless support without limits can unintentionally communicate that someone else will always absorb the consequences when things become difficult.

Independence usually requires some degree of pressure. Adults often change behavior only when remaining the same becomes uncomfortable enough to force adjustment. Healthy support should therefore move children toward greater stability and self-sufficiency rather than extending dependence indefinitely. Helping is valuable when it creates movement forward. It becomes harmful when it prevents adulthood from fully arriving. Helping feels good in the moment, but the effect on retirement decides whether it was sustainable.

CHAPTER 16

# RAISING *Capable* ADULTS

*It takes more power to say no out of love than to say yes out of weakness. This notion is at the very heart of establishing a healthy relationship with your money.*

– SUZE ORMAN

The ultimate goal of parenting is not permanent dependency. It is preparing children to function independently, responsibly, emotionally, and financially in adulthood. Yet many modern parenting patterns unintentionally delay this process by extending support far beyond what is developmentally necessary. Parents naturally want to protect children from struggle, disappointment, and failure, but capability develops through participation, not constant rescue. Children need opportunities to manage money, solve problems, tolerate frustration, recover from mistakes, and gradually carry increasing responsibility as they mature. Loving support should build confidence and competence, not lifelong dependence. Every time adults step in to solve problems children are capable of handling themselves, they may unintentionally communicate a damaging message: you are not capable without me.

Modern parenting culture also creates enormous pressure to supervise, optimize, and manage childhood constantly. Many parents fear that one wrong decision, one setback, or one uncomfortable experience could permanently damage a child's future opportunities. This fear often leads to hyper involvement—monitoring schedules, academics, friendships, emotions, activities, and future planning with extraordinary intensity. But capable adults are not created through permanent supervision. They are created through gradually increasing trust, autonomy, accountability, and experience. Children need opportunities to practice adulthood before adulthood fully arrives. Financial capability matters especially because many young adults now enter adulthood without understanding budgeting, debt, saving, delayed gratification, taxes, investing, or long-term planning, despite those decisions shaping enormous portions of adult life.

Children also need emotional capability. They need to learn how to tolerate criticism, navigate conflict, recover from disappointment, solve practical problems, and function without immediate parental intervention every time life becomes difficult. Capable adults are not people who never struggle. They are people who believe they can work through struggle without collapsing emotionally. That confidence develops slowly through responsibility, experience, and trust. One of the most loving things parents can do is allow children to become increasingly responsible for their own lives while still remaining emotionally supportive and connected. Independence is not abandonment. It is evidence that parenting successfully prepared a child for adulthood.

Ultimately, the healthiest parent-child financial relationships are built on a balance of support, boundaries, responsibility, and emotional honesty. Children need generosity, but they also need opportunities to contribute. They need security, but they also need manageable struggle. They need help, but they also need belief in their own capability. Families become emotionally healthier when money is treated neither as a source of shame nor as proof of love. The goal is not raising children who fear money, worship money, or depend endlessly upon money from others. The goal is raising emotionally stable adults who understand how to earn, save, adapt, give, recover, and live within reality without losing their sense of self. Financial stability does not guarantee happiness, but it often creates the conditions where healthier emotional relationships can grow. Parents who manage money responsibly are not simply protecting bank accounts. They are protecting the emotional climate of the home. They are teaching children how to tolerate disappointment without despair, how to work without resentment, and how to build lives grounded in capability rather than dependency. Those lessons shape not only financial outcomes but emotional ones.

## Consumerism

Most parents do not intentionally teach consumerism. In fact, many families who drift into financially unhealthy patterns would strongly reject the idea that materialism defines their household. They see themselves as loving, supportive, generous, and devoted to giving their children opportunities they may not have had themselves. The problem is repetition. Children learn values not from lectures, but from observing what families normalize repeatedly over time.

A child watching adults constantly upgrade phones, chase trends, overspend on holidays, participate in retail therapy after difficult days, or treat spending as the primary reward system begins learning something powerful about adulthood. They learn that discomfort is solved through consumption. They learn that celebration requires spending. They learn that emotional expression often arrives through purchases. Even families who verbally criticize materialism can unintentionally model it behaviorally through constant lifestyle escalation.

Consumerism is especially persuasive because modern culture rarely presents it honestly. It is packaged as self-care, memory-making, empowerment, identity, enrichment, convenience, or love. Parents are constantly told that a better childhood requires better experiences, better schools, better camps, better vacations, better technology, better activities, and better opportunities. Ordinary life slowly begins feeling emotionally insufficient. Simplicity starts looking like deprivation rather than stability. Please ask the question of every purchase:

**Does this purchase genuinely improve our lives, or does it create additional maintenance, pressure, comparison, and financial obligations?**

Children raised in financially balanced households often develop a stronger relationship with gratitude because they are not constantly emotionally overstimulated through endless consumption. A child who occasionally waits for things, saves for things, or learns to enjoy ordinary experiences develops emotional muscles that consumer culture constantly tries to weaken. Simplicity creates perspective. Limits create appreciation.

## Emotional Resilience

One of the greatest modern parenting temptations is the desire to remove discomfort from childhood entirely. Parents naturally hate watching children struggle socially, emotionally, academically, or financially. Love creates a powerful instinct to protect, soften, and solve problems quickly. But protection can become overprotection when parents begin treating every frustration, disappointment, inconvenience, or emotional struggle as something that must immediately be fixed through money, rescue, or constant accommodation. Bored children receive tablets. Sad children receive gifts. Exhausted families purchase convenience after convenience because it feels like survival. Emotional discomfort slowly becomes financially managed rather than emotionally processed. Over time, children can unintentionally absorb the idea that difficult emotions should always disappear quickly instead of being tolerated, worked through, and understood.

The problem is that emotional resilience develops through experiencing manageable discomfort, not through avoiding it completely. Children who occasionally hear "no," wait for things, lose competitions, work through boredom, feel left out, or experience disappointment without immediate rescue develop emotional flexibility that becomes incredibly valuable later in life. Material comfort and emotional resilience are not always aligned. In fact, they can sometimes work against one another when children become too dependent on external comfort to regulate internal emotions. Parents often underestimate how emotionally capable children really are. Kids can survive ordinary birthdays, simpler vacations, not making elite teams, and hearing, "That is not financially wise for our family right now." What children often struggle with far more is growing up inside households weighed down by chronic financial stress, parental exhaustion, anxiety, or conflict created by years of overextension and unsustainable spending.

This does not mean children should experience unnecessary hardship or emotional neglect. Children absolutely deserve love, safety, support, and protection. But healthy development also requires opportunities to experience frustration, uncertainty, effort, delayed gratification, and occasional failure without collapsing emotionally or being rescued financially every time. Emotionally resilient children learn something incredibly important early: happiness is not fully dependent on constant optimization. Joy can exist inside ordinary life. Meaning can exist without extravagance. Relationships matter more than presentation. Adults who develop that kind of resilience are often better equipped for real life because real life eventually includes disappointment, limits, boredom, uncertainty, and hardship for everyone. Parents who constantly chase material comfort for children usually do so from genuine love, but long-term emotional strength may require giving children something different: the confidence that they can survive ordinary discomfort and still be okay.

## Delayed Gratification

One of the most important things parents can teach children is that not every desire must be fulfilled immediately. Delayed gratification creates resilience. The ability to wait, tolerate frustration, and work toward something gradually becomes one of the foundations of emotional maturity and long-term financial stability. In a culture built around instant access and immediate gratification, delayed gratification has become almost countercultural. Yet many of the most meaningful parts of life—healthy relationships, career growth, financial security, and retirement stability—are built slowly over time, not instantly.

Children who learn to tolerate waiting often develop greater patience, persistence, emotional regulation, and financial discipline later in life. They learn that boredom is survivable, disappointment is temporary and wanting something does not automatically mean it must happen right now. These experiences may feel small in childhood, but they shape how adults eventually handle money, stress, debt, work, and relationships.

The goal is not to raise deprived children or emotionally cold households. The goal is to raise adults who can balance desire with wisdom and emotion with restraint. Children do not need every wish fulfilled to feel loved. In fact, one of the greatest gifts parents can give is the confidence that happiness, security, and self-worth do not depend on constant consumption or immediate comfort.

## Difference Between Love and Consumption

Love and consumption are not the same thing. Love is emotional safety. Love is consistency. Love is presence. Love is guidance. Love is stability. Love is boundaries. Love is teaching children how to build meaningful lives. Consumption can temporarily imitate love because spending often produces excitement, gratitude, relief, or emotional stimulation. Children who grow up equating love with spending often struggle later because relationships become emotionally tied to consumption, gifts, status, or external validation. They may unconsciously seek emotional reassurance through purchases or expect love to arrive through material expression.

Healthy families teach something far more sustainable. **People remain valuable even when spending decreases.** Relationships remain meaningful even without constant upgrades or performances. Parents absolutely should celebrate children, create memories, enjoy experiences, and express generosity. The issue is not joy. The issue is dependency. When emotional connection becomes financially dependent, families lose freedom. The deepest irony of parenting is that many adults spend enormous amounts of money trying to create magical childhoods while simultaneously creating the financial stress that undermines family peace.

CHAPTER 17

# FINANCIAL *Health*

*Beware of*
*little expenses.*
*A small leak will*
*sink a great ship.*

– BENJAMIN FRANKLIN

Financial health is not just about income. It is about awareness, structure, honesty, and behavior repeated consistently over time. This chapter makes recommendations for living a financially intelligent and healthy life. Many families believe they have an income problem when they actually have a spending awareness problem. Money disappears through habits, convenience, emotional spending, subscriptions, debt payments, lifestyle inflation, and thousands of small decisions that feel harmless individually but become financially destructive collectively.

Before families can change their financial future, they must first become honest about their current reality. Be honest about the daily habits draining money from the household. The coffee, beer, and cigarette purchases. The emotional spending after stressful days. The impulsive Amazon orders. The upgraded phones. The convenience spending. The overspending on children disguised as love or opportunity. The inability to say no. Most financial problems are not hidden. They are normalized. Couples should be able to sit together and honestly assess where the money goes, and what emotional patterns are attached to spending. Financial health requires self-awareness before strategy. If your children are old enough, explain their role in the family's finances and the changes that the family is making.

## Emergency Fund

Before investing, families should build an emergency fund. Unexpected expenses are not emergencies because they are unexpected; they are emergencies because families are unprepared for them. Job loss, medical bills, home repairs, vehicle breakdowns, and family crises occur for everyone. A fully funded emergency reserve prevents families from turning to credit cards, personal loans, retirement withdrawals, or borrowing from relatives when life inevitably becomes difficult. Many financial professionals recommend maintaining three to six months of essential living expenses in a readily accessible savings account.

## Credit Cards

You should only have one credit card. Paid off every month. If you have to put something on credit and can't pay it off at the end of the month, you shouldn't be buying it. Credit must be understood rather than feared or ignored. Shop interest rates carefully and understand exactly how much interest is costing you over time. Credit scores matter because they affect mortgage rates, car loan interest rates, apartment approvals, utility deposits, insurance pricing, and sometimes even employment opportunities for positions involving travel, sales, or financial responsibility. Parents do not give your children credit cards. Children need to earn and manage their own credit gradually as they become adults.

## Debt

Debt should be confronted directly. List every debt clearly—credit cards, medical bills, personal loans, car loans, student loans, everything. Many people avoid looking at the full number because it creates anxiety, but avoidance never reduces debt. Call creditors directly and negotiate whenever possible. Many companies will reduce balances, lower payments, remove fees, or settle debts if families communicate instead of avoiding contact entirely. When paying down debt, eliminate very small balances quickly to create momentum, then focus larger payments on the highest interest rates. Most importantly, stop borrowing for things that you cannot afford. Do not borrow from retirement accounts to pay debt because that solves one financial problem while creating another much larger future problem.

Sometimes families may need debt consolidation or even bankruptcy to reset financially. Bankruptcy carries long-term consequences and can remain on credit reports for years, but there are situations where it becomes the healthiest financial option available. Families should also understand that student loans survive bankruptcy and may reduce Social Security income later in life through garnishment or offsets in one's Social Security payments. So don't ignore your student loans as they are a lifetime commitment.

## Avoid Lifestyle Inflation

One of the fastest ways to remain financially stuck is allowing spending to rise every time income increases. Promotions, bonuses, raises, and new jobs often create the illusion of wealth while expenses quietly expand to consume every additional dollar earned. Before increasing lifestyle expenses, families should first increase retirement contributions, emergency savings, debt reduction, or investment accounts. The goal is not simply to earn more money but to keep more of what is earned.

## Create a Retirement Plan

You must have a plan RIGHT NOW. Not tomorrow. RIGHT NOW.

Retirement planning cannot remain a vague future idea. It must become an active financial priority now. Financial experts commonly recommend saving approximately 10% to 15% of gross income toward retirement. For many middle-income households earning roughly $64,000 to $96,000 annually, that often translates to approximately $800 per month invested consistently over time. Money without direction disappears. **Money with a purpose and a plan creates freedom, flexibility, and long-term stability.** Families often believe they need dramatically higher incomes to improve their financial future, when in reality many simply need greater awareness, stronger boundaries, reduced emotional spending, and a clearer understanding of where their money is draining away.

A Roth IRA and a 401(k) both allow investments to grow through compound interest over time, but the major difference is when taxes are paid. With a Roth IRA, taxes are paid upfront so withdrawals in retirement are generally tax free, while a traditional 401(k) provides tax savings today but withdrawals are taxed later during retirement (see infograph).

Many financial advisors recommend contributing to your employer-sponsored 401(k) first only if your company offers a matching contribution. A company match is essentially free money and provides an immediate return on your investment that is difficult to replicate elsewhere. However, if no employer match is available, many investors prioritize maximizing annual contributions to a Roth IRA because it offers greater flexibility and allows qualified withdrawals to be taken tax-free in retirement. Index funds with no or low expenses have historically outperformed the majority of actively managed investment strategies over long periods of time.

Even small, consistent contributions matter. Whether a parent invests $800 a month or begins with just $25 a month in a Roth IRA, consistency and intentionality over time are what build wealth. Speak with a financial advisor to determine the best strategy for your personal financial situation. Most major investment firms, such as Fidelity or Vanguard, offer free initial advisory consultations to help families get started.

# ROTH IRA vs. 401(k)

## TAXES NOW vs. TAXES LATER

*Same growth rate. Different tax timing.*

### 1 WHAT IT REALLY COSTS TO INVEST

Example: 22% Tax Bracket

| | Roth IRA (After-Tax Dollars) | 401(k) (Pre-Tax Dollars) |
|---|---|---|
| Gross Income Needed | $9,615 (to net $7,500 after taxes) | $7,500 (full pre-tax amount) |
| Taxes Paid Today | $2,115 (22% of $9,615) | $0 |
| Amount Invested | $7,500 | $7,500 |
| Tax Benefit Today | None | Immediate deduction lowers taxable income |

**ROTH IRA** (After-Tax)

Paycheck $9,615 → TAXES 22% -$2,115 → Invested $7,500

**401(k)** (Pre-Tax)

Paycheck $7,500 → No taxes taken out now → Invested $7,500

*Traditional 401(k): You get a tax break today. Roth IRA: You get a tax break later.*

### 2 INVESTMENT GROWTH (7% ANNUAL RETURN)

30 YEARS OF ANNUAL CONTRIBUTIONS

| ROTH IRA | | 401(k) |
|---|---|---|
| Future Value **$708,041** Tax-Free Growth | = | Future Value **$708,041** Pre-Tax Growth |

The accounts grow similarly.
The difference is WHEN taxes are paid.

### 3 RETIREMENT WITHDRAWALS

10% ANNUAL WITHDRAWAL AT AGE 59½

**ROTH IRA**

| | |
|---|---|
| 10% Withdrawal | $70,804 |
| Taxes | $0 |
| You Keep | **$70,804** |

Every dollar you withdraw is yours.

**401(k)**

| | |
|---|---|
| 10% Withdrawal | $70,804 |
| Taxes (22%) | -$15,577 |
| You Keep | **$55,227** |

Taxes are paid when you withdraw.

### 4 WHAT IF YOU INVEST THE TAX SAVINGS?

Compare Using the SAME Gross Income: $9,615

| | ROTH IRA | 401(k) |
|---|---|---|
| Actual Gross Income Used | $9,615 | $9,615 |
| Amount Invested | $7,500 | $9,615 (includes tax savings of $2,115 invested) |
| Future Value After 30 Years (7% annual return) | $708,041 | $907,410 |
| After-Tax 10% Withdrawal (22% tax rate) | $70,804 | $90,741 |
| You Keep (After Taxes) | **$70,804** | **$70,778** |

If tax rates stay similar and the tax savings are invested, the accounts can become surprisingly close after taxes.

### 5 KEY TAKEAWAYS

**ROTH IRA**

- Pay taxes now.
- Tax-free growth and withdrawals.
- More flexibility with contributions.
- No required minimum distributions during your lifetime.
- Great for younger investors or those expecting higher future tax rates.

VS.

**401(k)**

- Reduce taxes today.
- Full contribution amount invested upfront (more investing power).
- Often includes employer match.
- Taxes paid during retirement.
- Great for higher earners seeking current tax relief.

**BOTH ACCOUNTS:**

- Powerful tax-advantaged retirement tools
- Benefit from compound growth
- Should be part of a smart long-term plan

★ There is no one "best" account—only the best account for YOUR situation.
Consider your income, tax bracket now vs. later, employer match, and financial goals.

## Vehicles

Most families normalize car payments as a permanent part of adult life. Families should understand that vehicles are depreciating assets. The brand-new car or truck will never be worth what you paid for it when you drove it off the lot. The car is losing value while interest continues increasing the total amount paid. The average new car loan in America now exceeds $40,000, with monthly payments commonly ranging from $700 to over $1,000 depending on the vehicle, loan term, and interest rate. Many buyers focus almost entirely on the monthly payment rather than the total long-term cost, stretching loans across six, seven, or even eight years simply to make the payment feel manageable. But interest compounds the real price of the vehicle. A $40,000 vehicle financed over several years can easily cost tens of thousands more once interest is included, especially in higher-rate lending environments.

Leasing can appear financially attractive because the monthly payments are often lower than traditional financing, but leases contain many hidden costs that consumers underestimate. Most leases require upfront money at signing, including down payments, taxes, fees, and security deposits. Drivers also face strict mileage limits, and exceeding those limits can result in substantial penalties at the end of the lease term. Wear-and-tear charges, accident damage, scratches, tire replacement requirements, and repair standards can create additional unexpected expenses when returning the vehicle. Most importantly, leasing creates a permanent subscription type payment cycle where the consumer continuously pays for vehicles without ever building ownership. At the end of the lease, the family often starts over with another down payment and another monthly obligation. Over decades, this cycle consumes hundreds of thousands of dollars that could have been invested differently.

For many families, one of the healthiest financial decisions is learning to separate transportation from identity, status, or emotional reward. A reliable used vehicle paid with cash creates more financial freedom than constantly upgrading to newer cars with long-term loans or endless lease payments. Driving a less expensive vehicle for several additional years may not feel exciting in the moment, but it dramatically reduces financial pressure, interest costs, insurance expenses, and dependence on monthly payments.

## Home Ownership

Home ownership can become one of the most stabilizing financial decisions a family makes. Unlike rent, which often continues rising indefinitely, a fixed-rate mortgage creates predictability. Over time, inflation may increase nearly every other household expense while the principal and interest portion of the fixed rate mortgage remains stable. That consistency allows families to plan more effectively long term while gradually building equity instead of permanently paying on a landlord's asset through rent.

Families should also understand the value of purchasing the least expensive home in a strong neighborhood rather than the most expensive home in an average one. This type of purchase can provide instant equity, and the home might just need some DIY paint and landscaping. Better neighborhoods often hold value more consistently, provide stronger schools and infrastructure, and create more long-term financial stability without requiring the pressure of maintaining the highest-cost home on the block. Buy into the best school district that is available to you. School rankings are available on greatschools.org and good public schools eliminate the use of private schools.

**Not all home ownership decisions are financially intelligent.** Families should pay close attention to **property taxes, insurance costs, and geographical risk zones** before purchasing. Flood zones, hurricane exposure, wildfire regions, and high-risk coastal areas can dramatically increase insurance premiums, sometimes making an otherwise affordable home financially burdensome. Buying just outside those high-risk zones can significantly reduce long-term housing costs.

In addition, the geographical location in which you choose to live shapes nearly every part of financial life. Housing costs, taxes, insurance, wages, transportation, childcare, healthcare, and overall cost of living vary dramatically across the country especially between rural and urban areas. Many people remain in locations simply because they always have lived there, because extended family is nearby, or because moving feels emotionally overwhelming. But relocation, while difficult, can sometimes change a family's financial future significantly.

## State Income Tax

Some states offer no state income tax including Florida, Texas, Tennessee, Nevada, Wyoming, South Dakota, Alaska, Washington, and New Hampshire. A family earning $100,000 can lose $4,000–$10,000 more per year simply because of geography. Over twenty years, that difference—if invested instead at 7%—could become hundreds of thousands of dollars in retirement savings. While taxes alone should not determine where a family lives, they should absolutely be part of the conversation. A lower-cost area with lower taxes, reasonable insurance rates, and manageable housing costs may create far more long-term freedom than remaining in a location that constantly requires higher income simply to maintain the same standard of living. Sometimes financial health is not only about earning more money. Sometimes it is about choosing a location where money stretches further, and life requires less financial pressure to sustain.

## Groceries

Grocery spending is one of the easiest places for families to regain financial control because small food decisions repeat constantly throughout the year. Americans now spend thousands annually eating outside the home, often because exhaustion, convenience, and overscheduling make cooking feel overwhelming. But restaurant meals, delivery fees, tips, drinks, and impulse purchases add up far faster than most families realize.

One of the smartest financial habits is learning to cook intentionally in bulk. Prepare larger meals and freeze half for the nights when everyone is exhausted and takeout would normally feel easier. That single habit can dramatically reduce restaurant spending while also lowering stress. Families should also buy frequently used pantry items in bulk when they are on sale, plan meals around discounts, and use farmer's markets or discount grocery stores when practical.

Even saving $150–$300 per month consistently on food spending can free up thousands of dollars annually for debt reduction, emergency savings, retirement investing, or simply reducing financial pressure inside the household. Grocery discipline may not feel exciting in the moment, but over time it becomes one of the clearest examples of how small, repeated decisions shape long-term financial health.

## Start a 529 Plan Early

If college assistance is a goal, one of the most effective steps parents can take is opening a 529 college savings plan as early as possible. Contributions grow tax-deferred, and qualified withdrawals for education expenses are generally tax-free. Many states also offer state income tax deductions or credits for contributions. The account owner maintains control of the assets, and if one child does not use the funds, the beneficiary can typically be changed to another child, or eligible family member without tax consequences. The greatest advantage of a 529 plan is time. Starting early allows compound growth to work for years, potentially reducing future student loans and greater flexibility for the entire family.

## Loaning Money

If you choose to help family or friends, give only what you can truly afford to part with as a gift, with no expectation of repayment. Never loan money unless you are fully prepared to lose both the money and the relationship. What often begins with sincere promises, and a few good-faith payments gradually fades into missed deadlines, uncomfortable conversations, and eventually silence about the debt altogether. Money given with expectations attached can turn generosity into resentment on both sides.

## Shop Interest Rates, Insurance Rates, Refinance

Families should aggressively shop interest rates, insurance policies, and mortgage refinancing opportunities on a yearly basis rather than remaining loyal to companies charging higher rates. Many households overpay simply because they never compare options.

## Estate Planning

Every adult should have a basic estate plan regardless of net worth. A will, healthcare directive, power of attorney, and updated beneficiary designations provide clarity when families face illness, incapacity, or death. Estate planning is not about expecting the worst. It is about reducing confusion, conflict, and unnecessary legal costs during already difficult moments. One of the greatest gifts parents can leave their children is organization rather than uncertainty.

## The Quick Math of Small Habits

Many financial advisors recommend redirecting your small habits such as coffee, beer, wine, lottery tickets, fast food lunches or other small convenience purchases into an investment account. But what does that math really look like? When the coffee money is redirected, it has the opportunity to grow and compound. For example, a five-dollar coffee purchased five days a week costs approximately $1,300 per year. If that same amount were invested and earned an average annual return of 7%, it could grow to more than $56,000 over twenty years, nearly $133,000 over thirty years, and more than $290,000 over forty years. See the Small Habits, Big Returns table for other examples.

The challenge with habits is that they are rarely about the habit itself. Most people do not buy a coffee, a lottery ticket, a vape, or a six-pack because they have carefully calculated the financial consequences. They do it because they are tired, stressed, bored, overwhelmed, or simply looking for a small reward. These purchases become release valves—small moments of comfort in a life filled with responsibilities, deadlines, bills, parenting demands, and uncertainty. In the moment, the purchase feels earned. It feels deserved. And often, it is.

The problem is not the occasional treat. The problem occurs when small comforts become automatic habits. What begins as an occasional reward slowly becomes a recurring expense that no longer feels like a choice. People become attached to the immediate emotional benefit while losing sight of the long-term financial tradeoff. The coffee provides relief today. The cigarette reduces stress today. The cost, however, is often paid by a future version of yourself.

One way to break this cycle is not to focus on what you are giving up, but on what you are moving toward. Instead of asking, "Do I want this coffee?" ask, "Do I want this coffee more than I want financial freedom?" Instead of seeing retirement savings as money being taken away, begin viewing it as a gift to your future self.

The goal is not to eliminate every pleasure from life. The goal is to become intentional about which pleasures are worth keeping. A comfortable retirement, financial independence, and the ability to make choices later in life are rewards as well. They simply arrive more slowly. The people who build wealth are often those who learn to want the bigger reward more than the smaller one.

# SMALL HABITS, BIG RETURNS

What a single habit could become if invested at 7% annually.

| HABIT | MONTHLY COST* | ANNUAL COST | 20 YEARS 7% RETURN | 30 YEARS 7% RETURN | 40 YEARS 7% RETURN |
|---|---|---|---|---|---|
| **CIGARETTES** $10 per pack, 1 pack per day | $304 | $3,650 | $158,449 | $372,675 | **$815,737** |
| **VAPING** $60 per week | $260 | $3,120 | $135,401 | $318,554 | **$697,792** |
| **FAST FOOD LUNCH** $10 per day, 5 days per week | $217 | $2,600 | $112,867 | $265,462 | **$581,493** |
| **BEER** $15 six-pack, 3 times per week | $195 | $2,340 | $101,581 | $238,916 | **$523,344** |
| **WINE** $15 bottle, 2 times per week | $130 | $1,560 | $67,720 | $159,277 | **$348,896** |
| **COFFEE** $5 per cup, 5 days per week | $108 | $1,300 | $56,434 | $132,731 | **$290,747** |
| **LOTTERY TICKETS** $20 per week | $87 | $1,040 | $45,147 | $106,185 | **$232,597** |

*Monthly costs are calculated by dividing annual spending by 12 and rounding to the nearest dollar.

**A SINGLE HABIT CAN HAVE A SIX-FIGURE OPPORTUNITY COST.**
The goal is not to eliminate every small pleasure.
The goal is to understand the long-term financial tradeoff of recurring spending decisions.

**ASSUMPTIONS**

- Money invested monthly instead of spent
- 7% average annual return
- Returns are hypothetical and not guaranteed

## The Quick Math of 30- or 40-Year Investments

The financial models presented throughout this book were intentionally built using conservative assumptions. In each chapter, the examples assume that money spent on a particular expense was instead redirected and invested, earning an average annual return of 7 percent. The twenty-year values shown in the chapter illustrations were selected to provide a realistic and easy-to-understand comparison, not to maximize the results. Retirement accounts, brokerage accounts, Roth IRAs, and other long-term investments are often held for thirty, forty, or even more years. A parent making spending decisions in their thirties or forties may not access those funds until their sixties or seventies.

**The summary table (See table: The True Cost of Choices) demonstrates, the power of time using the examples in the chapters.** The Total Investment column reflects the amount spent in each chapter example, while the Spending Period (Years) column shows the number of years over which that spending occurred. The 20-Year, 30-Year, and 40-Year Value columns illustrate what the same dollars could have grown to if they had been redirected and invested at a 7% average annual return. These calculations are intended to demonstrate the long-term opportunity cost of spending decisions and the powerful effect that compound growth can have over time. The longer money remains invested, the greater the potential difference between spending today and building wealth for the future.

What may appear to be a six-figure tradeoff after twenty years can become several hundred thousand dollars—or even millions of dollars—over thirty or forty years. The purpose of these examples is not to suggest that every expense should be avoided, but rather to illustrate the hidden long-term value of intentional financial choices. Time is one of the most powerful forces in investing, and the longer money remains invested, the more significant the difference between spending and saving becomes.

# THE POWER OF TIME

## THE SUMMARY TABLE DEMONSTRATES, THE POWER OF TIME USING THE EXAMPLES IN THE CHAPTERS.

The Total Investment column reflects the amount spent in each chapter example, while the Spending Period (Years) column shows the number of years over which that spending occurred. The 20-Year, 30-Year, and 40-Year Value columns illustrate what the same dollars could have grown to if they had been redirected and invested at a 7% average annual return.

| CHAPTER | TOTAL INVESTMENT (DOLLARS) | SPENDING PERIOD (YEARS) | 20-YEAR VALUE AT 7% RETURN | 30-YEAR VALUE AT 7% RETURN | 40-YEAR VALUE AT 7% RETURN |
|---|---|---|---|---|---|
| Designer Baby | $16,600 | 1 | $64,107 | $125,806 | **$246,161** |
| Preschool Prestige | $55,200 | 2 | $213,728 | $419,593 | **$820,918** |
| Toy Pendulum | $80,000 | 20 | $164,424 | $322,750 | **$631,703** |
| Clothing, Culture & Cost | $36,000 | 6 | $152,268 | $298,421 | **$583,811** |
| The Subscription Childhood | $16,800 | 12 | $45,673 | $89,567 | **$175,001** |
| Club & Travel Sports, Dance & Cheer | $78,000 | 6 | $239,785 | $470,076 | **$918,627** |
| The Car at Sixteen | $13,040 | 3 | $45,299 | $88,864 | **$173,429** |
| Vacation Memories on a Credit Card | $52,500 | 15 | $112,957 | $221,518 | **$433,280** |
| Allowance - the Illusion of Earned Money | $8,320 | 8 | $24,032 | $47,099 | **$92,154** |
| Cost of High School Failure | $52,000 | 3 | $172,000 | $337,491 | **$658,302** |
| Stadium Lights and Student Loans | $128,000 | 4 | $418,900 | $821,165 | **$1,603,341** |
| The College Experience | $283,000 | 5 | $890,000 | $1,746,701 | **$3,409,755** |
| Weddings and the Cost of Love | $150,000 | 1 | $295,072 | $579,739 | **$1,131,663** |
| The House That Mom Bought | $96,000 | 10 | $353,732 | $693,805 | **$1,354,271** |

**ASSUMPTIONS**

- 7% average annual return (compounded annually)
- Values represent redirected spending invested instead
- Figures rounded to the nearest dollar

**SPENDING PERIOD DEFINITION**

Spending Period (Years) reflects the number of years over which the original expense occurred before future value calculations were applied.

**THE MATH**

30-Year Value = 20-Year Value × $(1.07)^{10}$

40-Year Value = 20-Year Value × $(1.07)^{20}$

*Where 1.07 = 1 + 7% annual return*

Assumes 7% average annual return.
Values are hypothetical and for illustrative purposes only.

## Create Family Financial Values

Families should also create clear financial values together (see example). What matters most? Stability? Freedom? Experiences? Retirement security? Simplicity? Without shared values, money decisions become emotionally reactive and inconsistent. Every purchase should eventually pass through a simple question: does this align with the type of life we are trying to build? Financial values create structure during emotional moments when impulse spending feels justified.

**Our Family Values**

______________________________________________

______________________________________________

______________________________________________

______________________________________________

**Do I Spend Impulsively? On What?**

______________________________________________

______________________________________________

______________________________________________

______________________________________________

**What Am I Currently Teaching My Children About Money?**

______________________________________________

______________________________________________

______________________________________________

______________________________________________

**What Do I Need to Teach My Children About Money?**

______________________________________________

______________________________________________

______________________________________________

______________________________________________

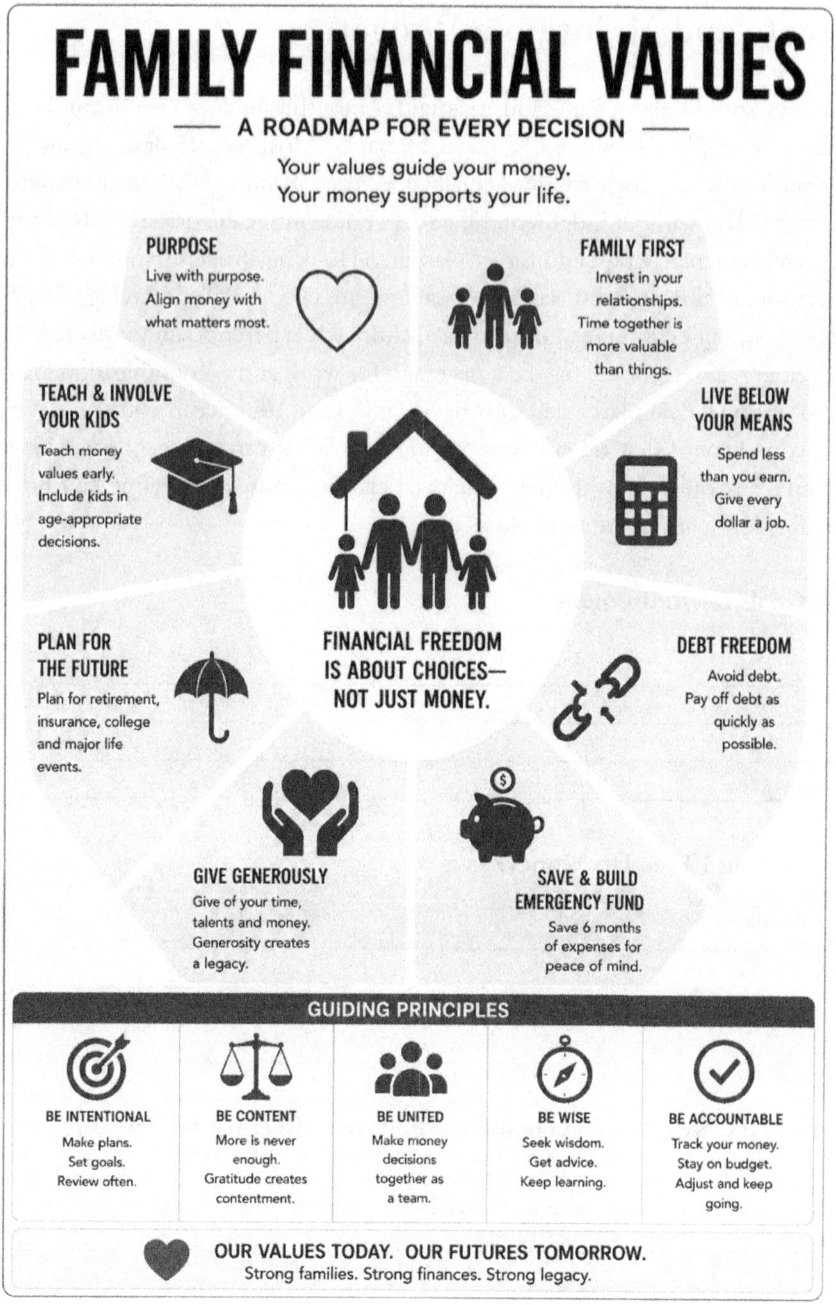
FAMILY FINANCIAL VALUES
A ROADMAP FOR EVERY DECISION
Your values guide your money.
Your money supports your life.
PURPOSE
Live with purpose. Align money with what matters most.
FAMILY FIRST
Invest in your relationships. Time together is more valuable than things.
TEACH & INVOLVE YOUR KIDS
Teach money values early. Include kids in age-appropriate decisions.
LIVE BELOW YOUR MEANS
Spend less than you earn. Give every dollar a job.
FINANCIAL FREEDOM IS ABOUT CHOICES—NOT JUST MONEY.
PLAN FOR THE FUTURE
Plan for retirement, insurance, college and major life events.
DEBT FREEDOM
Avoid debt. Pay off debt as quickly as possible.
GIVE GENEROUSLY
Give of your time, talents and money. Generosity creates a legacy.
SAVE & BUILD EMERGENCY FUND
Save 6 months of expenses for peace of mind.
GUIDING PRINCIPLES
BE INTENTIONAL
Make plans. Set goals. Review often.
BE CONTENT
More is never enough. Gratitude creates contentment.
BE UNITED
Make money decisions together as a team.
BE WISE
Seek wisdom. Get advice. Keep learning.
BE ACCOUNTABLE
Track your money. Stay on budget. Adjust and keep going.
OUR VALUES TODAY. OUR FUTURES TOMORROW.
Strong families. Strong finances. Strong legacy.

## Create and Maintain a Budget

Families should also create and maintain a monthly budget (see example). A budget is simply awareness organized on paper. Most people dramatically underestimate where their money actually goes each month. Track every expense for thirty days without judgment. Divide spending into categories: needs, wants, debt, retirement savings, and future planning. Housing, groceries, utilities, transportation, healthcare, and retirement savings are needs. College savings may be important, but children can borrow for school while parents cannot borrow for retirement. Your phone may be a necessity for work and communication. Your child's phone, data plan, or newest device is a want. Where can you save? What can you change? Get rid of? Stop paying for? What can you negotiate down? Where can you free up money? Financial clarity requires separating emotional justification from financial reality.

**My Goals for Retirement**

______________________________________________

______________________________________________

______________________________________________

______________________________________________

**Where Can I Free Up Money?**

______________________________________________

______________________________________________

______________________________________________

______________________________________________

**Do I Have Negative Psychological Patterns Affecting My Spending?**

______________________________________________

______________________________________________

______________________________________________

______________________________________________

# FAMILY BUDGET TEMPLATE

**PLAN • PRIORITIZE • PROTECT**

Every dollar should have a purpose.

## MONTHLY INCOME

| | |
|---|---|
| Income 1 ________ | $ ________ |
| Income 2 ________ | $ ________ |
| Other Income ________ | $ ________ |
| **TOTAL MONTHLY INCOME** | $ ________ |

## NEEDS (ESSENTIAL)

Must-Have Expenses

| | |
|---|---|
| Housing (rent/mortgage) | $ ________ |
| Utilities (electric, water, gas) | $ ________ |
| Phone (cell phone) | $ ________ |
| Groceries | $ ________ |
| Transportation (car payment, insurance, fuel, maintenance) | $ ________ |
| Insurance (health, auto, home, life) | $ ________ |
| Child Care / Education | $ ________ |
| Healthcare (medical, dental, vision) | $ ________ |
| Debt Payments (loans, credit cards) | $ ________ |
| Savings (emergency fund) | $ ________ |
| Retirement Fund | $ ________ |
| Taxes (federal, state, property) | $ ________ |
| **TOTAL NEEDS** | $ ________ |

## WANTS (NON-ESSENTIAL)

Nice-to-Have Expenses

| | |
|---|---|
| Dining Out / Takeout | $ ________ |
| Entertainment / Streaming | $ ________ |
| Shopping / Personal Items | $ ________ |
| Vacations / Travel | $ ________ |
| Hobbies / Recreation | $ ________ |
| Children's Phones (upgrades, gadgets) | $ ________ |
| Gifts / Miscellaneous | $ ________ |
| College Savings | $ ________ |
| Other Wants | $ ________ |
| **TOTAL WANTS** | $ ________ |

## PARENTING & FAMILY PLANNING

| Pregnancy / Birth | Child Care | Education (PreK–12) | College | Activities / Lessons | Health & Wellness |
|---|---|---|---|---|---|
| $ ________ | $ ________ | $ ________ | $ ________ | $ ________ | $ ________ |
| $ ________ | $ ________ | $ ________ | $ ________ | $ ________ | $ ________ |
| $ ________ | $ ________ | $ ________ | $ ________ | $ ________ | $ ________ |

## MONTHLY SUMMARY

| | |
|---|---|
| Total Monthly Income | $ ________ |
| Minus Total Needs | $ ________ |
| Minus Total Wants | $ ________ |
| Equals (Surplus / Shortfall) | $ ________ |

## BUDGET TIPS

- Needs come first, then savings, then wants.
- Adjust wants to stay on track.
- Review monthly.
- Plan weekly.
- Dream long-term.

**LIVE WITH FINANCIAL INTELLIGENCE**

Budget with purpose. Live with freedom.

## Every Dollar Needs a Destination

Budgeting and redirected spending requires more than simply choosing not to spend money. Many people assume that avoiding a purchase automatically improves their financial future, but that is only half of the equation. The other half is making a conscious decision about where that money will go instead. Money without a purpose has a way of disappearing. It gets absorbed into everyday expenses, convenience purchases, upgrades, subscriptions, and countless small decisions that rarely feel significant in the moment. Without intention, the savings from one choice often become the spending for another.

Building wealth requires a different mindset. **Every dollar should have a purpose BEFORE it arrives.** When a family chooses not to spend money on one expense, they must also decide to redirect those dollars toward a specific financial goal, whether that is retirement, a Roth IRA, a brokerage account, debt reduction, or another long-term objective. This process requires intentionality, self-discipline, and focus. The true financial benefit comes not from what you avoided spending, but from what you intentionally chose to do with the money. Wealth is rarely built through deprivation alone. It is built through consistent decisions to redirect resources away from short-term consumption and toward long-term financial independence. Over time, those deliberate choices compound into opportunities, flexibility, and freedom that far exceed the temporary satisfaction of most purchases

# CONCLUSION

# REDEFINING *Successful* PARENTING

*I am the master of my fate:*
*I am the captain of my soul.*

– WILLIAM ERNEST HENLEY

Healthy parenting may have far less to do with creating exceptional children and far more to do with raising emotionally capable adults. Can the child tolerate discomfort without collapsing emotionally? Can they delay gratification? Can they maintain relationships? Can they work through setbacks? Can they handle ordinary life without constant stimulation, praise, or rescue? Those skills often matter far more over decades than early achievement markers.

The deepest forms of parental success are often invisible during childhood. A financially responsible adult. A kind spouse. A resilient employee. A grounded friend. A person who can tolerate ordinary life without constant emotional chaos. A person capable of gratitude, boundaries, and healthy relationships. Those outcomes matter enormously, yet they are rarely celebrated publicly the way trophies, scholarships, or admissions letters are.

Many parents spend years chasing visible parenting victories while unintentionally sacrificing the emotional and financial stability children actually need most. Children benefit from seeing adults who model balance, self-control, thoughtful decision-making, healthy financial behavior, emotional regulation, and perspective.

Perhaps the goal is not raising children who appear extraordinary from the outside. Perhaps the goal is raising adults who can build meaningful, stable lives without requiring constant external validation to feel valuable.

Eventually, every parent must answer:

**Are we building independence—or creating dependence?**

What we allow, what we fund, what we prioritize, and what we normalize all send messages that are far more powerful than anything we say out loud. Children do not grow up in our lectures; they grow up in our patterns. And whether we realize it or not, those patterns are shaping not only their expectations, but their future relationship with responsibility, money, and independence.

Many parents struggle deeply with the willingness to let responsibility belong to the child at the appropriate time. It means allowing space for discomfort, delayed gratification, emotional resilience, accountability, and learning through experience instead of constant protection. Without that gradual transition, independence becomes delayed even when intentions are loving.

**Are we protecting our children's wants at the cost of our retirement?**

Prioritizing retirement savings is not selfish—it protects your future independence and reduces the likelihood that your children will one day have to carry the burden of supporting you financially. Even if money feels tight, creating space to save consistently, no matter how small the amount, allows time and compound growth to work in your favor. Families who plan ahead give themselves more choices, more security, and greater peace of mind for the future.

This book does not ask families to become perfect. It asks them to become honest. Because once you clearly see the emotional and financial patterns operating inside your family, it becomes much harder to pretend those tradeoffs are not real. And once you cannot unsee them, every decision becomes slightly more intentional.

Made in the USA
Monee, IL
04 November 2026

67391558R00128